HMH Florida Science

Grade 5

This Write-In Book belongs to

_____

Teacher/Room

_____

The giant manta ray can be found in Florida's coastal waters. It is the world's largest ray and averages about 7 meters in width.

Houghton Mifflin Harcourt.

MW01255193

Consulting Authors

Michael A. DiSpezio
Global Educator
North Falmouth, Massachusetts

Marjorie Frank
*Science Writer and Content-Area Reading
  Specialist*
Brooklyn, New York

Michael R. Heithaus, Ph.D.
*Dean, College of Arts, Sciences & Education
Professor, Department of Biological Sciences*
Florida International University
Miami, Florida

Houghton Mifflin Harcourt.

Cover: manta ray ©Steve Woods Photography/Getty Images; water ©UnderTheSea/Shutterstock

Florida Standards courtesy of the Florida Department of Education.

Printed in the U.S.A.

ISBN   978-1-328-79360-7

12 13 14 15 16 0607 28 27 26 25 24 23 22 21
4500838780   DEFG

Contents

©Mariana Bazo/Reuters/Corbis

© Houghton Mifflin Harcourt Publishing Company

EARTH AND SPACE SCIENCE

UNIT 3 – THE SOLAR SYSTEM AND THE UNIVERSE

PHYSICAL SCIENCE

UNIT 5 – THE NATURE OF MATTER

UNIT 6 – FORMS OF ENERGY 303

BIG IDEA 10: FORMS OF ENERGY

UNIT 7 – WORKING WITH ELECTRICITY 361

BIG IDEA 11: ENERGY TRANSFER AND TRANSFORMATIONS

©Nigel Cattlin/Photo Researchers, Inc.

© Houghton Mifflin Harcourt Publishing Company

© Houghton Mifflin Harcourt
Publishing Company

Safety in Science

Doing investigations in science can be fun, but you need to be sure you do them safely. Here are some rules to follow.

1. Think ahead.
Study the steps of the investigation so you know what to expect. If you have any questions, ask your teacher. Be sure you understand any caution statements or safety reminders.

2. Be neat.
Keep your work area clean. If you have long hair, pull it back so it doesn't get in the way. Roll or push up long sleeves to keep them away from your experiment.

3. Oops!
If you spill or break something, or if you get cut, tell your teacher right away.

4. Watch your eyes.
Wear safety goggles anytime you are directed to do so. If you get anything in your eyes, tell your teacher right away.

5. Yuck!
Never eat or drink anything during a science activity.

6. Don't get shocked.
Be especially careful if an electric appliance is used. Be sure that electrical cords are in a safe place where you can't trip over them. Never pull a plug out of an outlet by pulling on the cord.

7. Keep it clean.
Always clean up when you have finished. Put everything away and wipe your work area. Wash your hands.

Scientists at Work

FLORIDA BIG IDEA 1

The Practice of Science

FLORIDA BIG IDEA 2

The Characteristics of Scientific Knowledge

A shark swims off the coast of Florida.

I Wonder Why

Why do some scientists work outdoors and others work inside a laboratory? *Turn the page to find out.*

Here's Why

Scientists work to answer questions. Some questions can be answered with outdoor investigations. Others require tools in a lab.

Essential Questions
and Florida Benchmarks

© Houghton Mifflin Harcourt Publishing Company

Photo credit text to come

SC.5.N.1.6 Recognize and explain the difference between personal opinion/interpretation and verified observation. SC.5.N.2.1 ... science is grounded in empirical observations that are testable; explanation must always be linked with evidence. SC.5.N.2.2 ... when scientific investigations are carried out, the evidence produced by those investigations should be replicable by others.

ESSENTIAL **QUESTION**

What Is Science?

Engage Your Brain

Find one answer to the following question in this lesson and write it here.

What are some science skills you could use when studying fish in an aquarium?

_____

_____

_____

ACTIVE **READING**

Lesson Vocabulary

List the terms. As you learn about each one, make notes in the Interactive Glossary.

_____

_____

_____

_____

Use Headings

Active readers preview headings and use them to pose questions that set purposes for reading. Reading with a purpose helps active readers focus on understanding what they read in order to fulfill the purpose.

What All Scientists Do

Digging up fossils. Peering through telescopes. Mixing chemicals in a lab. Using computers to make weather predictions. These are only a few of the things scientists do.

ACTIVE READING As you read these two pages, turn the heading into a question in your mind, and underline sentences that answer the question.

Does solving puzzles and searching for buried treasures sound like fun? If so, you might like being a paleontologist. Paleontologists are scientists who study the history of life on Earth. Like all scientists, they try to explain how and why things in the natural world happen. They answer questions by doing investigations. An **investigation** is a procedure carried out to carefully observe, study, or test something in order to learn more about it.

In addition to knowing a lot about living things of the past, paleontologists have to use many skills. In fact, all scientists use these skills. All scientists **observe**, or use their five senses to collect information. And all scientists **compare**, finding ways objects and events are similar and different.

Observe

Write one observation you could make about the fossil.

_____

_____

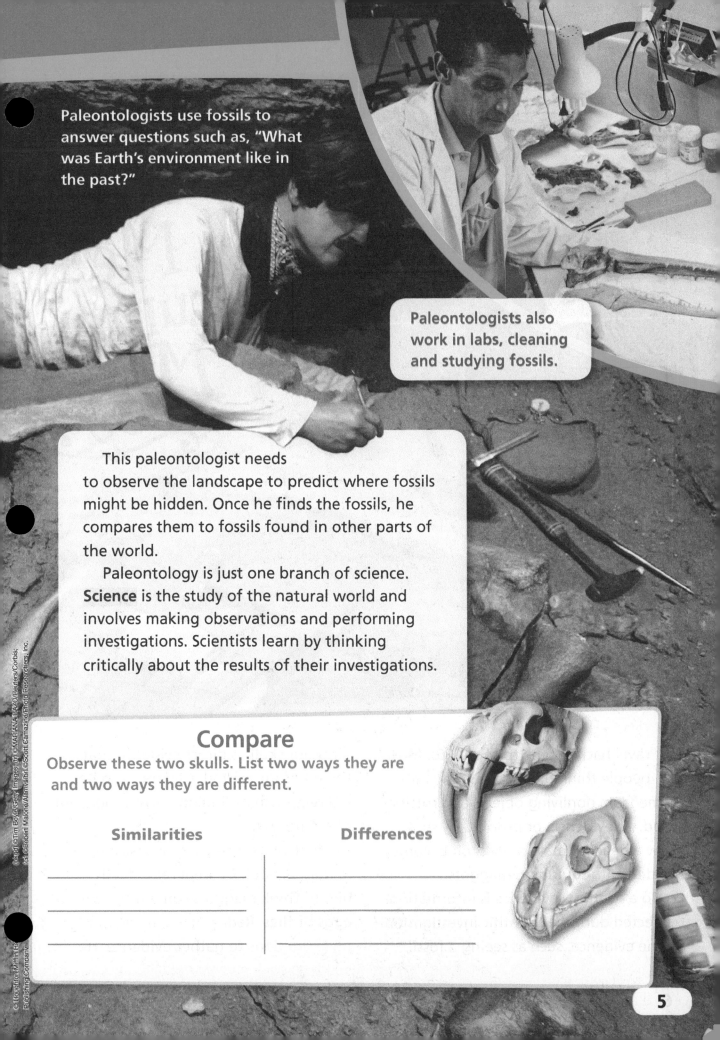

Paleontologists use fossils to answer questions such as, "What was Earth's environment like in the past?"

Paleontologists also work in labs, cleaning and studying fossils.

This paleontologist needs to observe the landscape to predict where fossils might be hidden. Once he finds the fossils, he compares them to fossils found in other parts of the world.

Paleontology is just one branch of science. **Science** is the study of the natural world and involves making observations and performing investigations. Scientists learn by thinking critically about the results of their investigations.

Compare

Observe these two skulls. List two ways they are and two ways they are different.

Similarities

Differences

_____ | _____

_____ | _____

_____ | _____

Prove It!

In the 1600s, there were not many ways to keep meat fresh. Rotting meat quickly filled with squirming, worm-like maggots. Yuck! Where did the maggots come from?

ACTIVE READING On these two pages, circle the examples of evidence.

Rotten Meat turns into Maggots!

▶ Draw a large X through the explanation that was shown *not* to be true.

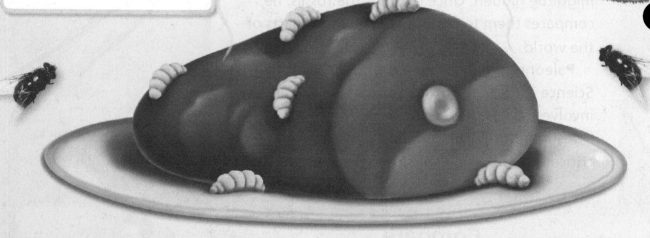

Travel back in time to the 1660s. Most people think flies, worms, and mice come from nonliving objects and rotting food. As evidence, or proof, they show how a dead animal's body soon becomes loaded with squirming maggots.

To a scientist, **evidence** is information collected during a scientific investigation. Some evidence, such as seeing a fossil dinosaur skull, is direct evidence that the dinosaur existed. Evidence can be indirect, such as finding a fossil footprint of a dinosaur.

Meet Dr. Francesco Redi, a scientist in Italy. A book Dr. Redi reads leads him to think maggots come from the eggs of flies. Redi **plans and conducts investigations** to gather evidence. He

6

The meat in the open jar soon became "wormy," while the meat in the sealed jar did not.

Redi placed fresh meat in two jars. He covered one jar and left the other jar uncovered.

▶ Fill in the blanks in this sequence graphic organizer.

Make observations and ask
_____.

↓

Plan and conduct
_____.

↓

Use _____ to make claims.

traps some maggots inside jars with pieces of meat. He watches the maggots turn into adult flies. He observes adult flies laying eggs and more maggots come out of these eggs.

Redi then sets up an experiment. He places meat in several jars. Some jars are sealed and others are left open to the air. Redi observes that only the meat in jars he left open have maggots.

Redi experiments many times over. He tries dead fish, frogs, and snakes. All the evidence supports his claim: Living insects can only come from other living insects.

Maggots Hatch from eggs that flies lay.

A Sticky Trap

Humans are too big to get stuck in a spider's web. But there are some sticky traps you need to avoid when thinking like a scientist.

ACTIVE READING As you read these two pages, turn the main heading into a question in your mind. Then underline sentences that answer the question.

▶ Look at the words in the spider web below. Star the things you *should* use to draw conclusions properly. Cross out the others.

How to Draw Conclusions

Scientists **draw conclusions** from the results of their investigations. Any conclusion must be backed up with evidence. Other scientists judge the conclusion based on how much evidence is given. They also judge how well the evidence supports the conclusion.

Don't jump to conclusions too quickly. That's a sticky trap in science! As Dr. Redi did, repeat your investigations. Think about what you can **infer** from your observations. And then—only then— draw your conclusions.

Suppose you spend a week observing spiders. You might conclude that all spiders build webs to catch their food. This may be true of the spiders you observed, but it's not true of all spiders. Some spiders, such as wolf spiders, hunt for their prey instead.

Opinions

Favorites

Observations

Inferences

Evidence

Feelings

© Houghton Mifflin Harcourt Publishing Company

(bkgd) Colin Zeal/Alamy

8

Observation	
Observation Information collected by using the senses	The insect is stuck in the spider web.
Inference An idea or a conclusion based on an observation	A spider is going to use the bug for food later.
Opinion A personal belief that does not need proof	Spiders are really gross!

Opinion or Evidence?

An **opinion** is a belief or judgment. It doesn't have to be proved, or backed up with evidence. It might be your opinion that spiders are gross and disgusting. Others may disagree, but you are welcome to stick with your opinion!

Personal feelings and opinions should not affect how you do investigations. Nor should they affect your conclusions. It's hard to do, but science is about keeping an open mind. For example, don't ignore evidence just because you don't like what it means.

▶ Write one observation, one inference, and one opinion about what you see in the photo.

Observation	
Inference	
Opinion	

Knowledge Grows

How is a man investigating electricity and wires almost 300 years ago connected to the latest video game release?

Stephen Gray, a scientist born in 1666, was working at home when he discovered that electrical energy could move along a short metal wire. Gray carried his materials to friends' homes. He showed them how the materials worked and, together, they made the wire longer and longer.

Today there are so many ways for scientists to **communicate**, or share, the results of investigations. When scientists communicate clearly, others can repeat their investigations. They can compare their results with those of others. They can expand on one another's ideas. In these ways, scientific knowledge grows.

DATA

Communicate
List several ways you can communicate.

_____

_____

_____

_____

1729 Stephen Gray shows that electrical energy can be carried through a wire.

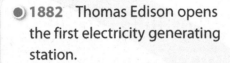

1882 Thomas Edison opens the first electricity generating station.

Knowledge grows when it is communicated. Each science discovery leads to new questions. More is learned and new things are invented.

The first video game was invented in 1958. The inventor was a scientist named William Higinbotham. The reason? To make Visitor's Day at his lab more interesting for the public! Hundreds of people lined up to play the game.

Take a look at the timeline. The science behind Higinbotham's game goes back hundreds of years or more.

1947 The transistor, needed to make radios and computers, is invented.

1953 The first computer is sold.

1958 William Higinbotham invents the first video game.

1967 First handheld calculator invented.

The first arcade games were not very complex.

1971 First coin-operated arcade video games in use.

1972 The first home video game systems are sold.

1977 The first handheld video games are sold.

2015 Video games are quickly moving from systems to cloud-based apps.

The video games of today are fast, complex, and interactive.

Meet Scientists

There are more people working as scientists today than ever before in history. Yet, there are plenty of unanswered questions left for you to answer!

ACTIVE READING As you read these two pages, underline what each type of scientist studies.

Astronomer

Astronomers ask questions about how the universe works. Because novas, black holes, and galaxies are so far away, they use time/space relationships to investigate them. For example, astronomers measure space distances in units called light-years. That's how far light can travel in one Earth year.

 DO THE MATH

Use Fractions

Earth and Mars travel around the sun. Each time Earth makes one complete trip, Mars makes about $\frac{1}{2}$ of its trip.

1. How many trips does Earth make around the sun in the time it takes Mars to make one trip?

_____

2. In the drawing below, put an *X* where Mars will be after Earth completes five trips around the sun.

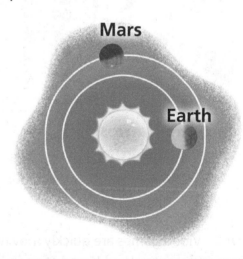

You don't have to be a pro to do astronomy. People have discovered many comets and exploding stars using telescopes in their back yards!

Order

When you **order**, you place objects or events one after another in the correct sequence. Write the numbers *1, 2, 3,* and *4* to show the order of the images below.

_____   _____

Botanist

Botanists investigate questions about plants. For example, some botanists study how environmental conditions affect a plant's life cycle.

Taxonomist

Taxonomists are scientists who identify types of living things and classify them by how they are related. When you classify, you organize objects or events into categories based on specific characteristics.

Classify

Look at the butterflies on this page. What are some ways you could classify them?

_____

_____

_____

Doxopoca agathina
America

Prepona dexamenes
America

Marpesia petrous
America

Sum It Up >>

Read the summary, and fill in the missing words.

The goal of a scientist is to understand the natural world. To do this, a scientist plans and conducts 1. _____ .

Scientists use the 2. _____ they gather to draw 3. _____ .

A good scientist does not let his or her personal beliefs, or 4. _____, influence his or her study.

There are many important skills that scientists use. For example, when scientists 5. _____ , they use their observations and prior knowledge to determine what is happening.

Read each of the statements below. Write the science skill that each student used.

6. Angela made a list of how the two planets were alike.

_____

7. Krystal sorted the rocks into five groups based on their color.

_____

8. Robbie explained the results of his investigation to his classmates.

_____

9. Dmitri noted how the feathers looked and felt.

_____

10. Juan organized the steps of the process from first to last.

_____

Name _____

Vocabulary Review

1 **Draw a line from each term to its definition or description.**

1. evidence*

A. the study of the natural worldthrough investigation

2. inference

B. collecting information by using the senses

3. classify

C. an idea or conclusion based on an observation

4. investigation*

D. facts and information collected over time

5. knowledge

E. to put things into groups

6. opinion*

F. to arrange things by when they happened or by their size

7. observing

G. the sharing of information

8. communication

H. the observations and information that support a claim

9. science*

I. the process of studying or testing something to learn more about it

10. order

J. a belief or a judgment

*Key Lesson Vocabulary

Apply Concepts

2 Compare these two birds. List how they look similar and different.

Similarities:

_____

_____

Differences:

_____

_____

3 Suppose someone tells you they saw a bird never before seen in your state. What kinds of evidence would you ask for?

_____

_____

_____

4 What, in your opinion, is the scariest animal on Earth? How should this affect your investigations?

_____

_____

_____

_____

5 One morning you see an outdoor garbage can tipped over. Plastic bags are torn open. What could you infer?

_____

_____

_____

 **Take It Home!** See *ScienceSaurus®* for more information about scientific investigations

Ask a Zoologist

Q. Do all zoologists work in a zoo?

A. Some, but not all, zoologists work in zoos. Zoologists are scientists who study animals. The word "zoo" comes from the Latin word for animal.

Q. Do zoologists get to play with animals?

A. No. Most zoologists study wild animals in their habitats. They try to observe animals without disturbing them.

Q. Do zoologists get to have wild animals as pets?

A. Wild animals do not make good pets. Zoologists do not take wild animals home. Pets such as cats and dogs have grown used to living with people. Wild animals have not.

Now It's Your Turn!

What question would you ask a zoologist?

_____

_____

_____

_____

Wombats live in Tasmania and southeastern Australia.

Animals That Start with "K"

Some zoologists study animal behavior, or how animals act. A zoologist spotted some interesting behaviors in Australia and wrote these journal entries. Match the sentences with the pictures by entering the day of the journal entry near the picture it describes.

Day 1   This afternoon we saw an adult koala carrying a young koala on its back.

Day 2   Today our team saw a kangaroo. It had a joey (a young kangaroo) in its pouch.

Day 3   Our team saw a kangaroo hopping quickly. We measured its speed—nearly 24 kilometers per hour!

Day 4   This morning we saw a koala. It was eating leaves from a eucalyptus tree.

Day 5   We saw two kangaroos boxing with each other.

Day _____

Day _____

Day _____

Day _____

Day _____

SC.5.N.2.1 Recognize and explain that science is grounded in empirical observations that are testable; explanation must always be linked with evidence.

INQUIRY
LESSON 2

Name _____

How Do Scientists Learn About the Natural World?

Materials
origami weather
predictor sheet
scissors
pencil
weather forecast
from a newspaper

EXPLORE

Scientists learn about the natural world by making observations and performing investigations. In this activity, you'll compare predictions made with—and without—using scientific evidence.

Before You Begin—Preview the Steps

① Tear out the origami weather predictor sheet from your student book. Think about the weather where you live. Write eight different weather predictions. One prediction might be *sunny, windy,* and *hot.*

② Follow the directions to make the origami weather predictor.

③ Use the origami predictor to forecast, or predict, the weather for the next week. Then, find the forecast made by a scientist. Record both forecasts.

④ For one week, compare the actual weather to both forecasts.

Set a Purpose

What will you learn from this experiment?

_____

_____

_____

_____

_____

Think About the Procedure

How did you choose what predictions to write on your origami predictor?

_____

_____

_____

_____

Name _____

Record Your Data

In the table below, record your results.

Date	Origami Prediction	Weather Service Prediction	Actual Weather

Draw Conclusions

Of the two kinds of weather predictions, which one was more likely to be correct? Explain.

_____

_____

_____

_____

_____

Claims • Evidence • Reasoning

1. Interpret your data. Write a claim about how your results would look if you continued your investigation for a month.

_____

2. How do you think the weather service makes its predictions?

_____

3. Provide reasoning for why is it important that scientists make good weather predictions?

_____

_____

_____

4. The line graph shows average October air temperatures in Houston, TX. Can you use this evidence to predict the air temperature in Houston next October?

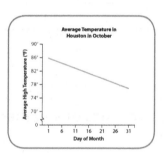

_____

_____

_____

5. What else would you like to find out about how scientists make predictions? Write each idea as a question.

_____

_____

_____

_____

Name _____

Directions

1. Carefully tear this page out of your book.

2. Cut out the square below. You will use it to make your origami weather predictor.

3. On each set of lines, write a weather prediction.

4. Follow the instructions on the back of this page to fold and use your origami weather predictor.

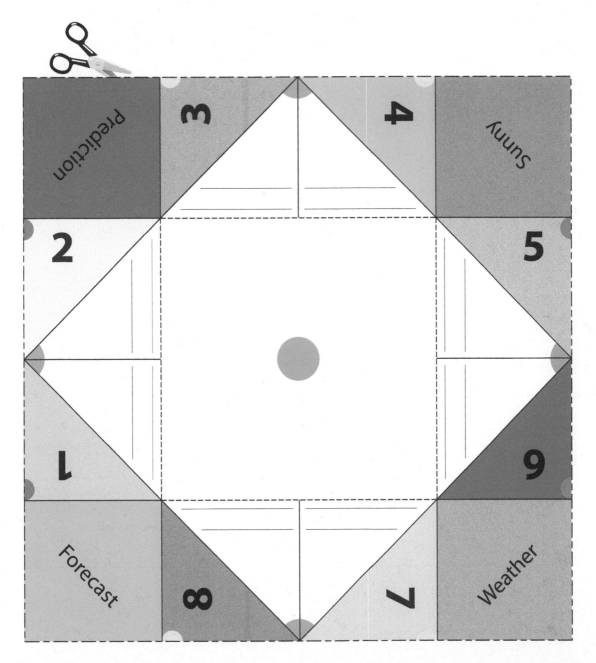

Directions (continued)

5. Fold the blue dots into the blue circle. Turn the paper over, and fold the green dots into the green circle.

6. Fold the paper in half so that the yellow dots touch each other. Make a crease, and unfold the paper. Fold it in half again, so that the pink dots touch each other.

7. Put your fingers under the colorful squares. With your group, make a plan to use this tool to predict the weather.

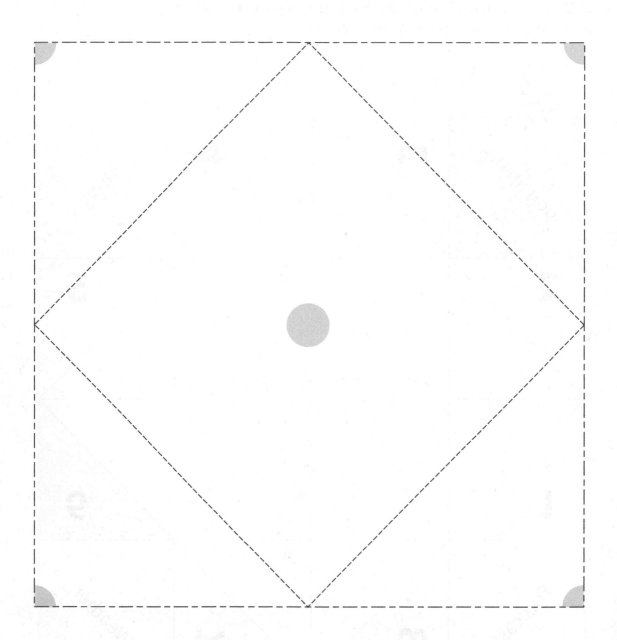

SC.5.N.1.1 ... plan and carry out scientific investigations.... SC.5.N.1.2 Explain the difference between an experiment and other types of scientific investigation. SC.5.N.1.3 Recognize and explain the need for repeated experimental trials. SC.5.N.1.4 Identify a control group and explain its importance.... SC.5.N.1.5 ... scientific investigation frequently does not parallel the steps of "the scientific method."

LESSON 3

ESSENTIAL QUESTION

What Are Some Types of Investigations?

Engage Your Brain

Find the answer to the following question in this lesson and record it here.

What did this scientist do prior to starting her experiment with plants?

_____

_____

_____

_____

ACTIVE READING

Lesson Vocabulary
List the terms. As you learn about each one, make notes in the Interactive Glossary.

_____

_____

_____

_____

Main Ideas
The main idea of a paragraph is the most important idea. The main idea may be stated in the first sentence, or it may be stated elsewhere. Active readers look for main ideas by asking themselves, What is this paragraph mostly about?

A Process for Science

Testing bridge models, mapping a storm's path, searching the sky for distant planets—each of these investigations uses scientific methods.

ACTIVE **READING** As you read these two pages, draw a line under each main idea.

How does the shape of the room affect the sound of a voice?

How does having a cold affect a person's singing?

How high a note can a singer sing?

Can a human voice shatter glass?

Start with a Question

Scientists observe the world and then ask questions that are based on their observations. But not all questions are the same. A good scientific question is one that can be answered by investigation. A scientific investigation always begins with a question.

Plan an Investigation

Once a scientist has a testable question, it is time to plan an investigation. **Scientific methods** are ways that scientists perform investigations. There are many ways that scientists investigate the world. But all scientific methods use logic and reasoning.

▶ Suppose you've just heard an opera singer warm up her voice. Write your own science question about the sounds a singer makes.

_____

_____

Experiments

In an experiment, scientists control all the conditions of the investigation. Scientists study what happens to a group of samples that are all the same except for one difference.

Repeated Observations

Scientists use repeated observation to study processes in nature that they can observe but can't control.

Using Models

Scientists use models when they cannot experiment on the real thing. Models help scientists investigate things that are large (like a planet), expensive (like a bridge), or uncontrollable (like the weather).

Investigations Differ

The method a scientist uses depends on the question he or she is investigating. An **experiment** is an investigation in which all of the conditions are controlled. Models are used to represent real objects or processes. Scientists make repeated observations to study processes in nature without disturbing them.

Drawing Conclusions

Whatever scientific methods are used, scientists will have results they can use to draw conclusions. The conclusions may answer the question they asked before they began. They may point to other questions and many more ideas for investigations.

▶ Write the type of investigation you should use to answer the following questions.

How do different bridge designs react to strong winds?

_____

How fast does the wind blow where a bridge will be built?

_____

Which type of paint works best to keep a bridge from rusting?

_____

Explosive Observations

How does a hurricane affect animals? Are coral reefs dying? How do whales raise their young? These are some science questions that can be answered with repeated observation.

ACTIVE **READING** As you read these two pages, place a star next to three examples of repeated observation.

Old Faithful

Some science questions can only be answered by making observations. This is because some things are just too big, too far away, or too uncontrollable for experiments. However, much can be learned from repeated observation.

In Yellowstone National Park, heated water and steam shoots out of holes in the ground. This is called a geyser. Old Faithful is a famous geyser that erupts about every hour. Observations of the geyser collected over many years can be used to predict when the next eruption will occur. A prediction is a statement, based on information, about a future event.

The time until Old Faithful's next eruption is affected by how long the previous eruption lasted. Suppose the last eruption was at 3:05 p.m. and lasted 3 minutes 15 seconds. Predict when it will erupt next.

How long an eruption lasts	1 min 30 sec	2 min	2 min 30 sec	3 min	3 min 30 sec	4 min	4 min 30 sec	5 min
Time until next eruption	50 min	57 min	65 min	71 min	76 min	82 min	89 min	95 min

The first observation of a whale is often its spout.

Scientists have many questions about whales—the largest mammals on Earth. How long do whales live? How do they communicate? How do they care for their young? How far can they travel in a year? These questions can be answered with repeated observation.

For example, the tail flukes of whales are different from one whale to another. Scientists take photos of the flukes and use them to identify individual whales. Once they know which whale is which, they can recognize them each time they are seen in the ocean.

Predict

Scientists have observed and recorded volcanic eruptions for hundreds of years. The map to the left shows that data. Which location—A, B, or C— is most likely to have a volcanic eruption? _____ Why do you think scientists call this region the "Ring of Fire"?

_____

_____

_____

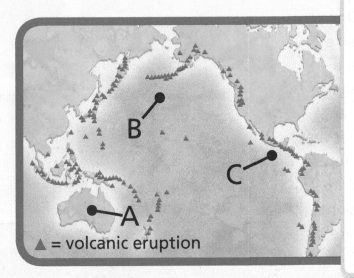

▲ = volcanic eruption

Super Models

How does a bat fly? How might Saturn's rings look close up? How does a heart work? These are some science questions that can be answered with models.

ACTIVE **READING** Circle different types of models that are described on these two pages.

When Modeling Is Needed

When scientists cannot experiment with the real thing, they can use models. Scientific models are needed to understand systems that have many hidden parts, such as an ant colony or the Internet. Scientists draw conclusions and make predictions by studying their models.

The closer the model represents the real thing, the more useful it is. So scientists change their models as they learn more.

Types of Models

Models are made in different ways. One way is to build a physical model. An earthquake shake table with model buildings on it is a physical model. Another way is to program computer simulation models. Scientists can speed up time in computer models so that they can see what might happen long in the future. Drawing diagrams and flow charts is a third way to make models. These two-dimensional models can be used to show how ideas are related.

Complex models can be made on a computer. This model shows where the most damage would occur if an earthquake were to strike.

Earthquakes are difficult to predict, and they can cause damage. New structures are designed to prevent damage.

Scientists build "shake tables" that model the motion of real earthquakes. This photo shows two types of houses being tested. Which house seems to be safer in an earthquake?

You can model the effects of an earthquake, using gelatin for the ground and buildings made of blocks.

Use Models

How is an earthquake model made of gelatin like a real earthquake? How is it unlike a real earthquake?

Alike: _____

_____

Different: _____

_____

_____

How to Excel *in* Experimentation

You're enjoying a frozen juice pop. The heat of your tongue melts the pop. As you slurp the liquid, you think about how different substances freeze.

ACTIVE **READING** As you read the next four pages, circle lesson vocabulary each time it is used.

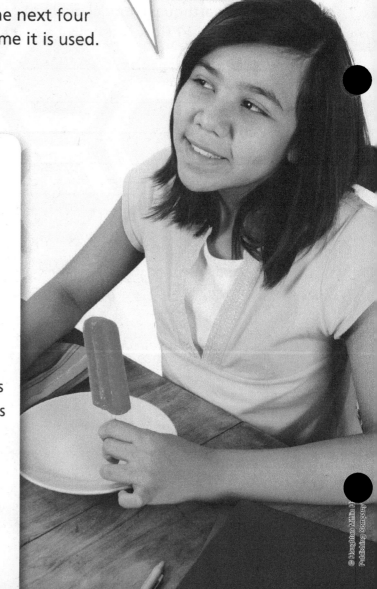

I know that water freezes at 0 degrees Celsius. How does adding other substances to water affect the temperature at which it freezes?

Ask Questions

You know a freezer is cold enough to freeze water. You also know that juice is mostly water. You ask "Does adding substances to water affect its freezing point?"

Many science questions, including this one, can be answered by doing experiments. An **experiment** is a procedure used to test a *hypothesis*. It's a good idea to make some observations before stating a hypothesis. For example, you might put a small amount of orange juice in a freezer. Then you'd check it every few minutes to look for changes.

Hypothesize

A hypothesis is a statement that can be tested and will explain what can happen in an investigation. In the case of the freezing question, you think about what you already know. You can also talk to other people. And you can do research such as asking an expert.

You find out that the freezing point and melting point of a material should be the same temperature. An expert suggests that it is better to measure the melting point than the freezing point.

Design an Experiment

A well-designed experiment has two or more setups. This allows you to compare results among them. For the freezing/melting experiment, each setup will be a cup of liquid.

A **variable** is any condition in an experiment that can be changed. In most experiments, there are many, many variables to consider. The trick is to keep all variables the same in each setup, except one. That one variable is the one you will test.

Among the setups should be one called the control. The **control** is the setup to which you will compare all the others.

You've decided to dissolve different substances in water and freeze them. Then you plan to take them out of the freezer and use a thermometer to check their temperatures as they melt.

Hypothesize

Fill in the blank in the hypothesis.

Any substance dissolved in water will _____ the temperature at which the mixture freezes and melts.

Identify and Control Variables

When you **identify and control variables**, you determine which conditions should stay the same and which one should be changed. Circle the variable that will be tested. Underline the variables that will remain the same.

- the kinds of cups
- the amount of water
- the material that is dissolved in the water
- the temperature of the freezer
- the types of thermometers
- the amount of time you leave the cups in the freezer

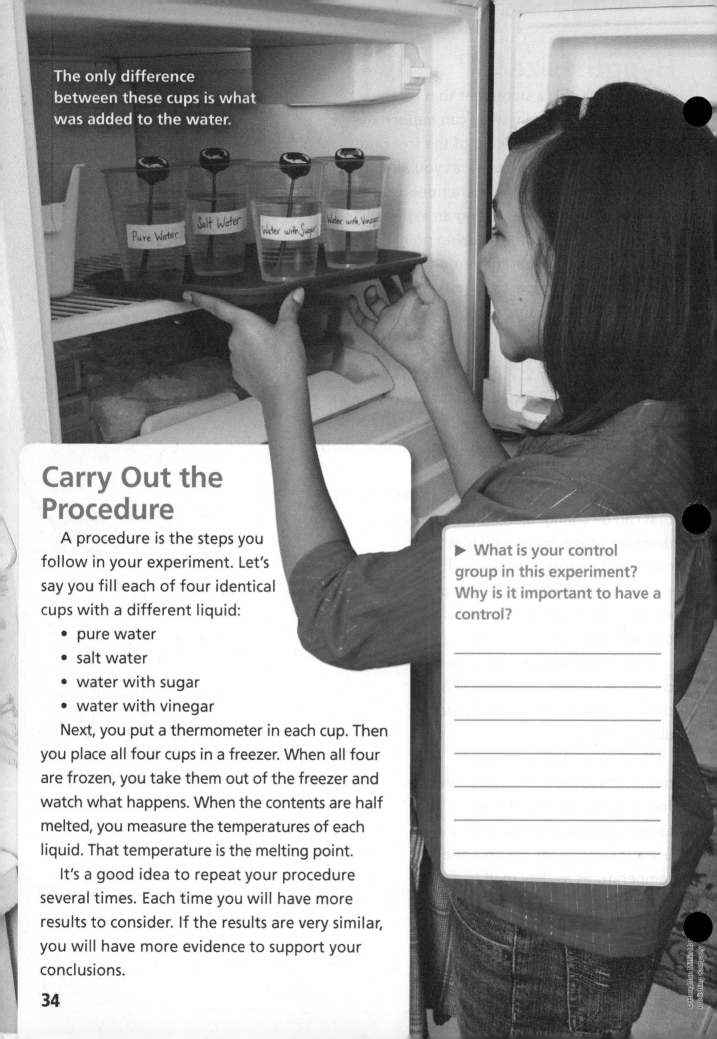

The only difference between these cups is what was added to the water.

Pure Water

Salt Water

Water with Sugar

Water with Vinegar

Carry Out the Procedure

A procedure is the steps you follow in your experiment. Let's say you fill each of four identical cups with a different liquid:

- pure water
- salt water
- water with sugar
- water with vinegar

Next, you put a thermometer in each cup. Then you place all four cups in a freezer. When all four are frozen, you take them out of the freezer and watch what happens. When the contents are half melted, you measure the temperatures of each liquid. That temperature is the melting point.

It's a good idea to repeat your procedure several times. Each time you will have more results to consider. If the results are very similar, you will have more evidence to support your conclusions.

▶ What is your control group in this experiment? Why is it important to have a control?

_____

_____

_____

_____

_____

_____

_____

Record and Analyze Data

You could write down your observations as sentences. Or you could make a table to fill in. No matter how you do it, make sure you record correctly. Check twice or have a team member check.

Once the experiment is completed and the data recorded, you can analyze your results. If your data is in the form of numbers, math skills will come in handy. For example, in the data table below, you'll need to know how to write, read, and compare decimals.

Melting Point Experiment	
Substance	Melting Point (°C)
Pure water	0.0
Salt water	−3.7
Sugar water	−1.8
Vinegar water	−1.1

Draw Conclusions and Evaluate the Hypothesis

You draw conclusions based on your results. Remember that all conclusions must be supported with evidence. The more evidence you have, the stronger your conclusion.

Once you've reached a conclusion, look at your hypothesis. Decide if the hypothesis is supported or not. If not, try rethinking your hypothesis. Then design a new experiment to test it. That's what scientists do—build on what they learn.

Draw Conclusions

What conclusion can you draw based on this experiment?

_____

_____

_____

_____

_____

_____

Special Delivery: Data Displays

Once you've completed a science investigation, you'll want to share it. What's the best way to communicate the data you collected?

As part of their investigations, scientists collect, record, and interpret data. There is more than one way to display, or communicate, your data. Some kinds of displays are more suited to certain kinds of data than others.

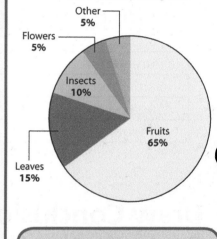

Food Eaten by Orangutans

Other 5%
Flowers 5%
Insects 10%
Leaves 15%
Fruits 65%

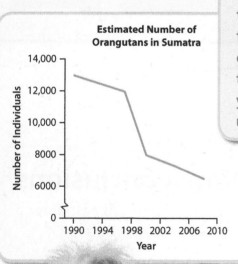

Estimated Number of Orangutans in Sumatra

Number of Individuals

14,000
12,000
10,000
8000
6000
0

1990 1994 1998 2002 2006 2010

Year

> Line graphs are suited to show change over time, especially small changes. If you want to show how much you grow each year, use a line graph.

> Circle graphs are suited to comparing parts to the whole. If you want to show fractions or percents, use a circle graph.

Orangutan Using Tool to Feed

> Diagrams are suited to show data that do not include numbers. This diagram shows how an orangutan uses a tool to eat seeds in fruit.

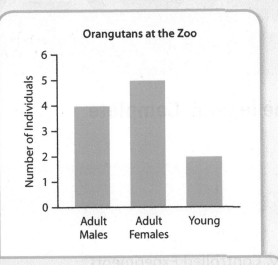

Orangutans at the Zoo

Bar graphs are suited to compare things or groups of things. When your data are in categories, use a bar graph.

 DO THE **MATH**

Draw a Bar Graph

Draw a bar graph on this page. Use the data in the table below. Decide whether you want the bars to be vertical or horizontal. Carefully label the intervals on each axis. Draw the bars. Then title and label all the parts of your graph.

Number of Orangutans Counted	
Day	Number
Monday	7
Tuesday	13
Wednesday	10
Thursday	2
Friday	6

Sum It Up »

The outline below is a summary of the lesson. Complete the outline.

I. Scientific Methods

    A. All start with a question

    B. Investigations differ

        1. experiments

        2. **①** _____

        3. **②** _____

    C. All have results from which to

        ③ _____

II. Repeated Observations

    A. Some things are just too big, too far away, or too uncontrollable for experiments

    B. Examples

        1. volcanoes

        2. **④** _____

III. Using Models

    A. Needed to understand systems that have many hidden parts

    B. Types of models

        1. diagrams and flow charts

        2. **⑤** _____

        _____

        3. **⑥** _____

IV. Controlled Experiments

    A. Ask questions

    B. Hypothesize

    C. **⑦** _____

    D. Carry out the procedure

    E. **⑧** _____

    F. Draw conclusions

V. Organizing and Displaying Data

    A. Data displays help communicate

    B. Kinds of data displays

        1. circle graphs

        2. **⑨** _____

        3. **⑩** _____

        4. **⑪** _____

Brain Check

Name _____

Vocabulary Review

1 **Use the clues to fill in the missing letters of the words.**

1. _____ t i ___ ___ h o __   all the ways scientists do investigations

2. _ o _____   These should be as similar as possible to the real thing.

3. ____ t r __   the part of an experiment used to compare all the other groups

4. _ s _ _____ n _   what scientists do that is the basis for their investigations

5. _____ b __   any condition in an experiment that can be changed

6. _ i __ __ a __   a type of graph suited to show change over time

7. _ y _____ e ____   a statement that can be tested and that explains what you think will happen in an experiment

8. ___ o ____ u __   the steps you follow in your experiment

9. p _____ t   to use patterns in observations to say what may happen next

10. _____ m e __   an investigation that is controlled

Apply Concepts

2 For each question, state which kind of investigation works best: repeated observations, using models, or controlled experiments. Then explain how you would do the investigation.

What kinds of birds visit a feeder at different times of the year?

_____

_____

_____

_____

Does hot water or cold water boil faster?

_____

_____

_____

_____

What are the parts of an elevator and how does it work?

_____

_____

_____

How does the length of a kite's tail affect the way it flies?

_____

_____

_____

_____

3 Ryan hypothesizes that darker colors heat up faster. He places a thermometer inside a red wool sock, a green cotton glove, and a black nylon hat. What's wrong with his procedure?

_____

_____

_____

_____

Take It Home! Help your family enjoy a healthy snack. Design an experiment to find out if coating apple slices in lemon juice can stop them from turning brown. What is your control group in this experiment? What are your variables? Why is it important to identify a control? Perform your experiment and record your results.

SC.5.N.1.2 Explain the difference between an experiment and other types of scientific investigation. SC.5.N.1.5 Recognize and explain that authentic scientific investigation frequently does not parallel the steps of "the scientific method."

Name _____

ESSENTIAL QUESTION

How Do You Perform a Controlled Experiment?

Materials

small ball
meter stick
various floor
surfaces

EXPLORE

A controlled experiment takes thought, care, and time. Let's see if you have what it takes!

Before You Begin—Preview the Steps

1. Place a meter stick against a wall so that the 0-cm mark touches the floor. Record what the floor is made from.

2. Drop the ball from the 100-cm mark. Record the height the ball bounces. Do this five times.

3. Find two more types of surfaces to test. Repeat Steps 1 and 2.

4. For each surface, find the average of the five trials.

© Houghton Mifflin Harcourt Publishing Company

Set a Purpose

What will you learn from this experiment?

_____

_____

_____

Think About the Procedure

What is the tested variable in this experiment?

_____

Why is it important to control all other variables in an experiment?

_____

_____

Each time you try the same test, it is called a trial. Why is it important to do repeated trials of this experiment?

_____

_____

_____

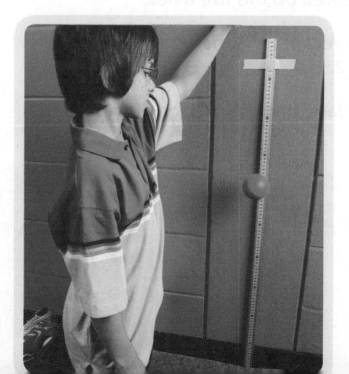

© Houghton Mifflin Harcourt Publishing Company

Name _____

Record Your Data

In the table below, record your results.

Surface Material	Height Ball Bounced					
	Trial 1	Trial 2	Trial 3	Trial 4	Trial 5	Average

Draw Conclusions

What can you conclude based on your experiment?

_____

_____

_____

_____

Claims • Evidence • Reasoning

1. Think about the materials the ball bounced on. Make a claim regarding how their characteristics affected the height of the bounce. Provide evidence to support your claim and explain how the evidence supports the claim.

_____

_____

_____

_____

2. What other floor materials could you test? What evidence could you use to predict the results?

_____

_____

_____

3. Tennis is played on three types of surfaces: grass, packed clay, and hard courts. Hard courts are often made from asphalt, the black road surface material, with paint on top. What evidence could you use to predict how these surfaces would affect ball bounces? Then, do some research. Find the pros and cons of each type of surface.

_____

_____

_____

4. What else would you like to find out about how balls bounce?

_____

_____

_____

_____

SC.5.N.1.1 Define a problem, use appropriate reference materials to support scientific understanding, plan and carry out scientific investigations of various types such as: systematic observations, experiments requiring the identification of variables, collecting and organizing data, interpreting data in charts, tables, and graphics, analyze information, make predictions, and defend conclusions.

LESSON 5

ESSENTIAL **QUESTION**

What Are Some Science Tools?

Engage Your Brain

Find the answer to the following question in this lesson and write it here.

This scientific equipment is filled with liquids. What tools can scientists use to measure the volume of a liquid?

_____

_____

_____

ACTIVE READING

Lesson Vocabulary
List the terms. As you learn about each one, make notes in the Interactive Glossary.

_____

_____

_____

_____

Compare and Contrast
Many ideas in this lesson are connected because they explain comparisons and contrasts—how things are alike and different. Active readers stay focused on comparisons and contrasts when they ask themselves, How are these things alike? How are they different?

Field Trips

If you like school field trips, you might want to become a field scientist. Field scientists travel around the world studying science in the wild. They pack their tools and take them along.

ACTIVE READING As you read these two pages, box the names of all the science tools.

Field scientists go "on location" to investigate the natural world. Their investigations are often in the form of repeated observations. They use tools to increase the power of their senses. Their choices of tools depend on the questions they ask.

Collecting Net

What kinds of animals swim near the shore of a pond? A scientist might use a collecting net and an observation pan to answer this question. By carefully pulling the net through the water, they can catch small animals without harming them.

Hand Lens

How does an ant move? How does it use its mouthparts? A hand lens might help answer these questions. Hold the hand lens near your eye. Then move your other hand to bring the object into view. Move the object back and forth until it is in sharp focus.

DO THE **MATH**

Estimate by Sampling

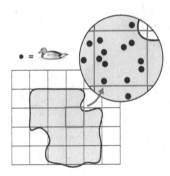

Scientists photograph ducks from a plane and then draw a grid over the photo. How many ducks do you estimate are on the whole lake?

_____

Why might your estimate differ from the actual number of ducks?

_____

_____

_____

Cameras

What do lion fish eat? How do they catch their food? To investigate, a scientist might use an underwater video camera. Cameras help scientists record events.

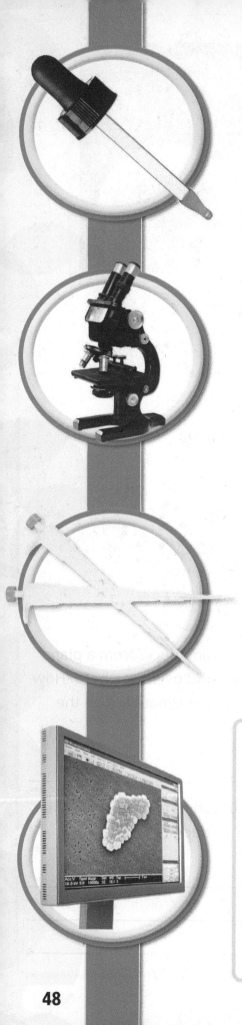

Into the Lab

What's living in a drop of pond water? Lots of tiny critters! Some behave like animals. Others are like plants. All are too small to be seen with only a hand lens.

ACTIVE **READING** As you read these two pages, draw lines connecting the pairs of tools being compared to each other.

Science tools can be heavy and expensive. If you want to observe the tiniest pond life, you'll need science tools that are too big or too delicate to be carried into the field. For example, scientists use computers to record and analyze data, construct models, and communicate with other scientists.

Use Numbers

Some tools help scientists count things. Some scientists estimate, while others perform complex mathematical calculations. All scientists must be comfortable **using numbers**.

▶ To find the magnification of a light microscope, multiply the power of the eyepiece lens by the power of the objective lens. The letter X stands for how many times bigger objects appear.

Eyepiece Magnification	Objective Magnification	Total Magnification
10X	40X	
15X	60X	
8X	100X	

Light Microscope

The tiny living things in pond water are **microscopic**, or too small to see with just your eyes. A light microscope magnifies things, or makes them look bigger. The object to be viewed is placed on a clear slide. Light passes through the object and two lenses. You look through the eyepiece and turn knobs to focus an image.

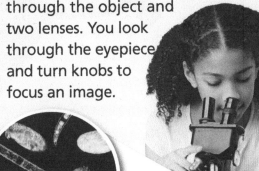

Dropper

A dropper is a tube with a rubber bulb on one end. Squeeze the bulb and then dip the tip into a liquid. Release the bulb, and the liquid will be sucked up the tube. When you slowly squeeze the bulb, the liquid drops out.

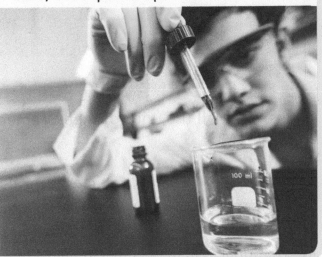

Electron Microscope

Light microscopes have been around for 500 years. But technology, or people's use of tools, has improved. Today a scanning electron microscope (SEM) can magnify an object up to one million times. The SEM shoots a beam of electrons at the object. An image of the surface of the object appears on a computer screen.

Pipette

A pipette is a tool like a dropper, but it's more exact. It is used to add or remove very small amounts of liquids. Pipettes often have marks on the side to measure volume. One kind of pipette makes drops so tiny that they can only be seen with a scanning electron microscope!

Measuring Up

What do a digit, a palm, a hand, a dram, a peck, a rod, and a stone have in common? They all are, or were at one time, units of measurement!

ACTIVE READING As you read the next four pages, circle all the units of measurement.

When you **measure**, you make observations involving numbers and units. Today most countries use the International System (SI) units in daily life. If you were to visit these countries, you'd purchase fruit or cheese by the *kilogram*. In the United States, most everyday measurements use units from the time when English colonists lived in America.

However, scientists around the world—including those in the United States—use the SI, or metric system.

The metric system is based on multiples of 10. In the metric system, base units are divided into smaller units using prefixes such as *milli-, centi-,* and *deci-.* Base units are changed to bigger units using prefixes such as *deca-* and *kilo-.*

Measuring Length

Length is the distance between two points. The base metric unit of length is the *meter*. Rulers, metersticks, and tape measures are tools used to measure length.

A caliper can be used to measure the distance between the two sides of an object.

Measuring Time

Time describes how long events take. The base unit of time is the second. Larger units are the minute, the hour, and the day. Smaller units include the millisecond and microsecond. Clocks, stopwatches, timers, and calendars are some of the tools used to measure time.

Measure Your Science Book

Use a metric tool and units to measure the length, width, and thickness of your science book.

Length: _____

Width: _____

Thickness: _____

Measuring Temperature

Temperature describes how hot or cold something is. Thermometers are used to measure temperature. Scientists measure temperature in degrees Celsius. So do most other people around the world. In the United States, degrees Fahrenheit are used to report the weather, to measure body temperatures, and in cooking.

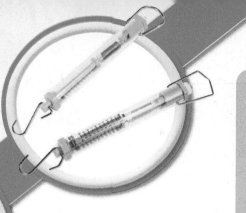

With this balance, you can directly compare the masses of two objects. Put one object in each pan. The pan that sinks lower contains the greater mass.

Pan Balance

A **balance** is a tool used to measure mass. *Mass* is the amount of matter in an object. The base unit of mass is the kilogram. One kilogram equals 1,000 grams.

To measure in grams, place an object in one pan.

Always carry a balance by holding its base.

Add gram masses to the other pan until the two pans are balanced. Then add the values of the gram masses to find the total mass.

This pan balance has drawers where the masses are stored.

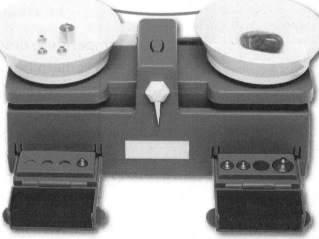

Three Beams

A triple-beam balance measures mass more exactly than the pan balance. It has one pan and three beams. To find the number of grams, move the sliders until the beam balances.

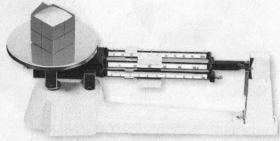

Digital Mass

An electronic balance calculates the mass of an object for you. It displays an object's mass on a screen.

How Strong?

A **spring scale** is a tool used to measure force. Force is a push or a pull. When an object hangs down from the scale, the force of gravity, or weight, is measured. When the spring scale is used to pull an object, it measures the force needed to move the object. Either way, the base unit is called a newton.

▶ **Draw lines to match the tools to what they measure and the units.**

Tool	What It Measures	Units
	• force •	• seconds, minutes, hours, days, years, etc.
	• temperature •	• grams, milligrams, kilograms, etc.
	• length •	• newtons
	• mass •	• degrees Celsius, degrees Fahrenheit
	• time •	• meters, kilometers, millimeters, etc.

More Measuring

It's a hot day and you're thirsty. How much lemonade would you like? 1,000 milliliters or 1,000 cubic centimeters? Not sure? Read on!

ACTIVE READING As you read the next two pages, circle important words that are defined, and underline their definitions.

Units of Volume

Volume is the amount of space a solid, liquid, or gas takes up. There are two base metric units for measuring volume. A *cubic meter* is one meter long, one meter high, and one meter wide. The *liter* is the base unit often used for measuring the volume of liquids. You're probably familiar with liters because many drinks are sold in 1-liter or 2-liter bottles. These two metric units of volume are closely related. There are 1,000 liters (L) in one cubic meter (m^3).

▶ One cubic centimeter (cm^3) is equal to 1 milliliter (mL). Both are equal to about 20 drops from a dropper. Which is greater—1,000 mL or 1,000 cm3?

1 cm

1 cm

1 cm

Finding Volume

You can find the volume of a rectangular prism by multiplying length times width times height. To find the volume of a liquid, use a measuring cup, beaker, or graduated cylinder. Use water to find the volume of an irregular solid. Put water in a graduated cylinder. Note the volume. Then drop the object in and note the new volume. Subtract the two numbers to find the volume of the object.

> The surface of a liquid in a graduated cylinder is curved. This curve is called a *meniscus*. Always measure volume at the bottom of the meniscus.

Accurate Measurements

When a measurement is close to the true size, it is **accurate**. Try to measure as accurately as you can with the tools you have. Make sure a tool is not broken and that you know how to use it properly. Also pay attention to the units on the tools you use. Accurate measurements are important when doing science investigations, when baking, and when taking medicines.

Follow these tips to improve your accuracy:

- ✓ Handle each tool properly.
- ✓ Use each tool the same way every time. For example, read the measurement at eye level.
- ✓ Measure to the smallest place value the tool allows.
- ✓ Measure twice.
- ✓ Record your measurements carefully, including the units.

▶ Write the math sentence for finding the volume of the toy.

_____

55

Sum It Up »

When you're done, use the answer key to check and revise your work.

There are many kinds of tools that scientists use. Tools help scientists observe, measure, and study things in the natural world.
Fill in the blank boxes with examples of tools that scientists use.

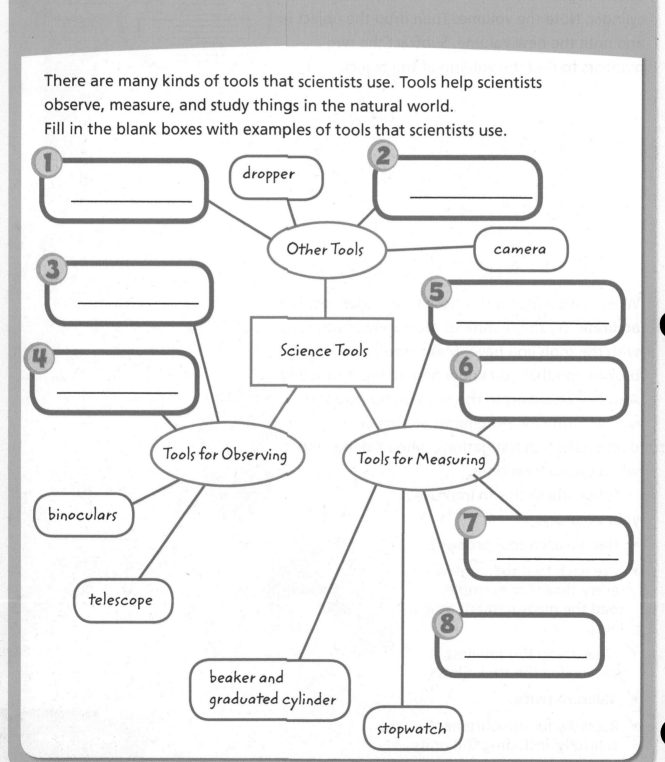

1 _____

dropper

2 _____

Other Tools

camera

3 _____

5 _____

Science Tools

4 _____

6 _____

Tools for Observing

Tools for Measuring

binoculars

7 _____

telescope

8 _____

beaker and graduated cylinder

stopwatch

Brain Check

Name _____

Vocabulary Review

1 **Put the scrambled letters in order to spell a science term.**

1. **treem** ◯_ _◯_ _   A metric unit of length

2. **amrg** _ _◯_   A metric unit of mass

3. **rdsgeee seCisul** _ _ _ _ _ _◯ _ _ _ _ _◯_   A metric unit for temperature

4. **taceurca** _ _ _ _◯_ _◯   A measurement close to the true size

5. **townne** _ _ _◯_ _   A unit used to measure force

6. **trile** _ _ _ _◯   A metric unit of volume

7. **pignrs ecsla** _ _ _ _ _ _◯_   A tool used to measure force

8. **nap cablane** _◯_ _ _ _ _ _ _ _   A tool used to measure mass

9. **dceson** ◯_ _ _ _ _   A metric unit of time

10. **veumol** _ _ _◯_ _   The amount of space a solid, liquid, or gas takes up

11. **tagurdade lycnidre** _ _◯_ _ _ _ _ _ _ _ _ _ _◯_   A tool used to measure volume

Riddle: Place the circled letters in order to solve the riddle below.

Why did the captain ask for a balance?
He wanted to _ _ _ _ _ _ _ _ _
the mass of the _ _ _ _ _ _ _ _ _ _ .

Apply Concepts

2 Tell how you use one or more of these tools to investigate each question.

How are two fossil teeth similar and different?

_____

_____

_____

Which kinds of butterflies are found in a field?

_____

_____

_____

What do scientists already know about the bottom of the ocean?

_____

_____

_____

Does the mass of a ball affect how far it rolls?

_____

_____

_____

3 Identify what each tool measures and the metric units it uses.

_____   _____   _____

_____   _____   _____

At your school or public library, find a book about how scientists work or the tools they use. Read and discuss the book with your family. Prepare a brief summary to present to your classmates.

SC.5.N.1.1 . . . plan and carry out scientific investigations of various types such as: systematic observation . . . SC.5.N.1.2 Explain the difference between an experiment and other types of scientific investigation.

INQUIRY
LESSON 6

Name _____

ESSENTIAL QUESTION

How Can Scientists Learn from Observations?

Materials

soil sample
white paper
measuring spoons
hand lens
measuring cup
coffee filter
pan balance
mesh sieve
small container
graduated cylinder
paper bag

EXPLORE

Sometimes you can't do an experiment. But you can still answer by investigating. In this activity, you'll learn about soils by simply making observations.

Before You Begin—Preview the Steps

1. On a sheet of white paper, place a teaspoon of soil. Use the hand lens to observe it. Record your observations.

2. Place 100 mL of soil in a coffee filter. Find and record its mass. Place the filter in a mesh sieve above a small container. Fill a graduated cylinder with 100 mL of water. Slowly pour water onto the soil. When the soil can no longer hold water, record the amount you poured.

3. Place 200 mL of soil in a paper bag, and record the mass of the bag. Place the bag in a dry place for a week. Then find the bag's mass again.

4. Compile your data in a class data table. In a small group, discuss ways to classify the soil samples.

Set a Purpose

What will you learn from this investigation?

_____

_____

_____

Think About the Procedure

What planning must I do before this investigation?

_____

_____

_____

_____

What tools are used in this investigation? What measurements, if any, are taken with them?

_____

_____

_____

_____

_____

Name _____

Record Your Data

In the space below, record your results.

Soil sample: _____

My observations:

Amount of water held by
100 mL of soil: _____

Mass before drying: _____

Mass after drying: _____

Draw Conclusions

Compare your data with the data from other groups. What can you conclude?

_____

_____

_____

_____

_____

Claims • Evidence • Reasoning

1. Make a claim about why it is important that soils be able to hold some water.

_____

_____

2. Why would a farmer want to know about the soil on his or her farm? Explain your reasoning.

_____

_____

_____

3. How was this investigation different from a controlled experiment?

_____

_____

_____

4. Make a claim about why it was important to know the mass of the soil before it was dried for one week.

_____

_____

_____

5. What else would you like to find out about different types of soils?

_____

_____

_____

Name _____

Vocabulary Review

Use the terms in the box to complete the sentences.

> balance
> control
> experiment
> variable

1. An investigation in which all conditions are controlled

   is a(n) _____.

2. Jane wants to measure the mass of a rock.

   The tool she should use is a(n) _____.

3. Any condition in an experiment that can be changed is

   a(n) _____.

4. The setup to which you compare all the others in an experiment

   is the _____.

Science Concepts

Fill in the letter of the choice that best answers the question.

5. Gabrielle counts the number of people who visit the community pool each day for 1 week. She displays her data using a bar graph.

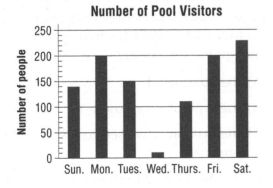

Number of Pool Visitors

How many more people did Gabrielle observe at the pool on Sunday than on Thursday?

(A) 20   (C) 75

(B) 30   (D) 100

6. Observations are made using our five senses. We can then use those observations to draw conclusions. Which of the following is an example of a conclusion?

(F) "The object is flat."

(G) "The flower smells like mint."

(H) "Crickets chirp to attract mates."

(I) "The food is both sweet and salty."

7. Asa watches his mom rub soap on her finger to help her get a ring unstuck. He thinks that soap must reduce friction. He designs an investigation to test his theory. He pulls a weight across a board and records the force with a spring scale. He then puts soap on the board and pulls the weight again. Which of the following variables is Asa measuring?

(A) the speed with which the weight is pulled

(B) the amount of weight being pulled

(C) the force needed to pull the weight

(D) the type of surface the weight is being pulled across

8. Erica is learning how to accurately read a thermometer. She places the following thermometer in the sun for 1 hour.

What temperature does Erica read on the thermometer?

(F) 38° Celsius

(G) 100° Celsius

(H) 38° Fahrenheit

(I) 105° Fahrenheit

9. Different systems for making measurements use different units. Which system of measurement is generally used by scientists?

(A) customary
(C) Imperial
(B) English
(D) metric

10. Joshua has been growing plants that receive ½ cup of water two times per week. Now, he wants to see what happens to the plants when the amount of water is reduced, as shown in the chart.

Plant	Amount of water
1	no water
2	½ cup once every two weeks
3	½ cup once per week
4	½ cup two times per week

Which plant is the control?

(F) 1
(H) 2
(G) 3
(I) 4

11. Scientists want to determine if walls that are painted a certain color will raise a person's blood pressure. They plan to set up four rooms. Which variable should change in each room?

(A) the color used

(B) the type of room used

(C) the instruments used to test the blood pressure

(D) the amount of time the person spends in the room

Name _____

12. Sandy observes the phases of the moon during a two-week period. She sketches and labels the phases and shares her drawings with the class. Which statement best describes Sandy's investigation?

(F) It involves modeling.

(G) It involves experimentation.

(H) It involves repeated observations.

(I) It involves both experimentation and repeated observations.

13. Scientists include controls in their experiments. Why is a control important?

(A) It helps scientists share results.

(B) It helps scientists form their first hypothesis.

(C) It helps scientists record their repeated observations.

(D) It helps scientists compare their results to a standard.

14. A teacher writes the following note on a student's experimental design: "You did not identify and control variables." Why is it important to identify and control variables?

(F) because a scientist must observe data

(G) because a scientist must form a hypothesis

(H) because a scientist must know which variable causes change

(I) because a scientist must know which variable to use for making a model

15. Michael rides a bike made by Company A. Luis rides a bike made by Company B. How can Michael and Luis determine in a scientific way whose bike has tires that last longer?

(A) Read information about the tires from each manufacturer.

(B) Ask ten classmates who ride each bike which tires last longer.

(C) Have each student ride their own bike for 25 days, then compare the tires.

(D) Use a machine to test the bikes in the same way for 25 days, then compare the tires.

16. A doctor says that drinking two glasses of milk in the morning will give students more energy. Which of the following would be good scientific evidence for or against the doctor's claim?

(F) a brochure from the doctor stating the benefits of milk

(G) data from scientific investigations about drinking milk in the morning

(H) a TV advertisement that drinking milk in the morning gives people plenty of energy

(I) statements from five people about how drinking milk in the morning gives them energy

17. When Andrew conducts an investigation, he repeats the investigation several times. Why does Andrew do this?

(A) to create inventions

(B) to get consistent results

(C) to do the work very safely

(D) to be sure the work is correct

Apply Inquiry and Review the Big Idea

Write the answers to these questions.

18. Aaliya knows that sliced apples turn brown when left out in the open air. She also knows that pouring certain liquids on them will keep this from happening. Aaliya thinks that water, ginger ale, or lemon juice may do the trick. How could Aaliya set up an experiment to gather evidence to support a claim about these liquids? What are the variables? What will she use as a control?

_____

_____

_____

_____

_____

_____

_____

_____

19. Yamil is observing a fossil insect preserved in amber.

What can Yamil learn about the fossil through observation? What tools might she use to make her observations?

_____

_____

_____

_____

The Engineering Process

The Practice of Science

These bags of sugar are being prepared to be sent to stores.

I Wonder Why

Mixers, rollers, cutters, tumblers, and hoppers, all run by electricity! I wonder why it takes so many machines to make sugar?

Here's Why

Food processing relies on technology. Machines produce treats that always have the same taste, color, smell, and size. When you buy sugar, you know exactly what you're getting!

Essential Questions and Florida Benchmarks

Science Notebook

Before you begin each lesson, write your thoughts about the Essential Question.

Photo credit: text to come

© Houghton Mifflin Harcourt Publishing Company

SC.5.N.1.1 Define a problem, use appropriate reference materials to support scientific understanding, plan and carry out scientific investigations of various types such as: systematic observations, experiments requiring the identification of variables, collecting and organizing data, interpreting data in charts, tables, and graphics, analyze information, make predictions, and defend conclusions. SC.5.N.1.5 Recognize and explain that authentic scientific investigation frequently does not parallel the steps of "the scientific method."

LESSON **1**

ESSENTIAL QUESTION

What Is the Design Process?

Engage Your Brain

Find the answer to the following question in this lesson and write it here.

What are the steps for designing technology such as the robot arm you see here?

_____

_____

_____

_____

_____

_____

📖 ACTIVE **READING**

Lesson Vocabulary
List the terms. As you learn about each one, make notes in the Interactive Glossary.

_____   _____

_____   _____

Problem–Solution
Ideas in this lesson may be connected by a problem–solution relationship. Active readers mark a problem with a *P* to help them stay focused on the way information is organized. When multiple solutions are described, they mark each solution with an *S*.

Works of Ingenuity

Did you brush your teeth this morning? Did you run water from a faucet? Did you ride to school in a car or bus? If you did any of those things, you used a product of engineering.

ACTIVE READING As you read these pages, underline the names of engineered devices.

Engineered devices, such as computers, help us solve many problems. Engineers use computers and hand-drawn diagrams to plan their designs.

Engineers are problem solvers. They invent or improve products that help us meet our needs. Engineers use their knowledge of science and mathematics to find solutions to everyday problems. This process is called **engineering**.

From the start of each day, we use the products of engineering. Engineered devices are found all around us. They include simple tools and complex machines.

Engineers work in many fields. Some design and test new kinds of materials. Some work in factories or on farms. Others work in medical laboratories. Engineers also design the engines that may one day fly people to Mars!

Devices like this CT scanning machine allow doctors to see inside the body without the need for surgery.

Sometimes engineers design devices with many purposes in mind.

Engineering Diary

List some of the engineered devices you use every day. Explain the need that each device meets.

Device	Need

The Right Tool for the Right Job

When you see or hear the word *technology*, you may think of things such as flat screen TVs, computers, and cell phones. But technology includes more than just modern inventions.

ACTIVE **READING** As you read these two pages, underline sentences that describe how technology affects our lives.

Stone tools, the wheel, and candles were invented a long time ago. They are examples of technology. **Technology** is any device that people use to meet their needs and solve practical problems.

Technology plays an important role in improving our lives. Tools and machines make our work easier or faster. Medicines help us restore our health and live longer. Satellites help us predict weather and communicate.

Technology changes as people's knowledge increases and they find better ways to meet their needs. For example, as people's knowledge of materials increased, stone tools gave way to metal tools. As people learned more about electricity, washboards and hand-cranked washing machines gave way to electric washers.

Centuries ago, many people washed their clothes on rocks in a river. The invention of the washboard allowed people to wash their clothes at home.

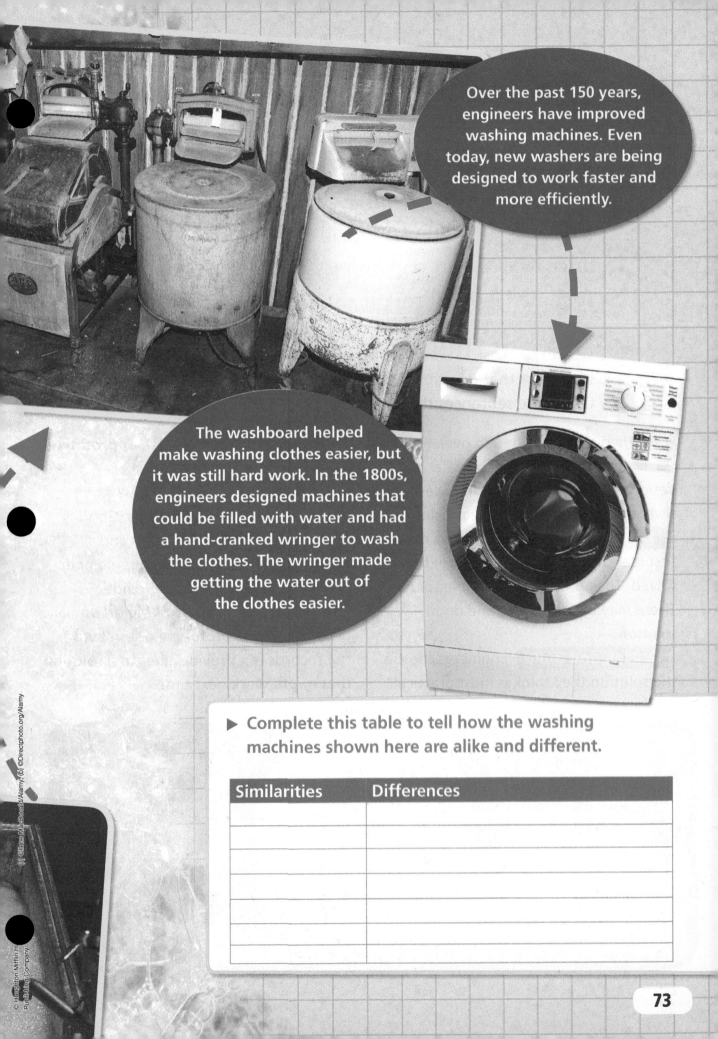

Over the past 150 years, engineers have improved washing machines. Even today, new washers are being designed to work faster and more efficiently.

The washboard helped make washing clothes easier, but it was still hard work. In the 1800s, engineers designed machines that could be filled with water and had a hand-cranked wringer to wash the clothes. The wringer made getting the water out of the clothes easier.

▶ Complete this table to tell how the washing machines shown here are alike and different.

Similarities	Differences

The Design Process (Part 1)

Technology is all over—video games, 3D TVs, microwaves. But technology doesn't just happen. It comes about through a step-by-step process.

ACTIVE READING As you read these pages, bracket sentences that describe a problem. Write *P* in the margin. Underline sentences that describe a solution. Write *S* by them.

When engineers design new technologies, they follow a *design process.* The process includes several steps. Here's how the process starts.

1. Find a Problem Engineers must first identify a need, or a problem to be solved. They brainstorm possible solutions. There may be more than one good solution.

2. Plan and Build Engineers choose the solution they think is most practical. They build a working model, or **prototype**, to test.

Throughout the design process, engineers keep careful records. Good records include detailed notes and drawings. Records help them remember what they have done and provide information to others working on similar problems. If the prototype doesn't work, the records can provide clues to a solution that *might* work next time.

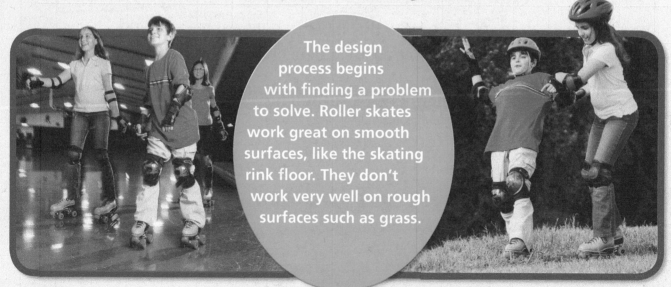

The design process begins with finding a problem to solve. Roller skates work great on smooth surfaces, like the skating rink floor. They don't work very well on rough surfaces such as grass.

Engineers make detailed drawings for their prototypes, as well as notes about the materials they plan to use. The notes and drawings are a record that they can study as they build and make changes to the prototype.

Engineers use their notes and drawings to build the first prototype. This prototype is a skate that is designed to work on rough surfaces.

Problem Solved!

The first step in the design process is identifying a problem and thinking up solutions. Complete the table with a problem or a solution.

Problem	Solution
Cord for the computer mouse keeps getting tangled	
	Watch face that lights up
	Hand-held electronic reader
Injuries in car crashes	

The Design Process (Part 2)

Do you get nervous when you hear the word *test*? A test is a useful way to decide both if you understand science and if a prototype works.

ACTIVE **READING** As you read these two pages, draw boxes around clue words that signal a sequence or order.

The skate designers are steadily working through the steps of the design process. They have found a problem and built a prototype. What's next?

3. Test and Improve After engineers build a prototype, they test it. **Criteria** are standards that help engineers measure how well their design is doing its job. The tests gather data based on the criteria. The data often reveal areas that need improvement.

4. Redesign After testing, engineers may decide that they need to adjust the design. A new design will require a new prototype and more testing.

A prototype is usually tested and redesigned many times before a product is made on a large scale and sold to consumers.

5. Communicate Finally, engineers communicate their results orally and in written reports.

Engineers use criteria to test a prototype. They may gather data on how fast someone can skate on a rough surface or the number of times the person falls. Speed and safety are two criteria in the test you see here.

The design is modified if it doesn't meet all criteria. An unsafe design will be reworked even if the design meets all other criteria. The engineers focus on improvements. They revise their drawings and keep notes on design changes.

DESIGN PROCESS STEPS
1 Find a Problem
2 Plan & Build
3 Test & Improve
4 Redesign
5 Communicate

This is the redesigned skate. It has larger wheels that work better on rough surfaces. The skater can skate faster for longer distances without falling.

DO THE MATH

Solve a Problem

Engineers tested a wheel that was 100 mm in diameter. Then they tested a wheel that was 15% larger.

Convert 15% to a decimal.

_____

What is the size of the larger wheel?

_____

If At First You Don't Succeed...

Suppose Thomas Edison asked himself, "How many times must I make a new prototype?" What do you think his answer was?

Many things affect how long it takes to reach the final product for new technology. The kinds of materials needed, the cost, the time it takes to produce each prototype, and safety are just some of the criteria engineers consider.

Thomas Edison tried 1,000 times to develop a light bulb that didn't burn out quickly. It took him nearly two years to develop a bulb that met the criterion of being long-lasting.

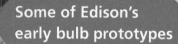

Some of Edison's early bulb prototypes

Cars must pass crash tests before they can be sold to the public.

Cars of the future may look different or run on fuels different from those of today. Years of testing and redesign occur before a new car is brought to market.

Finding materials that work well affects the design process. Edison found that the materials used to make light bulbs must stand up to heat.

Some technologies cost a lot of money to develop. For example, prototypes for many electronic devices are expensive to build. The cost of building the prototype, in turn, affects the cost of the final product.

It may take many years to develop new cars, because they must undergo safety and environmental testing. Environmental laws limit the pollutants that a car may release and determine the gas mileage it must get.

Criteria Match Up

Draw a line from the technology to criteria that must be considered during the design process.

Technology	Must Be Considered
Hydrogen car	Lightweight, sturdy
Laptop computer	Finding fuel
Bicycle	Portable, long battery life

Sum It Up »

In the blanks, write the word that makes the sentence correct.

engineering	technology

1. The things that engineers design to meet human needs are _____

2. _____ is the process of designing and testing new technologies.

3. Toothbrushes, washing machines, and computers are examples of _____

4. _____ uses math and science to test devices and designs.

Fill in the missing words to explain how engineers conduct the design process. Use the words in the box if you need help.

communicating	engineering	keep good records
needs	problem	prototype

5. _____ is the use of science and math to solve everyday problems. Engineers invent and improve things that meet human 6. _____.
The design process that engineers follow includes finding a
7. _____, building and testing a 8. _____, and
9. _____ results. During each step of the design process, engineers 10. _____.

Name _____

Vocabulary Review

1 **Beside each sentence, write *T* if the sentence is mostly about using technology. Write *E* if the sentence is mostly about the engineering design process.**

____ 1. Sarah sent a text message to Sam on her cell phone.

____ 2. The nurse used a digital thermometer to measure the patient's temperature.

____ 3. Henry tested three brands of blender. He wanted to see which one made the creamiest smoothies.

____ 4. Workers at the factory use machines to bottle spring water.

____ 5. Jessica invented a better mousetrap. She patented her invention.

____ 6. Eli used math to figure out how much weight a bridge could hold.

____ 7. The nurse is using a new x-ray machine.

____ 8. Mayling is designing a refrigerator that uses less electricity.

____ 9. Guillermo's new snowblower makes snow removal faster and easier.

____ 10. Laptop computers are designed to be smaller, lighter, and easier to carry.

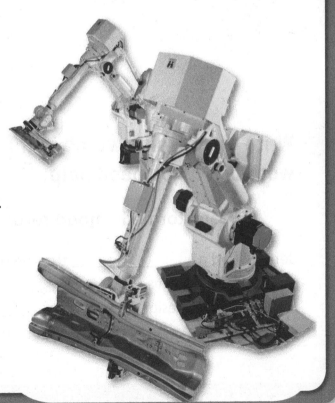

Apply Concepts

2 **Match the picture of the technology to the need it fulfills. Draw a line from the picture to the matching need.**

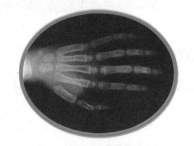

go to school

get up on time

see clearly

make a cake

fix a broken bone

keep papers together

3 **Write the missing words in the sentences below. Use the word box if you need help.**

brainstormed	good records	problem	prototype

Jeremy had a _____ that he wanted to solve—his go-cart was too slow. Jeremy and his friend Todd _____ ideas to make it faster. Together, they designed a _____ and tested it. They kept _____ that showed that the go-cart really was faster.

4 Circle the words or phrases that are criteria for designing skates that will be safe. Cross out those that are *not* criteria for safety.

roll smoothly   brake easily   come in different styles

fit snugly   come in different colors   sturdy

5 Look at the flow chart showing the steps of the design process. Then read the list of steps for designing a thermos. These steps are not in order. Write the letter of each step in the appropriate box of the flow chart.

The Design Process

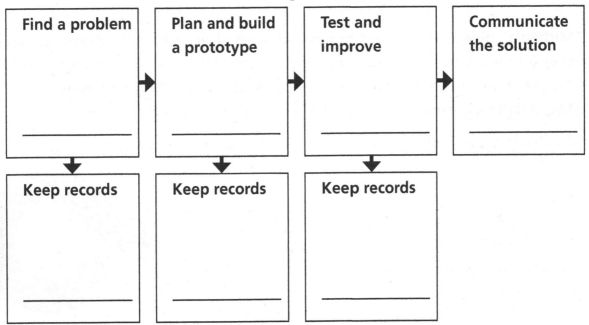

Find a problem	Plan and build a prototype	Test and improve	Communicate the solution
_____	_____	_____	_____
Keep records	Keep records	Keep records	
_____	_____	_____	

Steps for Designing a Thermos

A Keep data tables.

B Write a report

C Write down ideas.

D Make drawings.

E Measure the temperature inside the container.

F Keep hot things hot and cold things cold.

G Use insulating materials to make a container.

6 Sylvia is an engineer. Her friend Martin is an artist who paints with oil paints. Martin tells Sylvia that cleaning oil paint out of brushes takes a lot of time. It's messy, too. Write three or more sentences explaining what Sylvia would do to engineer a solution to Martin's problem.

_____

_____

_____

_____

_____

_____

7 Michaela's grandparents used to have a record player. When they were her age, they listened to songs recorded on vinyl records. Michaela's parents listened to cassette tapes when they were young. Later, they got a CD player. Now, Michaela's family members upload music onto MP3 players.

Explain how these changes are examples of engineering and technology.

_____

_____

_____

_____

Take It Home! See *ScienceSaurus®* for more information about science and engineering.

SC.5.N.1.1 Define a problem, use appropriate reference materials to support scientific understanding, plan and carry out scientific investigations of various types such as: systematic observations, experiments requiring the identification of variables, collecting and organizing data, interpreting data in charts, tables, and graphics, analyze information, make predictions, and defend conclusions.

Name _____

ESSENTIAL QUESTION

How Can You Design a Solution to a Problem?

Materials

balance
modeling clay
plastic container
    with water in it
10 or more pennies
paper towels

EXPLORE

Suppose you wanted to build a raft to carry a heavy load. What would you do? In this activity, you will design and test a model of a raft.

Before You Begin—Preview the Steps

1. Measure 60 grams of modeling clay. Shape the clay into a raft. Test your raft in water. If your raft doesn't float, reshape it until it does.

2. Float your raft on water. Test it to see how much cargo it can hold. Carefully add pennies, one at a time, to your raft until it sinks.

3. In your notebook, sketch a diagram of your raft loaded with pennies.

4. Record how may pennies you added before your raft sank.

5. Find a way to carry more pennies. Try a different design for your raft, or place the pennies in a different way. Test your new design and record your observations.

SC.8.N.1.1 Define a problem...to support a scientific
...data and carry out an investigation of a natural...
...interpret data in charts, tables, and graphs, analyze...

Set a Purpose

What is the purpose of this investigation?

_____

_____

State Your Hypothesis

Sketch a raft with pennies on it to show what you think will be the best design. Write a brief description of your raft's key features.

_____

_____

_____

_____

Think About the Procedure

What variables can affect the results of this investigation?

_____

_____

_____

_____

Name _____

Record Your Data

In the space below, make a table in which you record your results. Be sure to include information about each raft design and the number of pennies and their placement.

Draw Conclusions

Why did some of your model rafts work better than others?

_____

_____

_____

_____

Claims • Evidence • Reasoning

1. Sketch a raft design you claim would NOT float. Provide evidence about why it will not float and explain your reasoning.

_____

_____

_____

2. Mary and Sarah built identical raft models. Mary's raft sank after adding only 6 pennies. Sarah's raft held 12 pennies before it sank. Make a claim about a possible reason for the difference.

_____

_____

3. Scientists often build and test models to solve problems. What are the advantages of solving problems in that way?

_____

_____

_____

4. Think of other questions you would like to ask about designing solutions to a problem.

_____

_____

SC.5.N.1.1 Define a problem, use appropriate reference materials to support scientific understanding, plan and carry out scientific investigations of various types such as: systematic observations, experiments requiring the identification of variables, collecting and organizing data, interpreting data in charts, tables, and graphics, analyze information, make predictions, and defend conclusions.

ESSENTIAL QUESTION

How Does Technology Improve Our Lives?

Engage Your Brain

Find the answer to the following question in this lesson and record it here.

It looks like a map of a city with streets and buildings of all sizes. But all those bumps and lines are actually the "brain" of a computer! How has the invention of technology such as computers changed the way people communicate?

_____

_____

_____

_____

📖 ACTIVE READING

Lesson Vocabulary

List the terms. As you learn about each one, make notes in the Interactive Glossary.

_____

_____

Cause and Effect

Some ideas in this lesson are connected by a cause-and-effect relationship. Why something happens is a cause. What happens as a result of something is an effect. Active readers look for effects by asking themselves, What happened? They look for causes by asking, Why did it happen?

The Technology Zone

Pick up your pencil, and look at it carefully.
You are holding technology in your hand.

ACTIVE READING As you read these two pages, draw boxes around the names of two things that are being compared.

Most of the things you use every day are *technology*. Pencils, bikes, light bulbs, even the clothes you wear are technology. Cooking food uses technology. What makes something technology is not how modern it is. Technology doesn't need to be complex or require electricity to operate.

What technology must do is meet a human need. A pencil lets you write your thoughts or work math problems. Think about what needs are being met as you read about the technologies on these two pages. How would you meet those needs without these items?

▶ Bike helmets and doorknobs are both technology. What need does each meet?

_____

_____

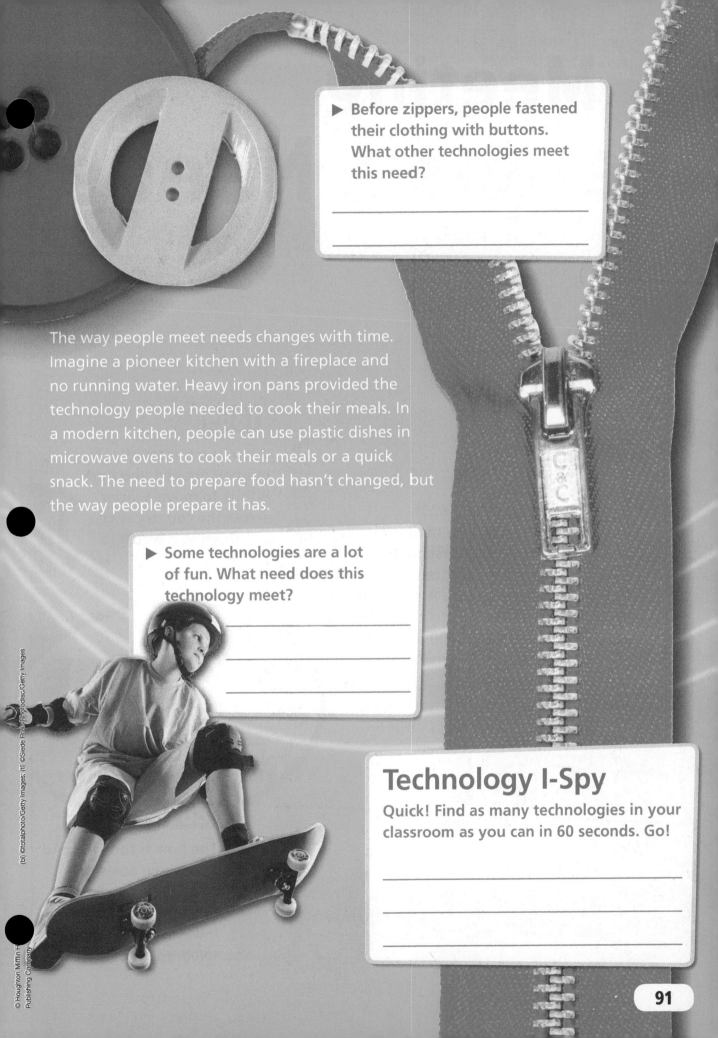

▶ Before zippers, people fastened their clothing with buttons. What other technologies meet this need?

_____

_____

The way people meet needs changes with time. Imagine a pioneer kitchen with a fireplace and no running water. Heavy iron pans provided the technology people needed to cook their meals. In a modern kitchen, people can use plastic dishes in microwave ovens to cook their meals or a quick snack. The need to prepare food hasn't changed, but the way people prepare it has.

▶ Some technologies are a lot of fun. What need does this technology meet?

_____

_____

_____

Technology I-Spy

Quick! Find as many technologies in your classroom as you can in 60 seconds. Go!

_____

_____

_____

Meeting People's Needs

It's 1860. You want to contact a distant friend. Today, you might send a text message. What about then?

ACTIVE **READING** As you read these two pages, draw one line under a cause. Draw two lines under its effect.

1858

In the early 1800s, long-distance mail was carried by horseback riders, steamboats, and stagecoaches. A stage coach took 25 days to carry a letter 3,000 km (1,700 mi) from St. Louis to San Francisco.

1869

When the transcontinental railroad opened, the time it took to move a letter across the country was cut down to a week or less.

1881

The time it took to send a message across the country was reduced to minutes with the invention of the telegraph.

In the early 1800s, communicating with someone far away might take weeks or months. Sometimes such communications were not possible at all. As people began to move westward across the growing United States, the need for reliable communication increased. The timeline on these pages shows ways technology changed in response to this need.

The time it took to communicate with someone across the country decreased as new technologies developed. What once took weeks, then days, then minutes now happens almost instantly! Today, people text back and forth almost as fast as they can talk in person. E-mails can be sent to many people at one time. New technologies for communicating seem to develop faster and faster. What could be next?

1915

Cross-country telephone service began in the United States.

1993

The first smart phone was developed.

DO THE **MATH**
Solve a Problem

Suppose you can send 2 text messages per minute. How many text messages could you send in the time it took to deliver a letter by stagecoach from St. Louis to San Francisco in 1858?

_____

_____

_____

07:00 AM

CONNECTED

1-

2 ABC   3 DEF

4 GHI   5 JKL   93

7 PQR

0

Technology Risks and Benefits

A cell phone lets you communicate from almost anywhere. What happens when the phone dies or a newer, better model comes out?

ACTIVE READING As you read these two pages, **underline** the things that are being contrasted .

Technology can have both positive and negative effects. Positive effects are called *benefits*. Benefits are the ways that a technology fills a need. For example, a cell phone lets friends and family communicate with you wherever you are. It might let you surf the Internet or download useful applications, too.

Negative effects are called *risks*. Cell phone technology changes fast, and some people switch to new models after just a few months. More resources are used up, and the old phones sometimes end up in a landfill. This risk is environmental.

No matter what the technology, there are both risks and benefits. Think about how each technology described here impacts your life. Are the benefits worth the risks?

Computers

BENEFITS	RISKS
Computers let you communicate with friends and family. They let you surf the Internet for information that can help with homework, and they let you play games.	Computer technology changes quickly, and many computers end up in landfills. Computers are expensive, and using the Internet can expose you to sites that are unsafe.

Automobiles

BENEFITS	RISKS
Cars allow personal freedom by letting you go almost anywhere. They carry heavy items that you could not move on your own.	Cars use gasoline that is made from a limited resource—oil. They cause air pollution, and they can be dangerous if not driven properly.

Audio Players

BENEFITS	RISKS
Audio Players let you download and listen to your favorite music without disturbing others.	Turning up the volume can damage your hearing. You may not be able to download some songs.

Risks Versus Benefits

Frozen foods and canned foods come prepackaged.
Write down some benefits and risks of using prepackaged foods.

BENEFITS	RISKS
_____	_____
_____	_____
_____	_____

Living Technology

The many branches of science are often connected. Engineered devices are sometimes used on living things. This connects engineering and biology.

This plant cleans waste water to make it safe to return to the environment.

Engineers who work with living things are called bioengineers. When bioengineers apply the engineering design process to living things, they are practicing **bioengineering**.

A bioengineer may design a fish farm to raise large numbers of fish for food or other uses.

An important part of bioengineering has to do with the environment. Bioengineers design tools to prevent or clean up pollution, for example. Any product used to benefit organisms or their environment is an example of **biotechnology**.

Bioengineering also deals with health and nutrition. For instance, plants can be engineered to grow faster or larger to feed more people. Food for livestock may be engineered to make the animals healthier.

Bioengineers also design biotechnology that helps detect or treat diseases. For example, scanners in hospitals can look inside the body. They let doctors see a diseased or damaged organ. Other devices help surgeons perform operations.

Some bioengineers design devices that replace human body parts. Artificial legs help people who have lost their own. Artificial skin helps people with burns. Bioengineers have even developed artificial hearts.

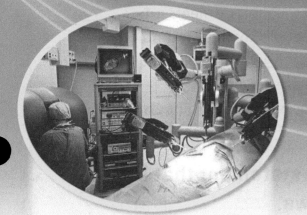

Surgeons today can use computer-assisted machines in delicate operations.

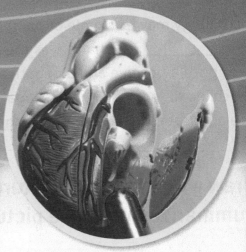

This artificial heart may not look like a real human heart, but it does the same job.

Bioengineering and Human Needs

Identify the human need met by each of these biotechnologies.

Biotechnology	Need
Water treatment plant	
Fish farm	
Robotic surgery	
Artificial heart	

Sum It Up »

Fill in the missing words to explain how technology improves our lives. Use the words in the box if you need help.

benefits	bioengineering	risks
effect	need	technology

Technology may be simple or complex, but all technology meets a 1. _____
2. _____ changes as the needs of people change. Technology may
have both a positive and a negative 3. _____ on people. Positive effects
are called 4. _____ . Negative effects are called 5. _____ .
The application of the engineering design process to living things is
6. _____ .

Draw a line from the picture to the statement that best summarizes what the picture shows.

7. Bioengineering may develop technologies that protect the environment, improve nutrition, or replace body parts.

8. A benefit of packaged food is convenience. A risk is an increase in the amount of trash.

9. Even a simple fastener is technology because it meets a human need.

10. Communication technology has changed greatly over time.

Name _____

Vocabulary Review

1 **Use the words in the box below to help you unscramble the highlighted words in each statement. Then, write the unscrambled word on the line.**

One irsk of using a computer is being exposed to unsafe Internet sites.

_____

A fish farm is an example of hetooblyincgo.

_____

otyleonchg is anything that meets a need or solves a problem. _____

Engineers work with living organisms in the process of nnneeeiiiggbor. _____

A nefetib of a car is that it allows personal freedom. _____

| benefit | bioengineering* | biotechnology* |
| risk | technology | |

* Key Lesson Vocabulary

Apply Concepts

2 Describe how changes in transportation have affected communication over long distances. Give an example.

_____

_____

_____

3 ## Name two benefits and two risks for each of these technologies.

Plastic Grocery Bags

BENEFITS	RISKS
_____	_____
_____	_____
_____	_____
	_____

Internet

BENEFITS	RISKS
_____	_____
_____	_____
_____	_____

Light Bulb

BENEFITS	RISKS
_____	_____
_____	_____
_____	_____
_____	

Television

BENEFITS	RISKS
_____	_____
_____	_____
_____	_____

Take It Home!
With a family member, identify five examples of technology in your home. Explain to the family member what needs are met by each of the technologies. Try to identify the risks and benefits of each one.

CAREERS **IN SCIENCE**

(1) Prosthetic designers help people who are missing a body part, such as a hand, arm, or leg.

(2) The people they help may have lost a body part from an injury or a disease. Or it may have been missing from birth.

(3) Prosthetic designers create the prosthesis that replaces the missing body part.

(4) To design a prosthesis, prosthetic designers need to study how the human body moves.

(5) A prosthetic designer looks for new ways to improve how a prosthesis is made.

(6) They use both computers and traditional tools including drills.

10 THINGS

YOU SHOULD KNOW ABOUT

Prosthetic Designers

(7) A prosthesis is made to meet the needs of each user.

(8) A person may need a special prosthesis to swim, run, bike, or golf.

(9) A prosthesis is designed to move easily, naturally, and under the wearer's control.

(10) Prosthetic designers can change people's lives!

Designing Sports Prostheses

For each image, write the number of the design criteria that meet each person's needs.

1 It should allow the leg to bend forward and the knee to lock.

2 It should fit comfortably at the knee and allow the ankle to rotate.

3 It should be lightweight, flexible, and resist high-force impacts.

4 It should be lightweight and able to rotate 180°.

5 It should be waterproof and allow the ankle to lock.

6 It should have attachments for gripping different objects.

7 It should be able rotate 90°and have good traction.

SC.5.N.1.1 Define a problem, use appropriate reference materials to support scientific understanding, plan and carry out scientific investigations of various types such as: systematic observations, experiments requiring the identification of variables, collecting and organizing data, interpreting data in charts, tables, and graphics, analyze information, make predictions, and defend conclusions.

Name _____

ESSENTIAL QUESTION

How Can You Use Engineering to Solve a Problem?

Materials

- 2 wood slats, with holes
- 2 pieces of sandpaper
- plastic tubing
- rubber belt
- masking tape
- glue
- wing nut and bolt
- small jar with lid
- medium jar with lid
- large jar with lid
- scissors

EXPLORE

You will use the engineering design process to design and build a prototype that solves the problem of a hard-to-open jar.

Before You Begin—Preview the Steps

1. With a partner, brainstorm how the materials provided could be used to make a jar opener. Sketch each of your ideas, and make notes as to how you think each design might work.

2. Choose the design you think will work best. Make a plan and build your prototype.

3. Test your prototype. Record how well it worked.

4. Make improvements to your design, if needed. Test your jar opener again.

© Houghton Mifflin H Publishing Company

Set a Purpose
What problem are you trying to solve?

_____

_____

Think About the Procedure
What is a prototype?

_____

_____

Describe two ideas for your prototype.

_____

_____

_____

_____

_____

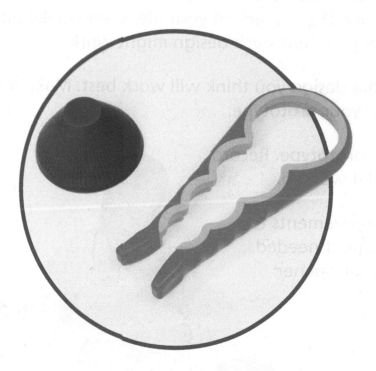

Name _____

Record Your Data

Draw a detailed plan for your jar opener. Label the
materials. Describe how it will work. Then, build
and test your prototype.

Draw Conclusions

What criteria did you use to test your prototype?

_____

_____

_____

Describe how you tested your prototype. Record any data you collected.

_____

_____

_____

Claims • Evidence • Reasoning

1. Describe the improvements you made to the prototype and your reasoning for making the changes.

_____

_____

_____

_____

2. Summarize how you designed and tested your jar opener. Provide evidence that your design worked.

_____

_____

_____

3. Make a claim about how the materials provided could be used to make a different jar opener.

_____

_____

4. Think of other designs you might make if you had different materials. How would that design work?

_____

_____

Name _____

Vocabulary Review

Use the terms in the box to complete the sentences.

bioengineering
biotechnology
criteria
engineering
prototype
technology

1. Any device that people use to meet their needs and solve

   practical problems is _____.

2. Using science and math for everyday purposes such as designing

   structures, machines, and systems is _____.

3. The standards for measuring how well a design does its job

   are _____.

4. The process of applying the engineering design process to living

   things is _____.

5. The working model on which tests are performed is

   a(n) _____.

6. Artificial legs are an example of _____.

Science Concepts

Fill in the letter of the choice that best answers the question.

7. Computer models, along with mathematical data, can help to provide which information to bioengineers?

   (A) which prosthesis is more appealing

   (B) which prosthesis would be less necessary

   (C) what kinds of changes need to be made to a prosthetic device

   (D) what kinds of adjustments need to be made to the marketing plan.

8. This foot x-ray is an example of which kind of science or engineering?

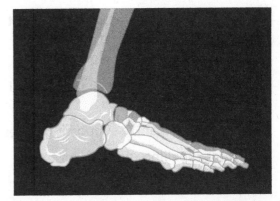

   (F) biotechnology   (H) prototype design

   (G) microbiology   (I) prosthetic devices

9. Suppose you are a bioengineer who is designing a prosthetic shoulder joint. You are building a prototype. Which is an **important** design criterion for a shoulder joint that you should include?

Ⓐ It should be realistic in color and appearance.

Ⓑ It should be capable of full movement within a shoulder socket.

Ⓒ It should keep the person for whom it is designed from injuring himself or herself again.

Ⓓ It should be stronger than a typical shoulder joint and support more weight.

10. A sports designer wants to produce a profitable product that will benefit the wearer. The data below show the result of a survey about students' favorite sport activities.

Sports Participation in High School	
Sport	Percentage of students
basketball	80
bicycling	60
soccer	50
swimming	30

Which can you infer would be the **most** needed product among the students surveyed?

Ⓕ a helmet to protect from accidental head injuries

Ⓖ high-impact, ankle-supporting shoes

Ⓗ water-repelling racing swim trunks

Ⓘ shorts with padded backs

11. You and your design team have designed a new waterproof wristwatch made of a soft, flexible, clothlike material. Which of the following prototypes could be tested to predict how well the watch would work in real life?

Ⓐ a graphic drawing of the watch

Ⓑ a computer model of the watch that actually moves

Ⓒ a wearable model of the watch made of plastic or cloth

Ⓓ a wearable version of the watch made of the new material

12. A company has developed a new skateboard that can more easily roll over gravel or grass. Some users of these new boards are wearing paths through the local park. What aspect of technology does this situation represent?

Ⓕ benefits and risks

Ⓖ design and redesign

Ⓗ computer models and prototypes

Ⓘ brainstorming and communication

Name _____

13. Bioengineers designed a prosthetic hand that is capable of grasping small objects between the thumb and index finger. The thumb was not one of the prosthetic hand's original design criteria. Which process was most responsible for including this feature in the final design?

Ⓐ troubleshooting after manufacture

Ⓑ safety concerns among doctors

Ⓒ brainstorming sessions within the design team

Ⓓ prototype testing and redesigning

14. You are determining the criteria you will use to decide how well your prototype racecar works. Which units would you use to determine the distance your car traveled?

Ⓕ grams

Ⓖ degrees

Ⓗ meters

Ⓘ liters

15. Engineers are investigating several materials that they think might be suitable for use in an artificial knee joint. They need to select a strong material that has a density (mass ÷ volume) in the range of 2.3–2.6.

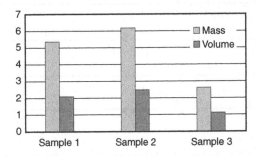

What can the engineers conclude using the data from the graph?

Ⓐ All of the samples meet the density criteria that the engineers identified.

Ⓑ Sample 3 has the least volume and should not be considered for the knee.

Ⓒ Sample 2 has the greatest mass per volume and is the densest material.

Ⓓ All samples are outside the acceptable range and show a mass of 5–6.

16. An engineering team is developing a device that will help individual farm families clean drinking water. The device must be inexpensive enough that families can afford to buy one. At what stage in the engineering process should the team take into account the need for the device to be affordable?

Ⓕ before they build a prototype

Ⓖ after the device is on the market

Ⓗ before they identify the problem

Ⓘ after the testing has been completed

Apply Inquiry and Review the Big Idea

Write the answers to these questions.

17. Building a prototype of a prosthetic human body part means that you must use materials in ways that will resemble the actions of the real body parts. For example, you can use rubber bands to simulate the action of muscles on bones in order to move them. Describe two ways that rubber bands can imitate muscles in a model of a human arm.

(1)_____

_____

(2)_____

_____

18. A fully loaded backpack should not exceed 20 percent of a student's weight. However, most doctors recommend a 15-percent weight limit. These data are shown in the table below.

Body weight (lb)	Recommended limit of 15% (lb) port	Maximum weight of 20% (lb)
70	$10\frac{1}{2}$	14
80	12	16
90	$13\frac{1}{2}$	18
100	15	20
110	$16\frac{1}{2}$	22
120	18	24

Materials that are often used to make backpacks have the following properties:

Material	Cost	Durability	Weight
plastic	low	low	low
canvas	moderate	average	medium
leather	high	high	high

a. What is the maximum weight a student who weighs 70 lb should carry?

_____

b. What is the range of weights for a student who weighs 80 lb?

_____

_____

c. Make a claim about the best material for a backpack that will be used by a 70 lb student to carry 9 lb of books and materials. Give evidence for your answer.

_____

_____

© Houghton Mifflin Harcourt Publishing Company

The Solar System and the Universe

FLORIDA BIG IDEA 5

Earth in Space and Time

A telescope helps us see objects that are very far away.

I Wonder Why

You can see distant stars and planets through a telescope. Scientists send space probes into space. Why do scientists launch space probes? *Turn the page to find out.*

Here's Why

Space probes can take images and collect and analyze samples from objects in the solar system. They provide data that would not be possible to get from Earth with a telescope.

Essential Questions and Florida Benchmarks

 Science Notebook

Before you begin each lesson, write your thoughts about the Essential Question.

SC.5.E.5.2 Recognize the major common characteristics of all planets and compare/contrast the properties of inner and outer planets. SC.5.E.5.3 Distinguish among the following objects of the Solar System—Sun, planets, moons, asteroids, comets—and identify Earth's position in it.

ESSENTIAL QUESTION

What Objects Are Part of the Solar System?

Engage Your Brain

Find the answer to the following question in this lesson and record it here.

Which planets have rings, and what are the rings made of?

_____

_____

_____

ACTIVE READING

Lesson Vocabulary

List the terms. As you learn about each one, make notes in the Interactive Glossary.

_____   _____

_____   _____

_____

Compare and Contrast

Many ideas in this lesson are connected because they explain comparisons and contrasts—how things are alike and different. Active readers stay focused on comparisons and contrasts when they ask themselves, How are these things alike? How are they different?

The Solar System

The sun, Earth, and its moon form a system in space. Earth revolves around the sun. That means Earth travels around the sun in a path called an orbit. The moon revolves around Earth. Read on to learn about other objects in space.

ACTIVE READING As you read this page, underline two details that tell how all planets are alike.

Earth and its moon are part of a larger system in space called a solar system. A **solar system** is made up of a star and the planets and other space objects that revolve around it. A **planet** is a large, round body that revolves around a star. In our solar system, the planets and other objects revolve around a star we call the sun.

There are eight planets in our solar system. All of them rotate, or spin, about an axis. This is an imaginary line that goes through the center of a planet. Earth rotates on its axis once every 24 hours. This is the length of one day on Earth.

Unlike planets, some objects don't revolve directly around the sun. *Moons* are small natural objects that revolve around other objects. Many planets have moons. Earth has only one. It revolves once around Earth about every 27 days.

Earth is about 150 million kilometers from the sun!

Diagrams not to scale.

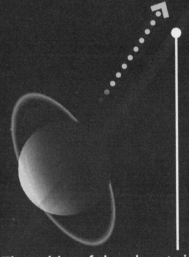

The planets in our solar system are very far from each other.

The orbits of the planets in our solar system are not perfect circles. They are oval-shaped, or elliptical [eh•LIP•tuh•kuhl].

Some planets have many moons. Earth has only one. Venus and Mercury have none!

Around and Around

Draw an orbit for the planet. Then draw a moon and its orbit.

sun

planet

The Inner Planets

At times, the brightest object in the night sky is not the moon or a star. It is Venus, one of Earth's closest neighbors in space.

ACTIVE READING As you read this page, underline ways in which the inner planets are alike.

Mercury

Mercury, the smallest planet in our solar system, is less than half the size of Earth. Its surface is filled with craters, much like Earth's moon. Mercury is the closest planet to the sun. On Mercury, the sun would look three times as large as it does on Earth.

Planets in our solar system can be classified based on their distance from the sun. The four inner planets are the closest to the sun. In order from closest to farthest, the inner planets are Mercury, Venus, Earth, and Mars.

The inner planets are very dense and rocky. They have thin atmospheres and small diameters. A planet's diameter is the distance from one side of the planet, through its center, to the other side. The inner planets have large solid cores at their centers. They have few moons, and their revolution times are short compared to the other planets in the solar system.

Venus

Venus is so hot that lead would melt at its surface! Thick clouds surround Venus, and its atmosphere is made up mostly of carbon dioxide. Lava flows from more than 1,000 volcanoes on Venus's surface.

Planets not to scale.

Earth

Earth is the third planet from the sun. It has an atmosphere made of mostly nitrogen, oxygen, and carbon dioxide. Earth is the only planet known to have abundant liquid water, which helps to keep Earth at temperatures that allow life.

No Home for Me

List three reasons why people could not live on Venus.

1. _____

_____

2. _____

_____

3. _____

_____

Mars

Sometimes you can see Mars in the night sky. Mars is known as the "Red Planet" because of its red, rocky surface. Giant dust storms often cover the entire planet, forming huge sand dunes. Mars, like the other inner planets, has many volcanoes.

The Outer Planets

On a clear night, Jupiter might appear to be a large, bright star in the night sky. But in fact, Jupiter is one of the outer planets in our solar system.

Great Red Spot

Jupiter

Jupiter is the largest planet in the solar system. In fact, all of the other planets would fit inside Jupiter! Its Great Red Spot is about as wide as three Earths. The red spots are massive, spinning storms. Jupiter's faint rings were discovered by the *Voyager 1* space probe in 1979.

Jupiter, Saturn, Uranus, and Neptune are the outer planets. In that order, they are the farthest planets from the sun. The outer planets are also called the gas giants, because they are huge and made up mostly of gases. They don't have a solid surface, and their cores are very small.

Because the gas giants are so far away from the sun, their surfaces are much colder than the inner planets. All of the outer planets have many moons and ring systems. Saturn's ring system is more visible than those of the other outer planets.

Planets not to scale.

Saturn

Saturn, the second largest planet, has thousands of rings around it. The rings are made up of ice and chunks of rock. Some of Saturn's moons are found inside these rings. Like Jupiter, Saturn has large storms.

What Makes Them Unique?

Write one thing that is unique about each of the outer planets.

Jupiter

_____

_____

Saturn

_____

_____

Uranus

_____

_____

Neptune

_____

_____

Uranus

The axis of Uranus is tilted so far that, compared to other planets, it rotates on its side. This makes seasons on Uranus last more than 20 years! Deep inside Uranus, heated gases bubble and burst onto the surface, causing bright clouds to form. Uranus has a system of at least 13 faint rings.

Neptune

Neptune is the windiest planet in our solar system. Its winds move at speeds of about 2,000 km/hr (1,243 mi/hr). These winds blow Neptune's Great Dark Spot around the planet. This spot is a storm, about the size of Earth, known to vanish and reform! Neptune has nine rings around it.

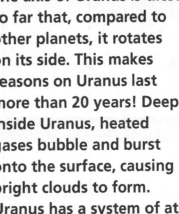

sun

Compare Inner and Outer Planets

Size, surface features, and distance from the sun are just some differences between the inner and outer planets. Look at this chart to learn about other differences.

Planet	Period of Revolution (in Earth days and years)	Period of Rotation (in Earth hours and days)	Temperature (°C) (inner planets: surface range; outer planets: top of the clouds)	Number of Moons	Density (g/cm³)	Diameter
INNER PLANETS						
Mercury	88 days	59 days	−173 to 427	0	5.43	4,878 km (3,031mi)
Venus	225 days	243 days	462	0	5.24	12,104 km (7,521 mi)
Earth	365 days	1 day	−88 to 58	1	5.52	12,756 km (7,926 mi)
Mars	687 days	about 1 day	−87 to −5	2	3.94	6,794 km (4,222 mi)
OUTER PLANETS						
Jupiter	12 years	about 10 hours	−148	67	1.33	142,984 km (88,846 mi)
Saturn	29 years	about 10 hours	−178	62	0.70	120,536 km (74,898 mi)
Uranus	84 years	about 17 hours	−216	27	1.30	51,118 km (31,763 mi)
Neptune	165 years	about 16 hours	−214	14	1.76	49,528 km (30,775 mi)

⊞ DO THE **MATH**

Find an Average

In the space below, find the average density of the four inner planets. Repeat for the four outer planets.

Inner planets:

Outer planets:

How do the average densities compare?

_____

_____

_____

The density of water is 1 gram per cubic centimeter (g/cm^3). Saturn would float because its density is less than the density of water. Earth would sink.

Patterns in Data

Look at the data table on the previous page. Describe two trends in the data between the inner and outer planets.

_____

_____

_____

_____

_____

The Flying Objects

Besides planets, there are many other bodies that orbit the sun. Let's find out more about some of them.

ACTIVE READING As you read these two pages, find and underline two facts about asteroids.

Moons

Other moons are very different from Earth's moon. Europa, one of Jupiter's moons, may have a liquid ocean under a layer of ice. Another of Jupiter's moons, Io [EYE•oh], has the most active volcanoes of any body in the solar system.

Io

Dwarf Planets

Pluto was once called a planet. But in 2006, it was reclassified as a dwarf planet. Dwarf planets are nearly round bodies whose orbits cross the orbits of other bodies. Most are found in a region of the solar system beyond Neptune's orbit called the Kuiper belt. These objects are far away and hard to study. Quaoar, shown above, was discovered in 2002.

Asteroids

Asteroids are rock and iron objects that orbit the sun. Millions of them are found in the wide region between Mars and Jupiter known as the *asteroid belt*. Some asteroids are as small as a city block. Others could fill up an ocean. Some asteroids even have their own moons!

(t) ©NASA/JPL/USGS; (b) ©Detlev van Ravenswaay/Photo Researchers Inc; (bl) ©M2
Photography/Alamy; (bkgd) ©Denis of Cless/Corbis

Meteoroids, Meteors, and Meteorites

Each day, tons of meteoroids hit Earth's atmosphere. *Meteoroids* are pieces of rock that break off of asteroids and travel through space. Most meteoroids burn up in Earth's atmosphere, causing a streak of light called a *meteor*. Meteoroids that reach Earth's surface are called *meteorites*.

Where's the Sun?

In the drawing of a comet, put an *S* to indicate the direction toward the sun. Put a *T* over each tail.

Comets

A comet is a chunk of frozen gases, rock, ice, and dust. Comets have long orbits around the sun. As comets pass close to the sun, part of their frozen surface begins to break away and turn into gases and dust. These particles reflect the sun's light and become visible as long tails. A comet's tails always point away from the sun.

Space Watch

Some objects in space cross each others' orbits. Often, nothing happens. But sometimes the objects hit each other. Scientists look out for objects that may cross Earth's orbit.

Pictures of the surface of the moon tell a story. Over millions of years, space objects such as comets, meteoroids, and asteroids have impacted, or hit, the moon. Impact craters of all sizes can be found on the moon's surface.

Space objects have also hit other bodies in the solar system. A comet named Shoemaker-Levy 9 impacted Jupiter in 1994. Pictures of the impact were taken by the *Galileo* space probe.

Scientists know that large objects have also hit Earth. In fact, a huge one impacted Earth about 65 million years ago. Many scientists think it caused changes in the environment that killed all the dinosaurs. Luckily, impacts like that one do not happen often.

Scientists use telescopes to scan space for near-Earth asteroids. These are objects that may cross Earth's orbit. Scientists keep track of their size, position, and motion. They analyze this data to determine if the objects could impact Earth.

The impact of Shoemaker-Levy 9 caused bubbles of hot gas to rise into Jupiter's atmosphere, as well as dark spots to form on its surface.

The Barringer Meteor Crater, in Arizona, was formed by a meteorite that struck Earth about 50,000 years ago.

Impacts can happen anywhere on Earth! This map shows some impact crater sites from around the world.

Impact Crater Diameter

- 10–25 km
- 25–50 km
- greater than 50 km

▶ On these pages, underline effects of impacts. Then circle a picture that shows evidence of an impact on Earth.

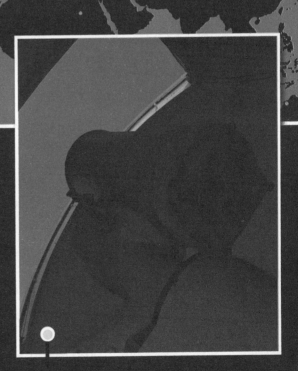

Observatories have powerful telescopes that enable scientists to track the movement of objects in space.

Sum It Up »

Read the summary, and then place the information in the list into the correct box below.

The sun is at the center of the solar system. Planets, dwarf planets, moons, and other smaller objects make up the solar system. The eight planets in the solar system can be divided into inner planets and outer planets. Each group has different characteristics.

small and dense	longer revolutions	many moons	few moons
giant size	closest to sun	gaseous surface	low density
rings	rocky surface		

① Inner Planets

② Outer Planets

Fill in the missing information to describe the object shown below.

③

Io

a. Object Type: _____

b. Space Neighbors: _____

c. Key Feature: _____

d. How It's Different from Earth: _____

_____

_____

Name _____

Vocabulary Review

1 Use each of the terms in the box to label the objects in the diagram below.

planet	comet	asteroid	solar system	dwarf planet
moon	orbit	gas giant	sun	* Key Lesson Vocabulary

(x 1) • ● **Pluto**

9. _____

1. _____

Neptune

(x 27) **Uranus**

•(x 13)

8. _____

7. _____

Jupiter

• (x 63)

Saturn

(x 61)

5. _____

← 4. _____

6. _____

Earth

Mercury

Mars

2. _____

3. _____

Venus

Apply Concepts

2 In the space below, draw pictures to show the key physical characteristics of an inner planet and an outer planet. Then describe your drawings.

_____   _____

_____   _____

_____   _____

3 Describe the features of a comet.

_____

_____

_____

_____

4 What is a meteoroid, and how does it become a meteorite?

_____

_____

_____

5 Identify each of the following large objects in the solar system. Write how you are able to identify each one.

_____

_____

_____

_____

_____

_____

_____

_____

6 A scientist discovers an object in the solar system. She describes it as bigger than an asteroid, smaller than Mercury, and farther from the sun than Neptune. What kind of object could it be? Explain.

_____

_____

7 Complete the Venn diagram in order to compare and contrast an asteroid and a comet.

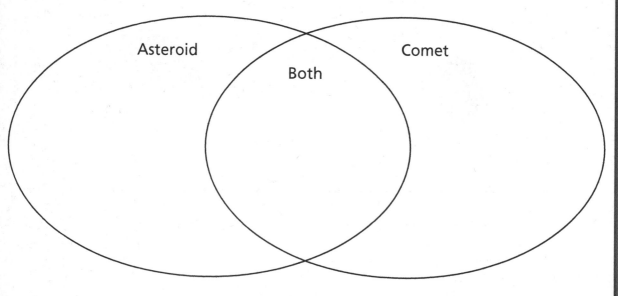

Asteroid   Both   Comet

8 Draw a picture of an object that might impact a planet. Label and describe the object. What evidence is there that these objects collide with planets and moons?

_____

_____

_____

Take It Home! See *ScienceSaurus*® for more information about the solar system and beyond.

SC.5.E.5.3 Distinguish among the following objects of the
Solar System—Sun, planets, moons, asteroids, comets—and
identify Earth's position in it.

Meet Two Space Explorers

Kalpana Chawla

On her first mission, Kalpana Chawla traveled more than six million miles in 15 days!

As a little girl in India, Kalpana Chawla dreamed about flying airplanes. She came to the United States and earned her degree in aerospace engineering. Chawla could fly many kinds of airplanes. Her dreams had come true! But she kept dreaming. She went to work for NASA and became an astronaut. Soon, Kalpana Chawla became the first Indian-born woman in space! Chawla's last mission was in 2003 on the space shuttle Columbia.

Claudia Alexander

Claudia Alexander explored outer space, too. But she never left Earth! She studied the moons of the planet Jupiter. She was in charge of NASA's Galileo mission. The mission sent an unmanned spacecraft to Jupiter. The spacecraft left Earth in 1989. It took six long years to reach Jupiter. Claudia Alexander directed it over 385 million miles! Under her command, Galileo was the first spacecraft to take detailed photos of Jupiter and its moons.

Galileo space probe

131

Two Ways to Study Space

Kalpana Chawla and Claudia Alexander study space in different ways. Write the statements that apply to each scientist in the correct circle.

Kalpana Chawla

_____
_____
_____
_____
_____

The *Hubble Space Telescope* sends scientists pictures of space from its orbit high above Earth.

- I led space missions without leaving Earth.
- I traveled on the space shuttle.
- I studied the moons of Jupiter.
- I grew up in India and learned to fly many types of airplanes.
- I studied objects in space.

Claudia Alexander

_____
_____
_____
_____
_____

Many scientists study space from Earth by using a telescope, such as this one, in an observatory.

SC.5.E.5.2... compare/contrast the properties of inner and outer planets. SC.5.E.5.3 Distinguish among ...Sun, planets, moons, asteroids, comets.... SC.5.N.1.2 Explain the difference between an experiment and other types of scientific investigation. SC.5.N.2.1 ... science is grounded in empirical observations....

Name _____

ESSENTIAL QUESTION

How Do We Observe Objects in the Solar System?

Materials

poster of solar
  system objects
binoculars

EXPLORE

In this activity, you will investigate ways scientists observe and record data about objects in the solar system. You will model different kinds of observations.

Before You Begin—Preview the Steps

① Observe your assigned object from far away. Make as many observations as possible. Record your observations in your Science Notebook.

② Use binoculars to observe the same object. Record your observations.

③ Pretend that one member of your group is a space probe. This student should walk to the poster and record observations. Have another student gather those observations and return them to your group's table.

④ Review the space probe's observations and write new questions about the object. Send the new questions to the space probe. Review the answers you receive.

SC.3.N.1.2 Computing the proper tools and methods to gather and solve problems... SC.3.N.3.3 Recognizing...
and about how scientists achieve... SC.3.N.1.3 Explain the difference between...
investigate and observe... SC.3.N.1.1 Raise questions about the natural world, investigate them in teams through free exploration and systematic observations, and generate appropriate explanations based on those explorations.

Set a Purpose

What do you think you will learn from this experiment?

_____

_____

_____

Think About the Procedure

Why do you think you will observe the object in different ways?

_____

_____

_____

_____

Why is it important that you work together as a team in this investigation?

_____

_____

_____

_____

Name _____

Record Your Data

In the space below, record the observations you
made, using all three methods.

Draw Conclusions

Think about how scientists view objects in space. What did observing the object
from far away represent?

_____

_____

What did using binoculars represent?

_____

_____

What did viewing the object up close represent?

_____

_____

Claims • Evidence • Reasoning

1. Make a claim about how your observations from far away differ from those made using binoculars. Provide evidence to support your claim.

_____

_____

2. Make a claim about how your observations made using binoculars differ from the observations made when a student walked to the poster. Provide evidence to support your claim.

_____

_____

_____

3. Use evidence from your investigation to explain how space probes help scientists learn about objects in space.

_____

_____

_____

4. Think about objects in the solar system. Make a claim about how scientists use time and space relationships to observe them. Explain your reasoning.

_____

_____

5. What other questions you would like to ask about how scientists study objects in space?

_____

_____

SC.5.E.5.1 Recognize that a galaxy consists of gas, dust, and many stars, including any objects orbiting the stars. Identify our home galaxy as the Milky Way.

LESSON 3

ESSENTIAL QUESTION

What Are Stars and Galaxies?

Engage Your Brain

Find the answer to the following question in this lesson and record it here.

Space is not completely empty. There are small particles in space. What happens when these particles come together?

_____

_____

_____

A nebula, such as the pelican nebula shown here, is a giant cloud of gas and dust.

ACTIVE READING

Lesson Vocabulary

List the terms. As you learn about each one, make notes in the Interactive Glossary.

_____

_____

_____

_____

Signal Words: Details

Signal words show connections between ideas. *For example*, *for instance*, and *such as* signal examples of an idea. *Also* and *in fact* signal added facts. Active readers remember what they read because they are alert to signal words that identify examples and facts about a topic.

TWINKLING STARS

You see stars as tiny points of white light in the night sky. Stars are not tiny, and they are not all white. Find out how scientists study stars.

ACTIVE **READING** As you read these two pages, draw boxes around words or phrases that signal a detail or an added fact.

People have always looked at objects in the sky. **Astronomy** is the study of objects in space and their characteristics. *Astronomers* are scientists who study space and everything in it. They use many types of telescopes to observe objects in space, such as stars and planets.

Stars are huge balls of hot, glowing gases that produce their own heat and light. The sun is the star you know the most about. It seems much larger than other stars only because it is much closer to Earth.

DO THE **MATH**

Dividing by 3-digit Numbers

A small telescope magnifies objects 150 times. A large observatory telescope magnifies an object 3,300 times. How many times as great is the magnification of the observatory telescope than the small telescope?

_____

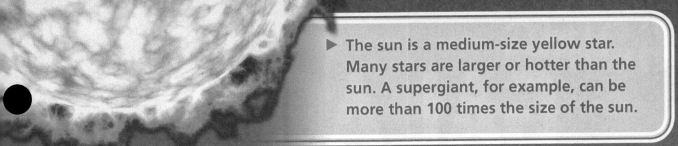

> The sun is a medium-size yellow star. Many stars are larger or hotter than the sun. A supergiant, for example, can be more than 100 times the size of the sun.

A STAR IS BORN

Stars form when gravity causes gas and dust particles found in space to pull together. These particles are squeezed together under great pressure. Eventually, energy stored in the particles is released as heat and light. A star is born.

Stars are classified by their color, temperature, brightness, and size. The color of a star can tell us about its temperature. For example, blue stars are the hottest. A blue star's average temperature is about 15,000 °C.

Stars have a wide range of sizes. White dwarf stars, for instance, can be as small as a planet. Giant and supergiant stars are many times bigger than the average-size star. The largest stars are also usually the brightest. A star's brightness is related to the amount of visible light it gives off.

Super Hot and Just Hot

Draw a rectangle around the hottest stars in the diagram. Draw a circle around the brightest stars.

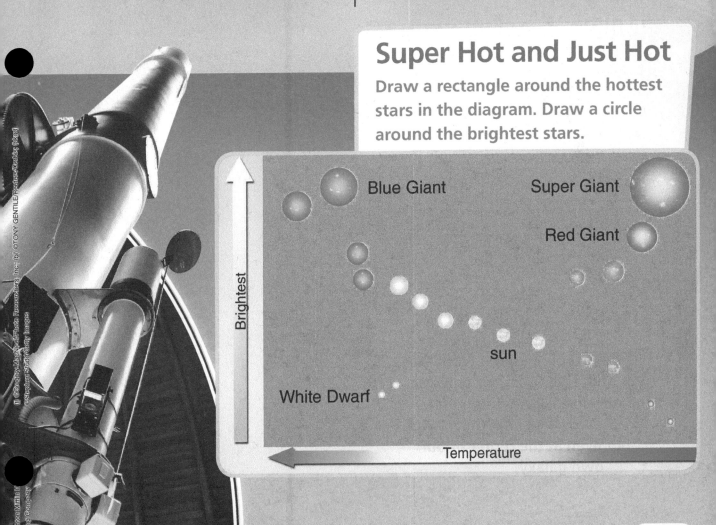

Blue Giant

Super Giant

Red Giant

Brightest

sun

White Dwarf

Temperature

GOING GALACTIC

Our solar system is huge. Yet it is only a tiny part of a much larger system in space. Our sun is one star in a group of billions of stars found in the Milky Way galaxy.

ACTIVE READING As you read the next four pages, circle details about the ages of stars in each type of galaxy.

Milky Way Galaxy

YOU ARE HERE

Once, people thought Earth was at the center of the universe. The universe is everything that exists. Now we know that we are not even at the center of our own galaxy!

▶ In the space below, describe the position of the solar system within the Milky Way.

_____

_____

_____

_____

FEATURES OF GALAXIES

A **galaxy** is a group of billions of stars, the objects that orbit the stars, gas, and dust. A galaxy is held together by gravity. There are billions of galaxies in the universe. Galaxies are separated by large distances. On a cloudless night, you might see what looks like a faint band of clouds among the stars. This is a part of our home galaxy, the Milky Way. Most other galaxies can be seen only by using powerful telescopes.

TYPES OF GALAXIES

In the 1920s, astronomer Edwin Hubble was the first to study galaxies. He classified them by shape. Through his telescope, Hubble observed pinwheel-like groups of stars that he called *spiral galaxies*.

Some spiral galaxies, called *barred spiral galaxies*, have a center shaped like a long bar. Recent evidence suggests that the Milky Way is a barred spiral galaxy.

SPIRAL **GALAXIES**

Spiral galaxies consist of a rotating disk of young stars, gas, and dust and a central bulge made of older stars.

BARRED SPIRAL **GALAXIES**

Barred spiral galaxies may have two or more spiral arms. Unlike regular spirals, there are young stars at the center of barred spiral galaxies.

MORE TYPES OF GALAXIES

Most of the brightest galaxies in the universe have spiral shapes. But spiral galaxies are not the only type of galaxy. In fact, they make up only about 20 percent of all galaxies. The dimmer *irregular galaxies* and *elliptical galaxies* make up about 80 percent of all galaxies in the universe.

IRREGULAR GALAXIES

Irregular galaxies do not have any particular shape. The stars are randomly scattered. There is lots of gas and dust to form new stars. About 20 percent of all galaxies are irregular. Some astronomers think that gravity from nearby galaxies causes irregular galaxies to form.

ELLIPTICAL GALAXIES

Elliptical galaxies are brightest at their center. About 60 percent of all galaxies in the universe are elliptical. They can be shaped like a perfect sphere or a flattened globe. Large ellipticals are made up of old stars and have too little dust or gas to form new ones.

COSMIC **CRASHES**

Sometimes galaxies collide, or crash together, in space! Why? Gravity pulls galaxies toward each other. Although galaxies may collide, single stars and planets almost never do.

Many things can happen when galaxies collide. Often, large amounts of dust and gas are pressed together. This causes a starburst, or rapid formation of many new stars. Sometimes, a smaller galaxy becomes part of a larger galaxy. A collision of galaxies can also form a large, irregular galaxy. Scientists believe that many irregular galaxies were once spiral or elliptical galaxies that were involved in a cosmic crash.

Galaxies do not stand still. They are always moving. Galaxies can move away from each other or toward each other.

▶ Look at pictures 1–5. Draw a picture to show what you think will happen next to these two galaxies. Write a sentence to describe it.

_____

_____

Sum It Up »

The universe is composed of billions of galaxies. Dust, gas, and billions of stars make up a galaxy. The idea web below summarizes information about stars and galaxies. Complete it using the words and phrases from the box.

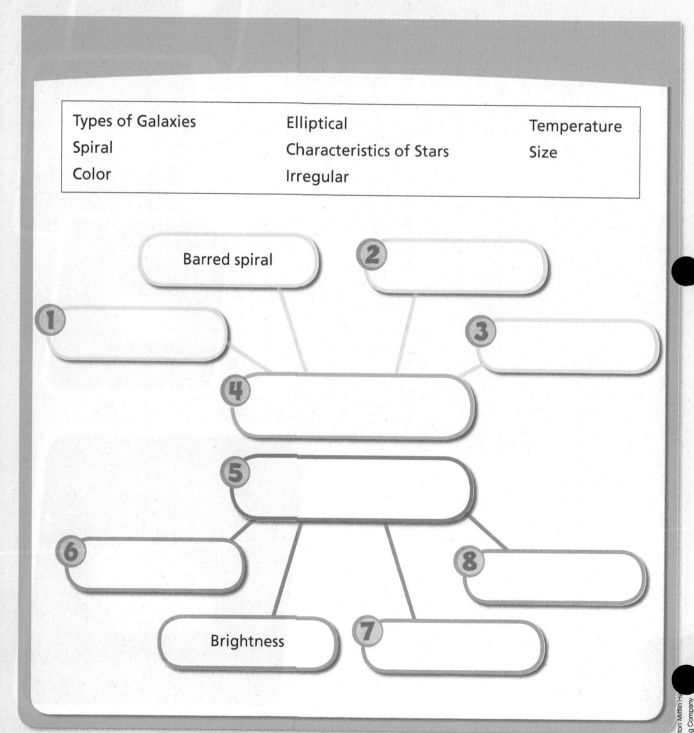

Types of Galaxies	Elliptical	Temperature
Spiral	Characteristics of Stars	Size
Color	Irregular	

Barred spiral

2

1

3

4

5

6

Brightness

7

8

Brain Check

LESSON **3**

Name _____

Vocabulary Review

1 Use the clues to unscramble the words in the boxes.

1. | oratsmreno | _____ A person who studies the universe

2. | rirarluge | _____ A galaxy with no particular shape

3. | loocr | _____ Characteristic that is related to a star's temperature

4. | rast | _____ A ball of hot, glowing gases

5. | prails | _____ A pinwheel-like galaxy

6. | xygaal | _____ A group of stars, dust, and gases

7. | plilelitca | _____ A galaxy shaped like a flattened globe

8. | eesrivun | _____ Everything that exists – planets, stars, dust, and gases

9. | mnooyrats | _____ The study of the objects in space and their properties

© Houghton Mifflin Harcourt Publishing Company

145

Apply Concepts

2 What are some ways in which galaxies differ?

_____

3 Look at this picture of a spiral galaxy.

Draw a picture of a barred spiral galaxy.

Tell how the two galaxies are alike and different.

_____

_____

4 Look at these two stars. Compare and contrast them using at least two properties.

red giant   blue star

_____

_____

_____

5 How do these stars compare to the sun?

_____

_____

 Find out which are the brightest stars that are visible this time of year in your area. With an adult, observe the stars. Make a diagram of the night sky showing where to find the brightest stars.

SC.5.N.1.5 Recognize and explain that authentic scientific investigation frequently does not parallel the steps of "the scientific method."

S.T.E.M.

ENGINEERING & TECHNOLOGY

Tools in Space

An astronaut often has to use screwdrivers or drills to fix things in space. The astronaut's tools are specially designed for a person wearing bulky gloves and floating in orbit. Hand tools must work in the extreme cold vacuum of space and be tethered so they don't float away. A robotic arm helps the astronaut move around outside. However, the astronaut's most important tool is the space suit that maintains an environment in which the astronaut can breathe.

TROUBLESHOOTING

Find the astronaut's drill. How is it similar to a drill used on Earth? How is it different?

_____

_____

_____

S.T.E.M. continued

You are used to doing everything under the pull of Earth's gravity. That's what makes it possible for you feel motions as up, down, and side-to-side. There is no "right side up" in space! It is harder than you might think to work in such an unfamiliar environment.

Turn your book so that the top of this page is closest to you.

_____

Hold your pencil near the eraser. Write your name on the line above so that it reads properly when you turn the page right side up again.

What made this task difficult?

_____

_____

How do engineers account for microgravity when designing the inside of a space station?

_____

_____

_____

_____

_____

Improvise It:
How High Is That Star?

An astrolabe is an ancient tool that was used by many cultures to study the sky. Using this instrument, you could measure the angle of a star above the horizon. That measurement could help you uncover your location and the exact time!

Now, it's your turn to build an astrolabe. Unlike the original astrolabes that were constructed of metal, the one you'll design will be made mostly of plastic. That's because you'll improvise this astronomical device using a familiar classroom tool called a protractor.

astrolabe

S.T.E.M. continued

What to Do:

DESIGN PROCESS STEPS
1 Find a Problem
2 Plan & Build
3 Test & Improve
4 Redesign
5 Communicate

1 Learn about historic instruments used to explore the sky. Study each tool's design to learn about it.

2 Find out how the elevation of the North Star above the horizon can be used to determine latitude.

3 Improvise an astrolabe using a classroom protractor. Identify the additional materials you'll need to construct the tool.

4 Draw your design.

5 Now build your astrolabe. Keep improving your design until you are satisfied with it.

6 In the evening, use your astrolabe to find the elevation of the North Star. Record this value.

7 Find out your latitude. Is it the same as the value you recorded in Step 6? Explain any difference.

8 Keep a record of your work in your Science Notebook.

Name _____

Vocabulary Review

Use the terms in the box to complete the sentences.

> asteroid
> comet
> galaxy
> solar system
> star

1. Together, a star and all the planets and other objects

   orbiting it form a(n) _____.

2. A chunk of rock or iron that orbits the sun is called

   a(n) _____.

3. A huge ball of very hot, glowing gases in space that can produce

   its own heat and light is called a(n) _____.

4. A group of solar systems that are held together by gravity and

   classified by shape is called a(n) _____.

5. The picture shows an example of

   a(n) _____.

Science Concepts

Fill in the letter of the choice that best answers the question.

6. Scientists use models to represent or explain things in the natural world. Why are models useful for the study of the solar system?

   (A) because models cannot be proven wrong

   (B) because models are always accepted by all scientists

   (C) because models describe the way things actually are

   (D) because models can be used to describe how things work

7. The illustration below shows several planets orbiting a star.

   What type of group is the figure illustrating?

   (F) constellation   (H) galaxy system

   (G) solar system   (I) universe

8. Galaxies are composed of many different objects. What kind of objects make up most of the visible matter in a galaxy?

Ⓐ asteroids   Ⓒ dust

Ⓑ planets   Ⓓ stars

9. Astronomers use the term *brightness* to describe how much light a star produces, not how bright a star appears from Earth. The diagram below compares the size, temperature, and brightness of some stars that can be seen from Earth.

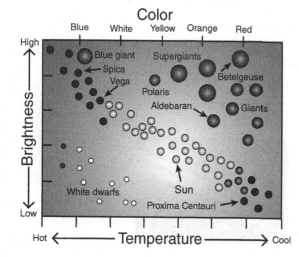

Which of these stars produces the most light?

Ⓕ Betelgeuse

Ⓖ Sun

Ⓗ Proxima Centauri

Ⓘ Vega

10. Some elliptical galaxies appear to be perfect spheres. How are the stars distributed within this kind of galaxy?

Ⓐ The stars are evenly distributed through the galaxy.

Ⓑ The center is very dense with many stars, and density decreases farther out.

Ⓒ Most of the stars are near the outside of the sphere, with dust clouds in the center.

Ⓓ The stars are spread throughout the sphere in bands that look like the arms of spiral galaxies.

11. There are many different colors of stars. Each of the images below shows two stars of the same color. Which picture and statement is correct?

Ⓕ

The larger star must be brighter.

Ⓖ

The smaller star must be hotter.

Ⓗ

The smaller star must be closer to Earth.

Ⓘ

Stars that are the same color are usually the same size.

Name _____

12. All the planets in the solar system orbit the sun. What is the main difference between the orbits of the inner and outer planets?

Ⓐ The inner planets travel a greater distance than the outer planets do.

Ⓑ The inner planets have almost round orbits, and the outer planets do not.

Ⓒ The outer planets rotate as they orbit the sun, and the inner planets do not.

Ⓓ The outer planets take longer to orbit the sun than the inner planets do.

13. The diagram below shows the orbit of Earth and the orbit of Borrelly.

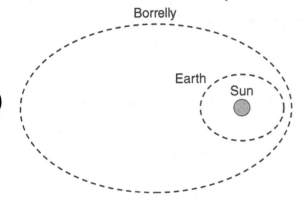

Which of these types of space objects is Borrelly most likely to be?

Ⓕ an asteroid

Ⓖ a moon

Ⓗ a comet

Ⓘ a star

14. Ming is doing a project on planets in other solar systems. She learns about a planet called Planet Z. Planet Z is very large, has a thick atmosphere, and has a low density. Which of these planets in our solar system is Planet Z most similar to?

Ⓐ Earth   Ⓒ Saturn

Ⓑ Mercury   Ⓓ Mars

15. Earth is part of the Milky Way galaxy. How does the Milky Way appear in the night sky from Earth?

Ⓕ a small, very dim group of stars

Ⓖ a faint band of clouds among the stars

Ⓗ a large number of stars in a broad, spiral shape

Ⓘ a large cloudy band of stars spreading across the sky

Apply Inquiry and Review the Big Idea

Write the answers to these questions.

16. When Galileo used his telescope to observe the Milky Way, the stars appeared as small points of light. Write a claim based on this evidence and explain how the evidence supports the claim.

_____

_____

_____

17. Describe the structure of our galaxy and the position of our solar system within our galaxy.

_____

_____

_____

18. Sofia observes an object in the night sky. What questions and observations can she use to determine whether the object is a planet or a star?

Questions _____

_____

_____

Observations _____

_____

19. People have developed models of the universe for thousands of years. Identify two observations that a model of the universe would need to explain in order to be useful.

a. _____

_____

_____

b. _____

_____

_____

© Houghton Mifflin Ha
Publishing Company

Weather, Climate, and the Water Cycle

Strong rains can quickly create flooding.

FLORIDA BIG IDEA?

Earth Systems and Patterns

I Wonder Why

Sometimes, the weather is stormy and cold. At other times, it is sunny and hot. Why does the weather change? *Turn the page to find out.*

Here's Why Weather changes because air moves constantly. Moving air changes local temperature and moisture—key factors affecting weather.

Essential Questions and Florida Benchmarks

© Houghton Mifflin Harcourt Publishing Company
Photo credit text to come.

SC.5.E.7.1 Create a model to explain the parts of the water cycle. Water can be a gas, a liquid, or a solid and can go back and forth from one state to another. SC.5.E.7.2 Recognize that the ocean is an integral part of the water cycle and is connected to all of Earth's water reservoirs via evaporation and precipitation processes.

LESSON **1**

ESSENTIAL **QUESTION**

What Is the Water Cycle?

Engage Your Brain

Find the answer to the following question in this lesson and record it here.

Where is all this water going?

_____

_____

_____

_____

ACTIVE **READING**

Lesson Vocabulary
List the terms. As you learn about each one, make notes in the Interactive Glossary.

_____

_____

_____

_____

Sequence
In this lesson, you'll read about a process of change called the water cycle. As you read about the water cycle, focus on the sequence, or order, of events in the process. Active readers stay focused on a sequence when they mark the transition from one step in a process to another.

Water on the Move

The water that you drink may have once been under ground or high in the sky. How does water get from Earth's surface to the air and back again?

▶ On the diagram, draw an X on three places where evaporation may take place.

ACTIVE READING As you read the next page, underline the main idea and circle details that provide information about it.

Earth's water is always being recycled. It evaporates from bodies of water, the soil, and even from your skin. Water exits plants' leaves through a process called *transpiration*. In the air, winds and clouds can help move water from one place to another.

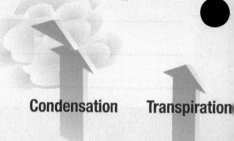

Condensation   **Transpiration**

Evaporation

After it rains, this birdbath is filled with water. When the sun comes out, its energy heats the water. The birdbath becomes empty as water changes to water vapor and returns to the atmosphere.

About three-fourths of Earth's surface is covered by water. Most of the water is stored in oceans. Water moves between Earth's surface and the atmosphere through a process called the **water cycle**.

The sun provides the energy for water to move through the water cycle. Sunlight heats up water particles near the ocean's surface. It causes water to evaporate.

Evaporation is the change from a liquid to a gas. When water evaporates, it forms an invisible gas called *water vapor*.

Water vapor rises into the atmosphere. The **atmosphere** is the mixture of gases that surrounds Earth. In the atmosphere, water vapor cools to form clouds. At any time, about three-fifths of Earth's surface is covered by clouds.

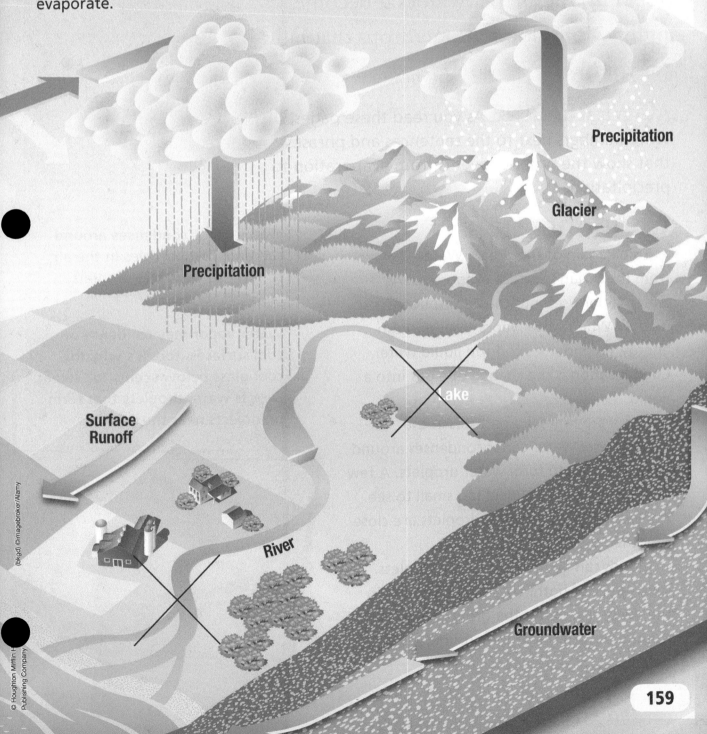

Precipitation

Glacier

Precipitation

Surface Runoff

Lake

River

Groundwater

What Goes Up Comes Down

What happens to water vapor after it rises into the air? How does it become puffy white clouds or raindrops that fall on your head?

ACTIVE **READING** As you read these pages, write numbers next to the sentences and phrases that show the order of events from evaporation to precipitation.

Condensation

Think again of the ocean. Water from the ocean's surface evaporates. As water vapor rises into the atmosphere, it cools. When water vapor loses enough energy, it condenses to form liquid water. **Condensation** is the change of a gas into a liquid.

There are tiny solid particles in the atmosphere. Water vapor condenses around these particles to form water droplets. A few water droplets are almost too small to see. However, when billions of droplets are close together, they form clouds.

Clouds can be made of water droplets, ice crystals, or both. They can form high in the sky or just above the ground. *Fog* is a cloud that forms near the ground.

Water vapor condenses around salt and dust particles in the air to form these water droplets.

Water vapor may condense on cool surfaces, too. It's why the cool glass below seems to "sweat." *Dew* is water droplets that form on objects near the ground.

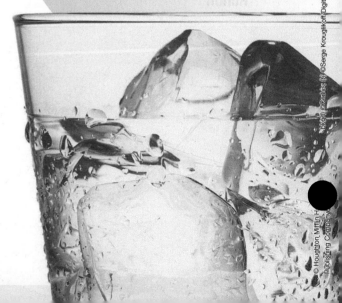

Water droplets in a cloud collide and join together. It takes many droplets to form a single raindrop.

Precipitation

Air currents keep water droplets in the air. But as droplets and snow crystals grow inside clouds, they become too heavy and fall to Earth as precipitation. **Precipitation** is water that falls from clouds to Earth's surface. Rain, snow, and hail are all forms of precipitation.

Precipitation that falls into the oceans may quickly evaporate back into the atmosphere. Precipitation that falls on land may be stored, it may flow across the land, or it may be used by living things. Depending on where it falls, water from precipitation may move quickly or slowly through the water cycle.

 DO THE **MATH**

Order Fractions

A raindrop is many times bigger than a water droplet and a dust particle. The table shows the size of droplets and dust particles in relation to the size of raindrops. Order the fractions from least to greatest.

Fractions	Ordered fractions
$\frac{1}{100}$	
$\frac{1}{1}$	
$\frac{1}{5000}$	
$\frac{1}{20}$	

Use the ordered fractions to correctly label the items on the diagram.

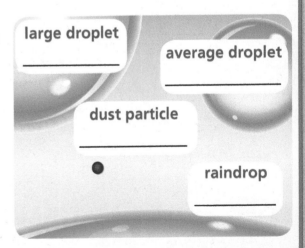

large droplet
_____

average droplet
_____

dust particle
_____

raindrop
_____

Where Does Water Go?

Most precipitation falls into oceans and evaporates back into the air. But some water takes a more roundabout path on its way through the water cycle.

ACTIVE READING As you read these pages, find and circle new key terms you need to know.

Imagine a rainstorm. Heavy rain falls on the ground. Some of this water will evaporate from shallow puddles quickly. It goes from Earth's surface directly back into the atmosphere.

Much of the rainfall will not reenter the atmosphere right away. Some will seep into the ground. Water that is stored underground is called **groundwater**. Groundwater can be found near the surface or very deep underground. Some groundwater may eventually return to the surface at places such as natural springs. Then it moves on through the water cycle.

As rainwater soaks into the ground, it fills up spaces between soil particles and cracks in rocks. Water that seeps deep underground becomes groundwater. Groundwater moves very slowly—if at all!

©Corbis

When glaciers melt, they quickly release stored water. Some of it may evaporate, some may seep into the ground, and some may move across the land as runoff.

Not all of the water that falls on land evaporates right away or seeps into the ground. **Runoff** is water that cannot soak into the ground and instead flows across Earth's surface. Too much precipitation may cause runoff. Runoff often flows into streams, rivers, and lakes. It may also flood low-lying areas.

Precipitation that falls in cold places may become part of a glacier. A *glacier* [GLAY•sher] is a large, slow-moving mass of ice. Water can be stored in glaciers for a very long time. Eventually, though, glaciers melt. Meltwater from glaciers can form lakes, flow into oceans, or become groundwater. Melting glaciers can increase the amount of runoff in a place.

Runaway Water

The picture shows runoff on a city street. In the space below, describe what might happen to this runoff.

_____

_____

_____

_____

_____

_____

A Precious Resource

Can you name all the ways that you use water? Water is an important resource used by all living things. People often need to share and conserve their sources of fresh, clean water.

ACTIVE READING As

you read these two pages, find and underline at least three facts about aquifers.

LEGEND
Floridan aquifer system

When you turn on a faucet, water flows out. Where does it come from? People can get fresh water from rivers or lakes. They can also get fresh water from aquifers. An *aquifer* [AH•kwuh•fuhr] is a body of rock that stores groundwater. People can drill into an aquifer and pump the water to the surface.

The water in aquifers can run low if people use more than can be replaced by precipitation. Human activities can also pollute aquifers. States that share aquifers work together to find solutions to these problems. They want to make sure there is enough fresh, clean water for everyone.

The Floridan Aquifer covers about 60,000 square kilometers. Billions of liters of water are pumped out of the Floridan Aquifer each day. Large cities, such as Savannah and Orlando, get water from this aquifer.

Where Does Your Water Come From?

Find out the source of your water at school or at home.

_____

_____

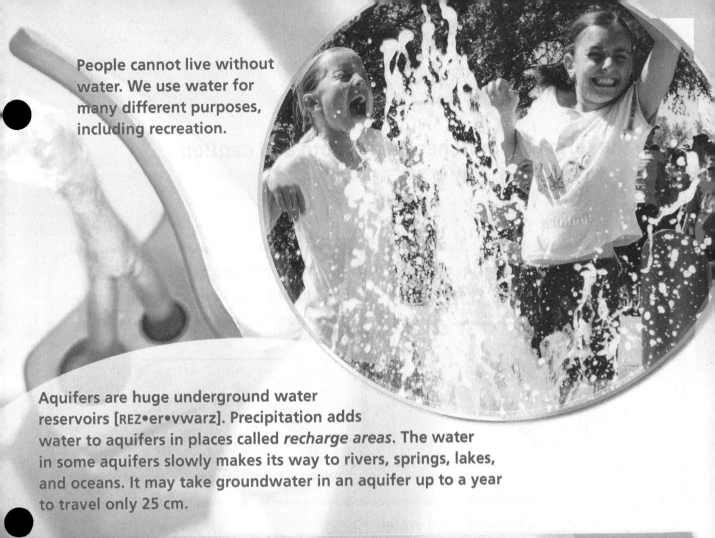

People cannot live without water. We use water for many different purposes, including recreation.

Aquifers are huge underground water reservoirs [REZ•er•vwarz]. Precipitation adds water to aquifers in places called *recharge areas*. The water in some aquifers slowly makes its way to rivers, springs, lakes, and oceans. It may take groundwater in an aquifer up to a year to travel only 25 cm.

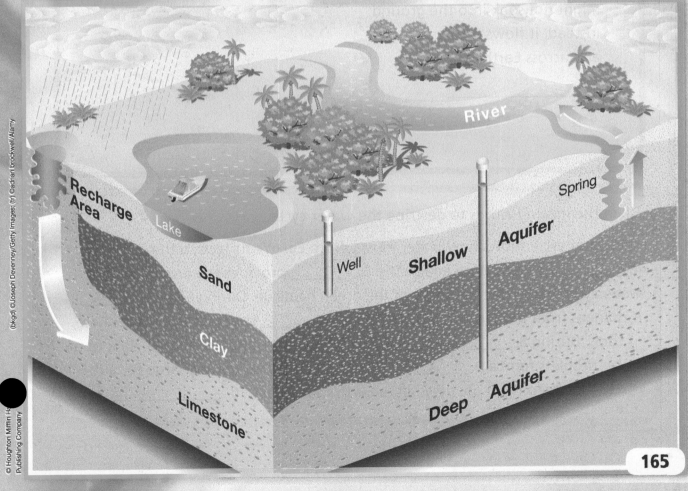

Recharge Area

Lake

River

Sand

Well

Shallow

Aquifer

Spring

Clay

Deep Aquifer

Limestone

Sum It Up »

Write the term that matches each photo and caption.

1 Water can be stored for a long time in a large, slow-moving mass of ice. _____

2 Water can also be stored underground between the spaces in soil particles or cracks in rocks.

_____

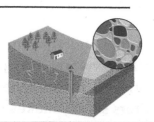

3 During heavy rains, some water might not soak into the ground. Instead, it flows down slopes and across Earth's surface.

_____

Fill in the missing words to describe the water cycle.

The water cycle shows how water moves from Earth's surface to the 4. _____ and back again. The 5. _____ provides the energy for the water cycle. Water on the surface of the ocean heats up. During 6. _____ , it changes from a liquid to a gas. As 7. _____ rises into the atmosphere, it cools. During 8. _____ , it changes from a gas to a liquid. Billions of water droplets form a 9. _____ . When the droplets get too large for air currents to keep them up, they fall to Earth's surface as 10. _____ .

Name _____

Vocabulary Review

① Use the clues to fill in the missing letters of the words.

1. g _ _ _ _ _ w _ _ ◯ _   Water stored underground
   10

2. _ o _ d _ _ _ _ _ _ _ _   The changing of water from a gas to a liquid

3. _ a _ _ _ _ ◯ c _ _   The movement of water from Earth's surface to the atmosphere and back again
   7

4. _ t _ _ _ p _ _ _ ◯   Mixture of gases that surrounds Earth
   4

5. _ r _ ◯ i _ _ _ _ _ t _ _ _   Water that falls from clouds to Earth's surface
   8

6. ◯ u _ _ _ _ _   Water that flows across Earth's surface
   5

7. g ◯ _ ◯ i _ _   A huge mass of frozen water that moves slowly
   9   6

8. _ r _ n _ _ i _ _ ◯ _ _ _   The process in which plants return water vapor to the atmosphere
   3

9. ◯ _ t _ _ _ _ a _ _ _   Water as a gas
   1

10. _ v _ _ o _ ◯ t _ o _   The changing of water from a liquid to a gas
    2

Bonus: Solve the Riddle!

Use the circled letters in the clues above to solve the riddle.

What is water's favorite way to travel?

On a ‾1‾ ‾2‾ ‾3‾ ‾4‾ ‾5‾   ‾6‾ ‾7‾ ‾8‾ ‾9‾ ‾10‾

167

Apply Concepts

2 The sentences below show the steps that lead to the formation of a cloud. Number the steps to place them in the proper order.

_____ Water vapor cools and condenses around tiny particles.

_____ Water is heated by the sun.

_____ Water evaporates into the air.

_____ Billions of water droplets join together.

3 In the picture below, show how groundwater can return to the atmosphere. Use arrows to show how the water moves and use wavy lines to show evaporation.

4 What would happen if water could not condense in the atmosphere?

_____

_____

_____

_____

5 In the spaces below, draw and label examples of water in the atmosphere as a solid, a liquid, and a gas. Hint: Wavy lines may be used to represent water vapor.

_____   _____   _____

_____   _____   _____

6 Label each of the following scenes as an example of evaporation, precipitation, or condensation. Then briefly describe what happens during each process.

_____   _____   _____

_____   _____   _____

_____   _____   _____

7 The picture shows stored water being used to irrigate crops. Circle and label the source of the water. How may this stored water be renewed?

_____

_____

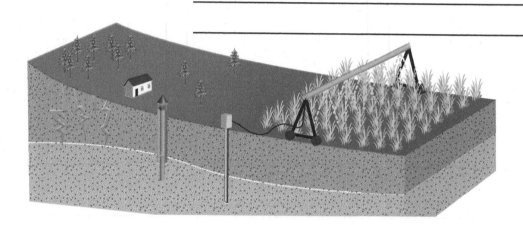

8 During an ice age, water is stored in glaciers. The picture below shows land area before and after an ice age. How are the land area and the oceans affected during an ice age?

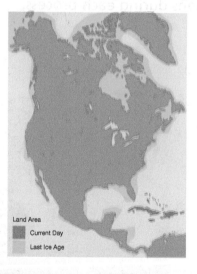

Land Area
Current Day
Last Ice Age

_____

_____

_____

_____

_____

_____

Take It Home!

See *ScienceSaurus*® for more information about water on Earth.

SC.5.E.7.1 Create a model to explain the parts of the water cycle... SC.5.E.7.2 Recognize that the ocean is an integral part of the water cycle and is connected to all of Earth's water reservoirs via evaporation and precipitation processes. SC.5.N.1.1 ... plan and carry out scientific investigations... SC.5.N.1.5 ... authentic scientific investigation frequently does not parallel the steps of "the scientific method."

Name _____

ESSENTIAL QUESTION

What Happens During the Water Cycle?

EXPLORE

What role does the ocean play in the water cycle?

Before You Begin—Preview the Steps

(1) Label the plastic containers A and B. Make two identical clay landform models. Include a lake in each model.

(2) Place the landform models on one end of each container. Each model should take up about 1/4 of the space in its container.

(3) Stir 2 teaspoons of salt into 2 cups of water. Pour the salt water into the empty area in container A. Add 3 drops of fresh water to the lake in each container.

(4) Cover both containers with plastic wrap. Use a large rubber band to hold the plastic wrap in place.

(5) Place a small weight on the plastic wrap above the land in each model. Place both containers on a sunny windowsill.

(6) Two hours later, observe the models. Record your observations.

© Houghton Mifflin H
Publishing Company

Set a Purpose

How do models help you study processes, such as the water cycle?

_____

_____

_____

Think About the Procedure

Why did the landform models take up only one-fourth of the containers?

_____

_____

Why did you add salt to the water?

_____

_____

Why did you put the containers on a sunny windowsill?

_____

_____

Name _____

Record Your Data

In the space below, write or draw your results.

| Observations of Model ||
Model without ocean water	Model with ocean water

Draw Conclusions

How did your models work?

_____
_____
_____
_____

Claims • Evidence • Reasoning

1. Make a claim about the role oceans play in the water cycle. Provide evidence to support your claim.

   _____

   _____

2. Suppose you kept the models under a lamp overnight. Make a claim about what would happen to the models. Explain your reasoning.

   _____

   _____

   _____

3. What evidence do you have about the role of the plastic wrap in the model? What does the plastic wrap represent?

   _____

   _____

   _____

4. Make a claim about what would happen if you left the models uncovered in the sunlight. Explain your reasoning.

   _____

   _____

5. Make a claim about what would happen if you left the models outdoors in a place with freezing temperatures. Explain your reasoning.

   _____

   _____

   _____

SC.5.E.7.3 Recognize how air temperature, barometric pressure, humidity, wind speed and direction, and precipitation determine the weather in a particular place and time. SC.5.E.7.4 Distinguish among the various forms of precipitation (rain, snow, sleet, and hail), making connections to the weather in a particular place and time.

ESSENTIAL QUESTION

How Do We Measure Weather?

Engage Your Brain

Find the answer to the following question in this lesson and record it here.

What is the weather like in this place and what tools could be used to measure it?

_____

_____

_____

_____

📖 ACTIVE **READING**

Lesson Vocabulary

List the terms. As you learn about each one, make notes in the Interactive Glossary.

_____

_____

_____

_____

Compare and Contrast

In this lesson, you will read about types of weather and the tools used to measure it. An author often compares and contrasts related things. Active readers ask themselves, How are these things alike? How are they different?

What's the Weather Like?

Crack! Boom! These are the sounds of a thunderstorm. Thunderstorms are one kind of weather. What other kinds of weather can you think of?

ACTIVE READING As you read these pages, connect two images that show similar types of weather.

Look outside. What is the weather like? It might be sunny or rainy. It might be stormy or windy. It might be hot or cold. **Weather** is what the atmosphere is like at a given time and place. Weather can change from day to day, or even from hour to hour.

Meteorologists [mee•tee•uh•RAHL•uh•jists] are scientists who study weather. They measure factors such as air temperature, amount of cloud cover, and how much precipitation falls from the sky. They analyze their measurements to make a weather report.

▶ Label the kind of weather shown in each photo on these pages. Then select one of the photos, and write a caption for it in the space below.

_____

_____

_____

Weather reports tell you what the weather will be like. They help you plan your day. For example, if the weather is cloudy and cold, you need to wear warm clothing to go outside. But if the weather is sunny and warm, you could wear a T–shirt and sandals.

Weather reports are helpful in other ways. Planes cannot fly in severe weather, so airports use weather reports to help schedule flights. Weather reports also help farmers care for their crops. They need to water their crops in dry weather. They need to protect their crops from freezing in cold weather.

Watching the Weather

You likely have used a thermometer before. Some of the tools shown on these pages might not be as familiar as a thermometer. But all are used to measure weather.

ACTIVE **READING** Before you read, turn the main heading into a question. As you read these pages, underline the sentences, terms, or phrases that answer your question.

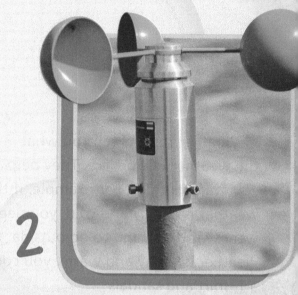

2

1

Meteorologists use tools to study the weather. You can use some of these tools, too, at home or at school.

- Weather balloons are used to carry weather tools high up into the atmosphere. Instruments attached to the balloon measure temperature, wind speed, and other weather conditions.

- A *wind vane* measures wind direction. It points in the direction from which the wind blows. Wind direction can be given as *N* for north, *S* for south, *E* for east, *W* for west, or as a combination such as *NE* for northeast.

- An **anemometer** measures wind speed. It has cuplike arms that spin when the wind blows. Wind speed is measured in kilometers per hour (km/hr).

- A **barometer** measures air pressure. It has a sealed metal chamber that expands and contracts when air pressure changes. Air pressure may be measured in inches of mercury (in. Hg) or in millibars (mb).

- A *hygrometer* measures the amount of water vapor in the air, or **humidity**.

The higher the temperature, the more water vapor air can hold. The amount of water vapor in the air compared to what it can hold at a given temperature is called *relative humidity*. Relative humidity is given as a percentage.

Which Tool Is Which?

▶ Look at the pictures on these pages. Identify the tool next to each number, and explain what it measures. Record your answers in the chart below.

	Tool	What It Measures
1		
2		
3		
4		
5		

Lying Low, Reaching High

You might see a cloud in the sky and think it looks like a fluffy dog. How would you go about classifying all the different clouds in the sky?

ACTIVE READING As you read these two pages, underline two characteristics used to classify clouds.

Clouds have different shapes and form at different heights in the atmosphere. Shape and height are two characteristics used to classify clouds.

Based on their shapes, clouds can be classified as stratus, cirrus, or cumulus.

- *Stratus* [STRAT•uhs] clouds form flat layers that cover most of the sky. They may signal rain.

- *Cirrus* [SIR•uhs] clouds are thin, white, and feathery. They are often signs of fair weather.

- *Cumulus* [KYOO•myuh•luhs] clouds are puffy and white. They may have flat bases. They can signal fair weather or stormy weather.

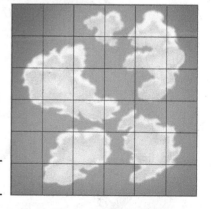

Stratus clouds form low in the sky. They look like a low, gray blanket. Fog is a kind of stratus cloud that forms near the ground.

 DO THE **MATH**

Estimating Fractions

Meteorologists look at the clouds in the sky to estimate cloud cover. Estimate the fraction of cloud cover in this model of the sky.

_____

_____

Cloud Identification Chart

High Clouds

Cirrocumulus

Cirrostratus
6,000 m

Altostratus

Middle Clouds

Altocumulus

2,000 m

Cumulus

Stratocumulus

Cumulonimbus

Stratus

Low Clouds

Nimbostratus

The chart on this page shows how clouds can also be classified by their heights.

- Low clouds are those formed below about 2,000 m (6,500 ft). Temperatures at this height are not very cold, so the clouds are mostly made of water droplets.

- Middle clouds are formed between 2,000 and 6,000 m (6,500 and 20,000 ft). Temperatures here can be cold, so the clouds are sometimes made of ice crystals. Altostratus [al•toh•STRAT•uhs] and altocumulus

[al•toh•KYOO•myuh•luhs] are examples of middle clouds.

- High clouds are formed above 6,000 m (20,000 ft). High clouds are often made of ice crystals because of the cold temperatures at these heights.

Notice that the tall cumulonimbus [kyoo•myuh•loh•NIM•buhs] cloud stretches from low heights to high heights. This kind of cloud has a flat top, and it often produces thunderstorms.

Cumulus clouds are usually made of water droplets. They resemble cotton puffs and often form at lower elevations. Sometimes they grow very tall and wide.

Cirrus clouds often form high in the atmosphere, where temperatures are cold. They are made up of ice crystals. They are often a sign that the weather is about to change.

It's Pouring
Solids and Liquids

Some precipitation falls as gentle flakes of snow.
Some precipitation falls as big drops of water.
Why isn't all precipitation the same?

ACTIVE READING As you read these two pages, underline the sentences that may help you contrast different kinds of precipitation.

*P*recipitation is solid or liquid water that falls from clouds to Earth's surface. Whether precipitation is solid or liquid may depend on the air temperature. Air temperature changes with the seasons, with elevation, and with location. Rain, snow, sleet, and hail are kinds of precipitation.

- *Rain* is liquid precipitation that falls through warm or cool air. It is the most common kind of precipitation.

- *Snow* is solid precipitation that falls through cold air.

- *Sleet* is precipitation that freezes near the ground. It often begins as rain or snow.

- *Hail* is solid precipitation made of layers of ice. It usually falls during thunderstorms.

Measuring Rain

▶ Look at the picture of the rain gauge. It shows the amount of rain that fell in an area. How much rain fell?

_____

1½ INCHES WHEN FULL

> **Rain** can start out high in the atmosphere as snow. A typical drizzle drop is about 0.1 mm in diameter. A raindrop that falls during a heavy storm can be as large as 6 mm in diameter. A rain gauge measures the depth of rain that falls in an area.

Sleet is made up of small pellets of ice. It may form when snow partially melts as it falls through a warm layer of air and freezes in a cold layer of air near the ground.

Hail forms inside large thunderclouds. First, wind carries raindrops high into the colder part of the cloud. The raindrops freeze and then fall through the lower, warmer part of the cloud. There, a new layer of moisture sticks to the hail particles, and wind carries them up again. This cycle repeats and the hail particles grow larger until they fall to the ground.

Snow forms when water vapor in the atmosphere turns directly into a solid. Like raindrops, when snow crystals become too large for air currents to keep them up, they fall to Earth. Snow falls in cold temperatures.

Sum It Up »

Write the term that matches each photo and caption.

1. This kind of cloud is usually found high in the sky. It is often made of ice crystals and signals fair weather.

   _____

2. This kind of cloud is found low in the sky. It often forms flat layers and produces rainy weather.

   _____

3. This kind of cloud is often found low in the sky. It has a flat base and can signal fair or rainy weather.

   _____

Use the terms below to fill in the graphic organizer about precipitation.

rain gauge   precipitation   snow   rain   air temperature   hail   sleet

Measured using a

5. _____

4. _____

Affected by

10. _____

Types of

6. _____

7. _____

8. _____

9. _____

Brain Check

Name _____

Vocabulary Review

Unscramble each word to match its definition.

1. **diytimuh**: A measure of the amount of water vapor in the air	
2. **threwae**: State of the atmosphere at a given place and time	
3. **teromerab**: Tool that measures air pressure	
4. **etomermane**: The water in a puddle changes to a gas through this process.	
5. **cruisr**: Thin, white, and feathery cloud	
6. **gfo**: Cloud that forms near the ground	
7. **lahi**: Precipitation made of layers of ice	

WORD BANK

barometer*	weather*	humidity*	cirrus
hail	anemometer*	fog	*Key Lesson Vocabulary

Apply Concepts

1 Complete the scene by drawing the type of precipitation that is most likely to fall based on the given air temperature. Label each scene with the type of precipitation.

25 °C

0 °C

−10 °C

_____   _____   _____

2 In the space below, draw the type of cloud that signals thunderstorms. Write a description of the cloud and the type of precipitation it produces.

_____

_____

_____

_____

_____

3 Draw a circle around the weather tool you would use to measure air pressure. Draw an X over the weather tool you would use to measure wind speed. Draw a square around the weather tool you would use to measure wind direction.

Take It Home! Share what you have learned about weather with your family. Go outside and look at the clouds. Describe the kinds of clouds that you see. Explain what kind of weather they usually signal.

SC.5.N.2.1 Recognize and explain that science is grounded in empirical observations that are testable; explanation must always be linked with evidence.

S.T.E.M.

ENGINEERING & TECHNOLOGY

Stormy Weather:
Beaufort Wind Scale

If you were a sailor on a ship, being able to measure wind speed would be very important. In the past, wind speed was estimated by observating its effect on things. Today, we use tools to measure wind speed. Read on to find out about ways to measure wind speed.

In 1805, Sir Francis Beaufort developed a scale to classify wind speed. This scale assigned levels based on sailors' observations. For example, a Force 3 wind describes a gentle breeze in which ships move steadily across the water. Force 6 describes a strong breeze that produces large waves, whitecaps, and spray. And Force 11 describes a violent storm.

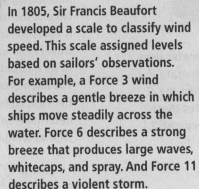

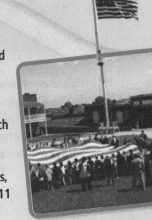

You can observe a flag to see how wind blows. A windsock shows the relative direction and speed of winds. The windsock droops during low wind speed. It flies straight out from the pole during high wind.

Use the text and reference materials to complete the table.

Beaufort Wind Force	Average Wind Speed (km/h)	Description	Beaufort Wind Force	Average Wind Speed (km/h)	Description
0	0	Calm		56	Near Gale
	3	Light Air			Gale
	9	Light Breeze		82	Severe Gale
		Gentle Breeze			Storm
	24	Moderate Breeze		110	
		Fresh Breeze	12	124	Hurricane
6	44				

S.T.E.M. continued

Today, wind speed is measured using anemometers.

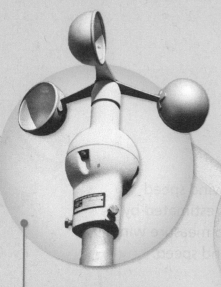

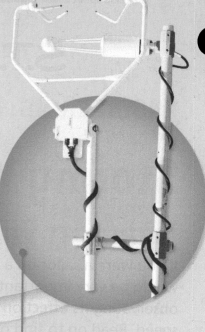

This anemometer uses cuplike devices to measure wind speed. The faster the wind blows, the faster the cups spin. The cups are attached to sensors that measure the actual wind speed.

This digital anemometer uses spinning fans to generate magnetic pulses. Then the instrument translates these pulses into measurements of the wind speed.

An ultrasound anemometer has pairs of sound speakers and microphones. Electronic circuits measure the time it takes for sound to travel from each speaker to its microphone. The anemometer uses the data collected to determine wind speed as well as wind direction.

Design Your Future

Use observations to design your own scale to measure something such as temperature, cloud cover, or amount or strength of rainfall. Write the process for using the scale and then try it out.

_____

_____

_____

_____

_____

ENGINEERING
DESIGN CHALLENGE

Design It:
Build a Wind Vane

Meteorologists use many tools to measure and predict weather. One of the most basic tools is called a wind vane. This tool points in the direction from which the wind blows. Knowing the wind's direction helps meteorologists make better weather predictions.

Some wind vanes have a base that shows the directions north, east, south, and west to help identify wind direction. How can you build a wind vane? Remember, an effective wind vane swivels easily when the wind direction changes!

S.T.E.M. continued

What to Do:

DESIGN PROCESS STEPS

1 Find a Problem
2 Plan & Build
3 Test & Improve
4 Redesign
5 Communicate

1 Research different types of wind vanes.

2 Identify everyday materials you could use to build a wind vane. List them here.

3 Think about the best ways to put these materials together to make a wind vane.

4 Identify the design criteria your wind vane must meet.

5 Make a diagram of your design.

6 Build and test your design.

7 Analyze the results of your test. Improve your wind vane until it meets your design criteria. What improvements did you make?

8 Use your wind vane to learn about weather in your community. What did you learn?

9 Keep a record of your work in your Science Notebook.

SC.5.E.7.3 Recognize how air temperature, barometric pressure, humidity, wind speed and direction, and precipitation determine the weather in a particular place and time. **SC.5.E.7.7** Design a family preparedness plan for natural disasters and identify reasons for having such a plan.

LESSON **4**

ESSENTIAL **QUESTION**

How Do Weather Patterns Help Us Predict Weather?

 **Engage Your Brain**

Find the answer to the following question in this lesson and record it here.

What do you think will happen when the dark cloud moves over this place?

_____

_____

_____

_____

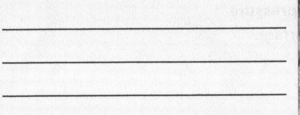 ACTIVE **READING**

Lesson Vocabulary

List the terms. As you learn about each one, make notes in the Interactive Glossary.

_____ _____

_____ _____

_____

Signal Words: Details

This lesson gives many details about predicting weather. Active readers look for signal words to identify examples and facts about a topic. Some words and phrases that signal details are for *example*, *also*, and *in fact*.

Windy Weather

You can't see air. But you can feel it each time the wind blows. What exactly is wind, and why does it blow?

ACTIVE **READING** As you read this page, circle common, everyday words that have a different meaning in science.

Air is made of matter. It has mass and volume. It presses on you from all sides. To understand wind, you must know more about air pressure. **Air pressure** is the weight of the atmosphere on Earth's surface.

The sun does not heat all parts of Earth's surface evenly. This uneven heating of Earth's surface causes differences in air pressure. The differences in air pressure cause air to move. **Wind** is moving air. In general, wind blows from areas of high pressure to areas of low pressure.

Lows

▶ What are two characteristics of air in a low pressure area?

_____

_____

_____

Air Pressure

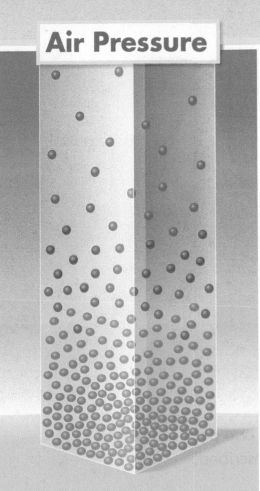

Local Winds Land heats up more quickly than water does. This means that during the day, the air above the land is warmer and has a lower density than the air above the water. Because of these differences, the warm air over the land rises and cool air over the water moves inland to replace it. This is called a *sea breeze*.

At night, the land loses heat faster than the water does. The cool air over the land has a greater pressure than the warm air over the water. So, the cool air moves out to sea to replace the rising warm air. This is called a *land breeze*.

The weight of air particles at the top of the atmosphere presses down on the air particles underneath. So, air pressure is greater near Earth's surface than high above it.

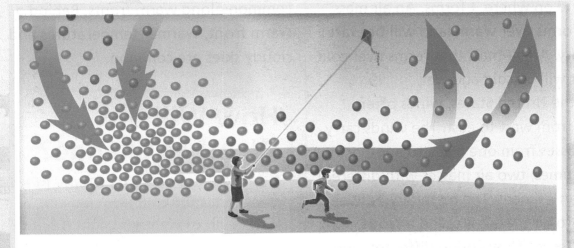

Temperature can affect air pressure. In cold temperatures, where air particles move close together and sink, the air pressure is high. In warm temperatures, where air particles move apart and rise, the air pressure is low. Across Earth's surface, air moves from high-pressure to low-pressure areas.

© Houghton Mifflin Harcourt Publishing Company

Battling Bodies of Air

When you take a shower, the air inside the bathroom becomes warm and wet. When you open the bathroom door, the warm, wet air meets cool, dry air. You've made a front! Read on to find out more about fronts and how they affect weather.

ACTIVE READING As you read these two pages, draw boxes around each type of front that is described.

Meteorologists call a large body of air that has the same temperature and moisture properties throughout an **air mass**. The properties of an air mass depend on where it forms. An air mass that forms over warm land will be warm and dry. An air mass that forms over cold water will be cold and wet.

In the United States, winds often blow from west to east. The winds carry air masses from one place to another. Sometimes, two air masses with different properties meet. The boundary between the two air masses is called a **front**.

Different fronts bring different types of weather. A cold front forms where a cold air mass moves under a warm air mass. Severe weather often forms along cold fronts. Sunny skies and cooler air that can be wet or dry usually follow a cold front. A warm front forms where a warm air mass moves over a cold air mass. Light rains and snow showers are common along warm fronts. Behind a warm front, warmer temperatures and cloudy skies are common.

How Will the Weather Change?

► Look at the map to the right. In which direction is the cold front moving, and what kind of weather might it bring?

_____

_____

_____

Warm air is lifted steeply upward along a cold front. Water vapor in the air cools and condenses into large cumulonimbus clouds. Hailstorms are possible.

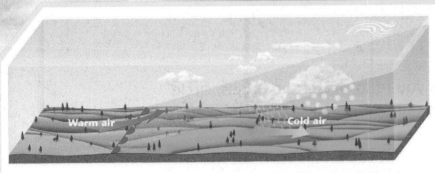

Warm air rises and cools slowly along a warm front. Cloudy skies can extend over large areas. Steady rain or snow can fall.

Weather forecasters use symbols to show fronts. The triangles and half-circles on these symbols point in the direction the front is moving.

LEGEND
△ cold front
◠ warm front

Hudson Bay

CANADA

ATLANTIC OCEAN

Cool dry air

Warm moist air

UNITED STATES

Gulf of Mexico

PACIFIC OCEAN

MEXICO

©John Lund/Corbis

© Houghton Mifflin Harcourt Publishing Company

Mapping the Weather

A flashing red hand on a traffic signal means *don't walk*. You use symbols each time you cross a busy street. Weather forecasters use symbols, too, to show weather conditions.

ACTIVE READING As you read these two pages, circle clue words or phrases that signal a detail such as an example or an added fact.

Maps are useful tools. A **weather map** is a map that uses symbols to show weather data. You already know the symbols for cold fronts and warm fronts. Weather maps also use symbols to show areas of high pressure (H) and areas of low pressure (L). They might also show temperature, cloud cover, and wind direction for different places.

How do meteorologists get the data they need to make weather maps? They use weather tools such as thermometers, barometers, and anemometers. These tools are placed in weather stations. A *weather station* is a structure that has tools for measuring and recording weather data at a given location. Weather stations are found all across the United States.

Meteorologists also get weather data from other sources. Satellites high above Earth send back information about cloud cover and storms. Doppler radar uses radio waves to track storms. Meteorologists look for patterns in the data they collect. For example, high pressure often brings fair weather. Low pressure often brings stormy weather. A weather report is based on the patterns that meteorologists find in the data they collect.

Predicting the Weather

▶ Use the weather map on the right to describe the weather for the city of Denver and to predict how it will change .

_____

_____

_____

_____

Weather maps can be used to help predict the weather. The map key shows what the symbols on the weather map represent.

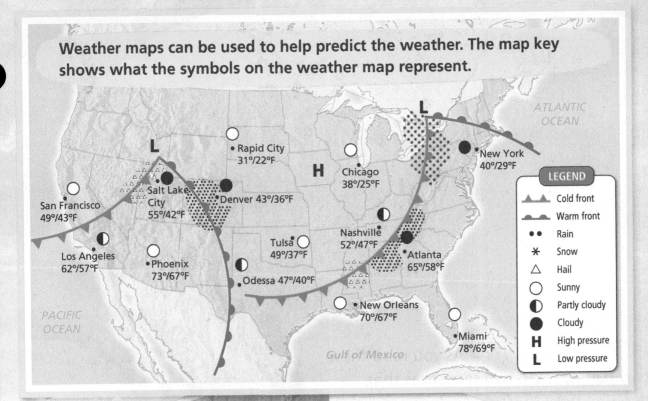

San Francisco 49°/43°F
Rapid City 31°/22°F
Salt Lake City 55°/42°F
Denver 43°/36°F
Chicago 38°/25°F
New York 40°/29°F
Los Angeles 62°/57°F
Phoenix 73°/67°F
Tulsa 49°/37°F
Nashville 52°/47°F
Atlanta 65°/58°F
Odessa 47°/40°F
New Orleans 70°/67°F
Miami 78°/69°F

ATLANTIC OCEAN
PACIFIC OCEAN
Gulf of Mexico

LEGEND
- Cold front
- Warm front
- Rain
- Snow
- Hail
- Sunny
- Partly cloudy
- Cloudy
- **H** High pressure
- **L** Low pressure

weather satellite

Meteorologists use satellites, Doppler radar, computer models, and weather stations to make weather reports. Using all of these tools, meteorologists are able to accurately track and predict the weather.

Doppler radar

weather station

When Disaster Strikes

Tornadoes. Hurricanes. Blizzards. Sometimes, the weather can turn dangerous. What should you do to stay safe when bad weather strikes?

ACTIVE READING As you read these two pages, circle two sentences that describe how to stay safe during a disaster.

A hurricane is a low-pressure storm. Its center, or eye, is calm. But wind speeds around the eye can be as fast as 250 km/hr. The strong winds cause much of the damage that a hurricane brings.

Thunder is crashing overhead. You look outside. You see a whirling column of air that stretches from a dark cloud to the ground. It's a tornado! Tornadoes, hurricanes, and blizzards are types of severe weather.

- A *tornado* has a funnel shape. Its strong winds can toss cars into the air. It can form from violent thunderstorms.

- A *hurricane* is a strong storm that forms over warm ocean water. When a hurricane moves over land, it can cause flooding, tornadoes, and thunderstorms. It is the most powerful storm of all.

- A *blizzard* is a strong winter storm. Blizzards have high winds and heavy snowfall.

Preparedness plans help people stay safe when disasters strike. Before and after a disaster, volunteers help provide assistance for people in need. They might help to sandbag riverbanks to prevent flooding or deliver water and food to those who need it.

Meteorologists track severe weather. They rank the storms by how strong the winds are or how much damage the storms might cause. They put out warnings so that people can seek shelter before a storm hits.

If possible, you should always go indoors when a storm is near. To prepare for severe weather, you can help your family put together an emergency kit. Your kit should have water, flashlights, batteries, canned food, first-aid supplies, and a radio. Listen to the radio for storm warnings.

 DO THE **MATH**

Solve Word Problems

The table shows how much water people of different ages should drink each day. Suppose a family wants to be sure they have enough water in case a natural disaster strikes. The family includes a mother, a father, a 10-year-old son, and a 6-year-old daughter. About how many gallons of water should they store to cover their needs for 3 days?

Remember: 16 cups equal 1 gallon.

Age Range	Amount of Water Needed Each Day
1 to 3 years	4 cups
4 to 8 years	5 cups
9 to 13 years	8 cups
14 years to adult	10 cups

_____

_____

_____

Sum It Up >>

Read the summary statements. Then match each statement with the correct picture.

①

1. During the day, cool, dense air from the ocean moves inland, replacing warm air over the land.

A

2. A cold air mass moves under a warm air mass.

B

3. During the night, cool, dense air over land moves out to sea, replacing warm air over the ocean.

C

4. A warm air mass moves gently over a cold air mass.

D

Fill in the Venn diagram about air pressure by writing the correct number in each category.

5. Shown as *L* on a weather map

6. Brings fair weather

7. Measure of the weight of the atmosphere on Earth's surface

8. Shown as *H* on a weather map

9. Brings stormy weather

High Pressure   **Low Pressure**

Both

Brain Check

Name _____

Vocabulary Review

1 ### Draw a line from each term to its definition or description.

1. wind*

2. sea breeze

3. front*

4. air mass*

5. weather map*

6. weather station

7. air pressure*

A. Body of air with the same properties throughout

B. Structure that houses weather tools

C. Boundary between two different air masses

D. Map that shows weather conditions

E. Measure of the weight of the atmosphere on Earth's surface

F. Breeze that blows from the sea to the land

G. Moving Air

*Key Lesson Vocabulary

2 The symbols below show weather data for a place. Write what each symbol stands for. Predict the kind of weather a place near the *H* will have.

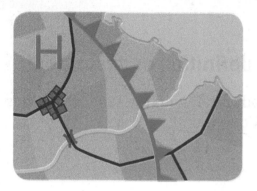

_____

_____

_____

_____

_____

3 Fill in the graphic organizer below to show how meteorologists get data to predict the weather.

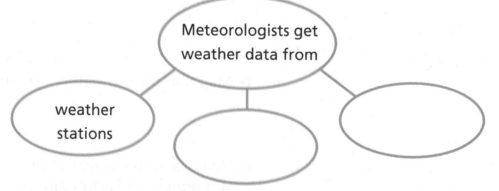

Meteorologists get weather data from

weather stations

4 Label the kinds of severe weather shown in the pictures below.

_____   _____   _____

5 Heated air inside a hot-air balloon causes it to rise into the sky. When the air cools, the balloon returns to the ground. When is the hot-air balloon behaving like an air mass in a high-pressure area? In a low-pressure area?

_____

_____

_____

_____

6 Label each picture with the type of air mass that would form over it.

_____   _____

_____   _____

7 Mountain and valley breezes are similar to land and sea breezes. During the day, the sun heats up a mountain's side more quickly than the valley below. In the picture below, draw arrows to show wind direction during the day.

8 Put a check mark (√) next to each item that should be part of an emergency kit.

Items	Emergency Kit
1. air conditioner	
2. portable radio	
3. electric blanket	
4. bottled water	
5. first-aid supplies	

 Share with your family what you've learned about preparing for bad weather. Work with a family member to make a safety plan. Gather supplies for an emergency kit. Review the plan with family members.

SC.5.E.7.3 Recognize how air temperature, barometric pressure, humidity, wind speed and direction, and precipitation determine the weather in a particular place and time. SC.5.E.7.4 Distinguish among the various forms of precipitation... SC.5.N.1.1 ... plan and carry out scientific investigations of various types... SC.5.N.1.6 Recognize and explain the difference between personal opinion/interpretation and verified observation.

INQUIRY LESSON 5

Name _____

ESSENTIAL **QUESTION**

How Can We Observe Weather Patterns?

Materials

thermometer
barometer
rain gauge
wind vane
cloud chart
hygrometer
anemometer

EXPLORE

Meteorologists use weather tools to observe and measure weather. They look for patterns in the data they collect to make weather predictions. How can we use these same tools to find weather patterns?

Before You Begin—Preview the Steps

1. With your teacher's help, practice taking measurements using weather tools. Make sure you know what each tool measures. Also, review the units of measurement for each tool.

2. As a class, select a place on the school grounds to set up a weather station. The place should be sheltered from the sun.

3. Set up the weather station using the tools listed in the materials section.

4. As a class, take turns and work in teams to measure weather data at the same times each day for five days. Use the cloud chart to identify cloud types. Record your weather observations.

5. After the fifth day, look for patterns in your observations. Predict the weather for the following three days.

205

Set a Purpose

Why is it helpful to observe the weather?

_____

_____

_____

_____

Think About the Procedure

Why should the chosen location for your weather station be sheltered from the sun?

_____

_____

_____

_____

Why would it be useful to measure the weather conditions at the same time every day?

_____

_____

_____

_____

Name _____

Record Your Data

Record your observations in the table below.

DAY	Weather Observations
	Weather Predictions

Draw Conclusions

How can we observe weather patterns?

_____

_____

Claims • Evidence • Reasoning

1. Describe weather patterns you can identify in your data.

_____

_____

2. Based on your data, make a claim about which weather conditions were most likely to change before the weather changed. Explain your reasoning.

_____

_____

_____

3. What were your weather predictions? On which weather pattern did you base them?

_____

_____

_____

4. Make a claim about whether your predictions were accurate. Provide evidence to support your claim.

_____

_____

5. What would have made your weather predictions more accurate?

_____

_____

_____

SC.5.E.7.5 Recognize that some of the weather-related differences, such as temperature and humidity, are found among different environments.... SC.5.E.7.6 Describe characteristics ... of different climate zones as they relate to latitude, elevation, and proximity to bodies of water.

LESSON 6

ESSENTIAL **QUESTION**

What Factors Affect Climate?

 Engage Your Brain

Find the answer to the following question in this lesson and record it here.

Giraffes live in warm places. How can there be snow near a giraffe's home?

_____

_____

_____

_____

📖 ACTIVE **READING**

Lesson Vocabulary

List the terms. As you learn about each one, make notes in the Interactive Glossary.

_____ _____

_____ _____

Visual Aids

A map adds information to the text that appears on the page with it. Active readers pause their reading to study maps and decide how their information adds to the text.

Climate vs. Weather

During the summer, the weather might be sunny one day and cloudy the next. But for most places, temperatures in the summer stay warm. The weather changes, but the overall weather pattern stays the same.

ACTIVE **READING** As you read the next two pages, draw a star next to what you consider to be the most important sentence, and be ready to explain why.

Your area has certain weather patterns during the year. These patterns make up the climate where you live. **Climate** is the long-term weather patterns of a place.

Climate is different from weather. *Weather* describes what the atmosphere is like at a given time and place. For example, on average, a desert might get only a few centimeters of rain each year. The desert has a dry climate. But the weather in the desert might be rainy one day and dry the next.

Scientists find the climate of an area by averaging weather conditions over a long period of time. They study an area's temperature, wind speed, wind direction, cloud cover, air pressure, and amount of precipitation. They find the average of these conditions for each month or year. They look at 30 years or more of data to determine the climate of an area.

©Houghton Mifflin Harcourt Publishing Company

DO THE MATH

Analyze Data

Use the data in the table to make a line graph. Then compare all the graphs to answer the questions below.

1. During which months in 2005 was Fargo's precipitation more than 20 mm below its long-term average?

_____

2. During which months in 2005 was Fargo's average temperature closest to its long-term average? Which month is most different?

_____

_____

_____

_____

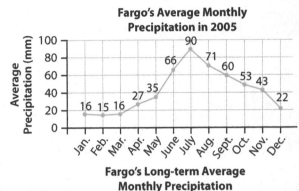

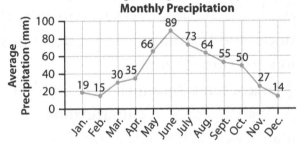

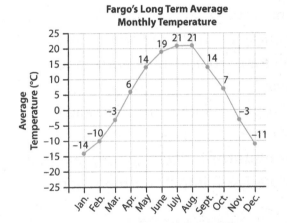

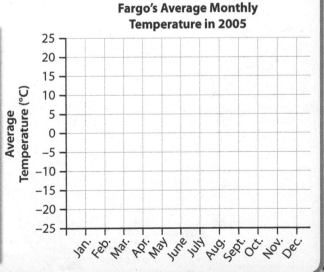

Average Monthly Temperature for Fargo, North Dakota, in 2005			
Month	Average Temp. °C	Month	Average Temp. °C
Jan	−13.0	July	22.0
Feb	−10.0	Aug	20.0
Mar	−2.0	Sept	14.0
Apr	7.0	Oct	7.0
May	14.0	Nov	−2.0
June	18.0	Dec	−8.0

Hot, Cold, and Medium

Is it hot year-round where you live? Or is it cold? What is the climate where you live? Look through these pages and find out!

KEY	
Temperate	☐
Tropical	■
Polar	■

ACTIVE **READING** As you read these two pages, underline the sentence that describes the temperature in each climate zone.

Places can be grouped into different climate zones. A **climate zone** is an area that has similar average temperatures and precipitation throughout. Three of Earth's climate zones are *tropical, temperate,* and *polar.*

Tropical climates are generally warm. They occur near the equator. The **equator** is the imaginary line that divides Earth into its northern and southern hemispheres, or halves.

Temperate climates are found in middle latitudes, between the tropical and the polar climate zones. **Latitude** is a measure of how far north or south a place is from the equator.

Polar climates are generally the farthest from the equator. They have cold temperatures year-round and low amounts of precipitation.

Temperate climate zones have moderate temperatures and varying precipitation. For most of the year, the temperature ranges from 10 °C to 18 °C. They usually have four distinct seasons. Much of the United States is found in this zone.

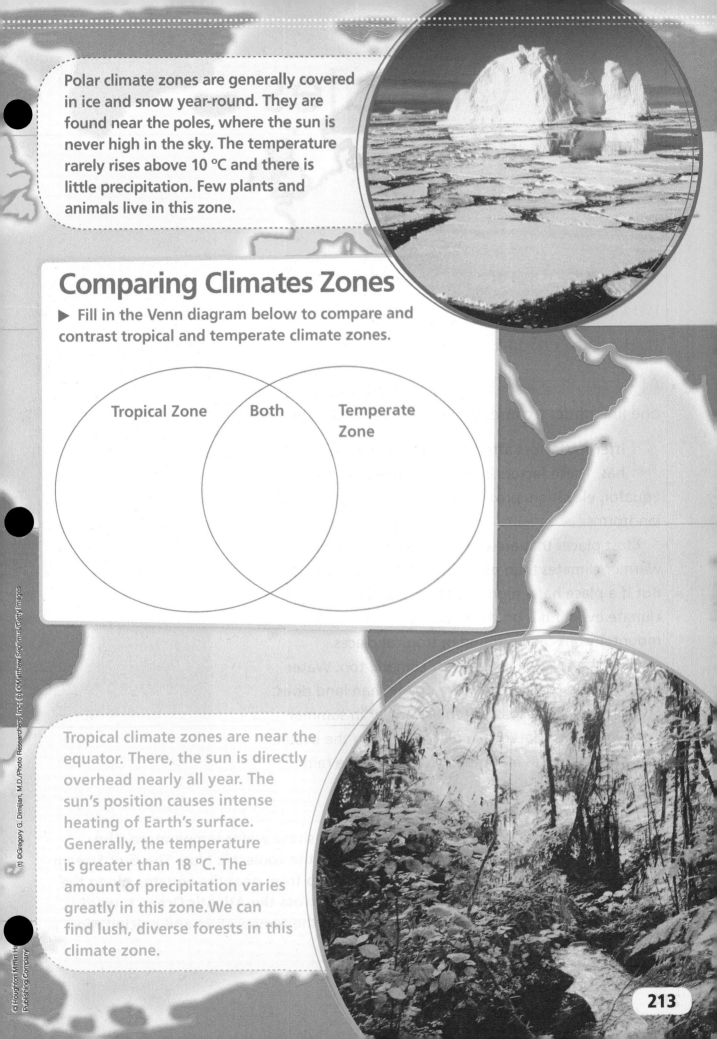

Polar climate zones are generally covered in ice and snow year-round. They are found near the poles, where the sun is never high in the sky. The temperature rarely rises above 10 °C and there is little precipitation. Few plants and animals live in this zone.

Comparing Climates Zones

▶ Fill in the Venn diagram below to compare and contrast tropical and temperate climate zones.

Tropical Zone   Both   Temperate Zone

Tropical climate zones are near the equator. There, the sun is directly overhead nearly all year. The sun's position causes intense heating of Earth's surface. Generally, the temperature is greater than 18 °C. The amount of precipitation varies greatly in this zone. We can find lush, diverse forests in this climate zone.

Why Climates Differ

Why does it rarely snow in Florida? Why isn't Alaska warm year-round? What things make one climate different from another?

ACTIVE READING As you read this page, draw one line under a cause. Draw two lines under the effect.

Different factors affect the kind of climate a place has. These factors include distance from the equator, elevation, proximity to bodies of water, and landforms.

Most places that are close to the equator have warmer climates than places that are farther away. But if a place has a high elevation, it will have a cool climate even if it is on the equator. That's why snowy mountaintops can be found in tropical places.

Oceans and large lakes affect climate, too. Water heats up and cools down more slowly than land does. So places near the coast often are cooler in summer and warmer in winter than places far from the ocean. Landforms, such as mountains, can affect the rain pattern of large areas.

Gulf of Mexico

Pacific Ocean

The different colors on the oceans show water temperature. The warmest water is colored red, and the coolest is blue. The *Gulf Stream* is a warm ocean current. It flows up from near the equator, along the east coast of North America, and across the Atlantic Ocean toward northern Europe. It deeply affects the temperature and precipitation amounts of nearby coastal areas.

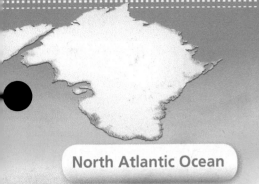

North Atlantic Ocean

The elevation of the mountain causes climate zones. As you go up in Earth's atmosphere, the air gets colder. So, the climate at the base of a mountain might be very hot, but as you go up, it gets colder and colder until you reach a zone where no trees grow at all. That is why mountains near the equator can have tropical rain forests at their base, but snow with no trees at all at the top.

Gulf Stream

A rain-shadow effect can happen when wet air that formed over the ocean rises up the side of a mountain. Clouds form and precipitation takes place on the ocean side of the mountain, giving it a wet climate. The air, now dry, moves down the far side of the mountain. This side has a dry climate. It's in a *rain shadow*.

Predicting Change

▶ Town A is located near the coast, along which a warm ocean current flows. Predict what would happen to the climate of Town A if the ocean current stopped flowing.

_____

_____

Cool Drier

Wind

Ocean

Warm Wet

Hot Dry

Climate and the Environment

Why do polar bears live in cold places, while elephants live in warm places? How does climate affect the living and nonliving things in a place?

ACTIVE READING As you read this page, find and underline examples of how climate affects living and nonliving things.

Climate affects where organisms can live. A polar bear has a thick layer of fat that keeps it warm in the polar climate where it lives. Maple trees have broad leaves to capture sunlight during the warm summer months. They shed their leaves during the cold, dry winter to prevent water loss.

Climate also affects the nonliving parts of the environment. Over time, wind-driven waves can reshape a continent's coastline. Rain, wind, and changes in temperature can cause rock to break. The broken bits of rock can mix with dead plant and animal matter to form soil.

Polar bears

216

Desert: A desert is a dry environment. Temperatures may vary greatly in deserts. It can be very hot during the day and cold at night. Living things in deserts need to be able to survive on little water. Cactuses have a waxy coating that helps them store water.

Swamp: Swamps can be covered by fresh water, salt water, or both. Swamps occur in places where the ground cannot soak in all the preciptation or runoff that reaches the area. Temperatures may be very hot in swamps for part of the year. But swamps may also occur in places that have cold winters. Many types of plants and animals live in swamps.

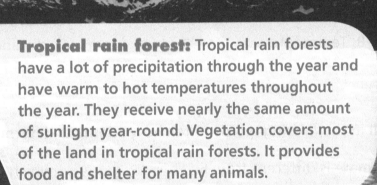

Tropical rain forest: Tropical rain forests have a lot of precipitation through the year and have warm to hot temperatures throughout the year. They receive nearly the same amount of sunlight year-round. Vegetation covers most of the land in tropical rain forests. It provides food and shelter for many animals.

▶ What effects might a long time with no rain have on these three environments?

_____

_____

_____

_____

Sum It Up »

Complete the outline below to summarize the lesson.

① I. Climate

    A. **①** _____

    B. determined by the long-term average precipitation and temperature

II. Main climate zones

    A. **②** _____

        1. warm year-round

        2. can be wet or dry

        3. found near the equator

    B. Temperate

        1. **③** _____

        2. different amounts of precipitation

        3. found in middle latitudes

    C. Polar

        1. usually little precipitation

        2. **④** _____

        3. found in high latitudes

III. **⑤** _____

    A. bodies of water

    B. landforms

    C. elevation

    D. distance from the equator

Fill in the missing words to tell how scientists determine the climate of a place.

Climate is different from 6. _____ , which describes what the atmosphere is like at a given time and place. Scientists find the climate of a place by averaging weather conditions over a 7. _____ period of time. They study an area's temperature, wind speed, wind direction, cloud cover, air pressure, and amount of 8. _____ .

They find the 9. _____ of these conditions for each month of the year. They look at 10. _____ years or more of data to find the climate of a place.

Vocabulary Review

1. Use the clues to unscramble the words in the box. Use the word bank if you need help.

1. **qaroeut**: the imaginary line that divides Earth into the northern and southern hemispheres, or halves	
2. **ertmpeate emlciat**: has moderate temperatures	
3. **taliecm noze**: an area with the same kind of climate conditions	
4. **dutlatei**: distance of a place from the equator	
5. **lopricta itleamc**: is warm year-round	
6. **rewaeth**: state of the atmosphere at a certain time and place	
7. **ropal atmlcie**: is cold year-round	
8. **catmile**: long-term weather patterns of a place	

latitude*   temperate climate   climate zone*   polar climate
climate*   equator*   tropical climate   weather

*Key Lesson Vocabulary

Apply Concepts

(2) The pictures below show different kinds of clothing to wear in the fall. In which climate zone would you wear each piece of clothing? Write your answers on the lines under the pictures.

_____   _____   _____

(3) Correctly label each statement below with a C if it refers to climate and a W if it refers to weather.

a. In Antarctica, the average yearly temperature is below freezing. ___

b. Cherrapunji, India, may be the rainiest place on Earth. ___

c. It hasn't rained for two weeks in Macon, Georgia. ___

d. Today's air temperature was the highest this week. ___

(4) In the picture below, add arrows to show how air moves to form a rain shadow. Add labels showing where you would find a dry climate and a wet climate.

5 Label the climate zones in the map below.

A _____

B _____

C _____

6 The graph below shows the long-term average monthly temperature of a place. In which climate zone is this place likely to be found? Explain.

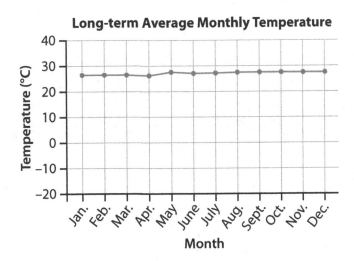

Long-term Average Monthly Temperature

_____

_____

7 Suppose the climate of a rain forest changes. Its temperature is now always near or below freezing, but its precipitation remains high. Draw and describe what this place would look like after a few years.

_____

_____

_____

8 The picture shows a landform. Label where the climate will be the coolest and where it will be the warmest on the landform.

SC.5.E.7.2 Recognize that the ocean is an integral part of the water cycle and is connected to all of Earth's water reservoirs via evaporation and precipitation processes.

⬡ CAREERS **IN SCIENCE**

1 Hydrology is the study of the quality and movement of water. A hydrologist is a person who uses hydrology in their everyday work.

2 The word *hydrology* comes from the Greek words *hydro* meaning "water" and *logos* meaning "study".

3 To make sure it is safe, hydrologists test the water you drink for pollutants.

4 Hydrologists need to know how soils and rocks may affect water quality.

5 They also care about the quality of the water in rivers, streams, and oceans.

10 THINGS
YOU SHOULD KNOW ABOUT
Hydrologists

6 Hydrologists can help decide where to dig wells for underground water.

7 A hydrologist can help farmers figure out how to get water for their crops.

8 Hydrologists help design dams to produce electricity and prevent floods.

9 They can use their knowledge to help predict floods and droughts.

10 A hydrologist can help design sewers and drainage systems.

Show What You Know About Hydrologists

Answer these five questions about hydrologists.

1 What part of a hydrologist's work do you find most interesting?

_____

_____

_____

_____

2 What do hydrologists study?

_____

_____

_____

_____

3 How do hydrologists help us?

_____

_____

_____

_____

4 Write the question that goes with the answer below.

_____

_____

_____

_____

5 Write and answer your own question about hydrologists.

_____

_____

_____

_____

©Comstock/Getty Images

Benchmark Review

Name _____

Vocabulary Review

Use the terms in the box to complete the sentences.

┌─────────────────┐
│ precipitation   │
│ evaporation   │
└─────────────────┘

1. The climate of a particular place is determined

   by temperature and _____.

2. Oceans receive freshwater from rain and rivers, but

   ocean levels do not change much because of constant

   _____ of water from the ocean's surface.

Science Concepts

Fill in the letter of the choice that best answers the question.

3. Deanna measured the temperature and humidity every afternoon for four days. She recorded the results in the table below.

Day	Temperature	Relative humidity (%)
Monday	28 °C (82 °F)	90
Tuesday	27 °C (81 °F)	79
Wednesday	24 °C (75 °F)	70
Thursday	28 °C (82 °F)	69

Which day could Deanna conclude was the most hot and humid?

(A) Monday   (C) Tuesday

(B) Wednesday   (D) Thursday

4. Kendell wants to determine if there is a trend in air temperature changes during April. Which of the following procedures should he follow?

(F) Measure the temperature every hour for 1 day.

(G) Measure the temperature at noon every day in April.

(H) Measure the temperature at the same time each Monday.

(I) Measure the temperature on the first and last day of April.

5. Most of the clouds in a photograph of a mountain scene are cirrus clouds. Where do cirrus clouds form?

(A) around mountains

(B) at high elevations

(C) near the ground

(D) over the oceans

6. The table below describes some weather conditions at two different weather stations.

	Station 1	Station 2
Temperature	10 °C (50 °F)	20 °C (68 °F)
Precipitation	3 cm	2 cm
Wind	3 km/hr west	8 km/hr east
Cloud cover	overcast	mostly cloudy

Which statement is correct?

Ⓕ Station 1 is experiencing more rain than station 2.

Ⓖ Both stations are experiencing freezing conditions.

Ⓗ Station 1 is experiencing stronger winds than station 2.

Ⓘ Both stations have wind traveling in the same direction.

7. The diagram below shows the water cycle.

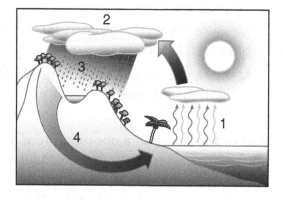

At which point does precipitation happen?

Ⓐ 1   Ⓒ 3

Ⓑ 2   Ⓓ 4

8. Which of the following is a cumulus cloud?

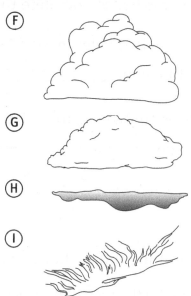

9. The following diagram shows a location where two air masses meet.

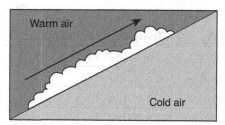

What is the weather like at this type of front?

Ⓐ cloudy and rainy

Ⓑ clear and cold

Ⓒ clear and warm

Ⓓ windy and cold

226   Unit 4

Name _____

10. The following diagram shows the pattern of air movement in a coastal area.

Which type of wind is illustrated in the diagram?

(F) valley breeze   (H) land breeze

(G) sea breeze   (I) mountain breeze

11. Where in a tropical climate are you most likely to find cooler weather and snow?

(A) at the top of a tall mountain

(B) at sea level near a cold ocean current

(C) in cloudy places near the center of the continent

(D) at the base of a mountain range that blocks air flow

12. Scientists study many factors that allow them to predict weather. Which factor **most directly** affects the movement of air?

(F) air pressure   (H) precipitation

(G) relative humidity   (I) temperature

13. Darnell read that the central part of Argentina has a climate that is very similar to that of the central part of the United States.

What information on the map provides the best explanation for the climates' similarities?

(A) Both countries are located to the east of the Pacific Ocean.

(B) There are large mountains in the western parts of both countries.

(C) The central parts of both countries are about the same distance from the equator.

(D) Both countries are very large compared to many of the countries in the Americas.

Apply Inquiry and Review the Big Idea

Write the answers to these questions.

14. Jamie sketched the following picture of the landscape he saw while he was on vacation. It included cacti and barren rock.

What can you conclude about what kinds of plants can grow in this climate? Explain how you know.

_____

_____

_____

15. The figure below shows how a puddle changes during the day.

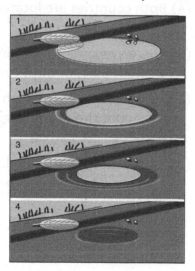

Make a claim about the process that is taking place. Support your claim with evidence.

_____

_____

_____

The Nature of Matter

Properties of Matter

Changes in Matter

Divers can see the bright colors of the coral reef.

I Wonder Why

Why are some kinds of materials better than others for making diving suits? *Turn the page to find out.*

Here's Why

Suits for scuba diving come in a variety of materials. Divers need suits to protect them against scrapes and stings. They also may need the suit to keep them warm in cold waters. The properties of the material used to make the suit will help divers choose the best suit for their purposes.

Essential Questions and Florida Benchmarks

SC.5.P.8.1 Compare and contrast the basic properties of solids, liquids, and gases, such as mass, volume, color, texture, and temperature.

LESSON 1

ESSENTIAL **QUESTION**

What Are Solids, Liquids, and Gases?

Engage Your Brain

As you read the lesson, look for the answer to the following question and record it here.

Bottled water and the snow from this snow machine are both water. How are these forms of water different?

_____

_____

_____

_____

_____

ACTIVE **READING**

Lesson Vocabulary
List the terms. As you learn about each one, make notes in the Interactive Glossary.

_____   _____

_____   _____

_____   _____

Compare and Contrast
Many ideas in this lesson involve comparisons and contrasts—how things are alike and different. Active readers stay focused on comparisons and contrasts when they ask themselves, How are these things alike? How are they different?

What's the Matter?

This book is made of matter, and so are you. You might think that matter can be seen and felt. But did you know that air is matter also? What is matter?

The large pencil has more matter than the smaller pencils. It has more mass and more volume.

ACTIVE **READING** As you read these two pages, draw two lines under each main idea.

Breathe in and out. Can you feel air hitting your hand? You can't see air, and you can't grab it. Yet air is **matter** because it has mass and it has volume. Matter cannot be created or destroyed. It might change form, but it is still matter.

Mass is the amount of matter in something. Each of the tiny particles that make up matter has mass, even though the particles are so small you cannot see them. **Volume** is the amount of space something takes up. When air is blown into a balloon, you can see that it has volume.

Name That Matter

Look at the matter in this picture.

1. What matter is soft and sticky?

_____

2. What matter is hard and sharp?

_____

Odor

Texture

Matter Has Properties

You might say that apple juice is gold in color, tastes sweet, and pours easily. These are properties of the juice, which means they are characteristics used to describe or identify it. All matter has properties.

All the properties shown on this page are physical properties. You can observe a physical property without changing the matter into a new substance. For example, texture is how something feels. In observing that sandpaper has a rough texture, you don't change the sandpaper.

Color

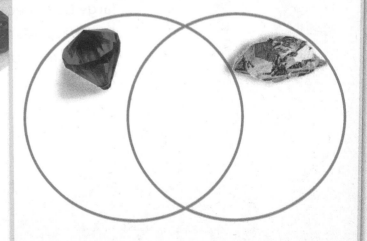

Comparing Stones

Complete the Venn diagram by comparing and contrasting the properties of the two stones.

More Properties

Color, texture, and odor are just a few physical properties. What are some other properties of matter?

ACTIVE READING As you read these two pages, circle common, everyday words that have a different meaning in science.

Temperature

Temperature is a measure of the energy of motion of the particles in matter. Melted glass has a very high temperature. Temperature can be measured by using a thermometer.

Volume

The food in the small bowl has less volume than the food in the large bowl because it takes up less space. Many tools can be used to measure volume.

Mass

A bowling ball and a basketball have about the same volume. The bowling ball has a greater mass because it contains more matter. Mass can be measured by using a balance.

Density

Density is found by dividing the mass of an object by its volume. The density of the gas in this balloon is less than the density of the air around it. That is why the balloon "floats" in air.

➗ DO THE MATH

Use Division

Use the data to find the density of each of these foods.

Determining Densities of Foods			
Food	Mass (g)	Volume (cm3)	Density (g/cm³)
gelatin	75	100	
pudding	90	100	
whipped cream	50	100	

235

Liquids

A **liquid** is a substance that has a definite volume but does not have a definite shape. The particles in a liquid move slower than the particles in a gas, and they slide by each other.

States of Matter

Another physical property of matter is its state. Solid, liquid, and gas are the most common states of matter on Earth.

ACTIVE **READING** As you read these two pages, draw boxes around the names of the three things that are being compared.

Gases

A **gas** is a substance that does not have a definite shape or volume. The particles in a gas move very quickly and are far apart from each other.

Matter is made of tiny particles. The particles in solids, liquids, and gases have different amounts of energy. The amount of energy affects how fast the particles move and how close together they are.

The shape and volume of something depends on its state. Because each particle in a gas is affected little by the other particles, gas particles are free to move throughout their container. Gases take both the shape and the volume of their container.

Particles in a liquid cannot move as freely. A sample of a liquid keeps the same volume no matter what container it is in. However because the particles slide by each other, a liquid takes the shape of its container.

The particles in a solid do not move from place to place, so solids keep the same shape and volume.

Solids

A **solid** is a substance with a definite shape and volume. The particles in a solid are very close to each other. They don't move from place to place. They just vibrate where they are.

The bubbles in the tank are a _____.

The water is an example of a _____.

The castle is a _____.

A Matter of Temperature

On a hot day, an ice cube melts. This change is caused by a change in temperature. When matter changes state, the type of matter is not changed.

ACTIVE **READING** As you read these two pages, draw one line under a cause. Draw two lines under the effect.

When matter takes in or releases energy, its temperature changes. When enough energy is taken in or released, matter can change state.

When a gas releases energy, its temperature goes down until it *condenses,* or changes to a liquid. When a liquid releases energy, its temperature goes down until it *freezes,* or changes to a solid.

When a solid takes in energy, its temperature rises until it *melts,* or changes to a liquid. When a liquid takes in energy, its temperature rises until it *evaporates,* or changes to a gas. Evaporation and boiling are similar—both turn liquids into gases. Evaporation is slower and happens only at a liquid's surface. Boiling is faster and happens throughout the liquid.

When a solid absorbs enough energy, the solid melts, changing to a liquid.

When a liquid absorbs enough energy, the liquid *boils*, or rapidly changes to a gas.

When a gas releases enough energy, the gas condenses, changing to a liquid. Particles of water vapor condense and form raindrops and dew.

When a liquid releases enough energy, the liquid freezes, changing to a solid. Dripping water that freezes can form icicles.

The temperature at which a certain type of matter freezes or melts is the same. The temperature at which a type of matter condenses or boils is also the same. For water, the melting and freezing points are 0°C. The condensation and boiling points are 100°C. Evaporation can happen at temperatures below the boiling point.

Lava is hot, melted rock that erupts from a volcano. Lava releases energy as it cools and becomes solid rock.

▶ Complete this graphic organizer.

As a solid takes in energy, its temperature _____.
Eventually, it will _____, changing to a _____.

If the liquid takes in enough _____, it will _____, changing to a _____.

Properties of Solids, Liquids, and Gases

Each different material has its own unique properties. However, properties can change depending on the state of the material.

ACTIVE **READING** As you read these two pages, find and underline facts about each state of matter.

Each state of matter has different physical properties. Liquids and gases both flow, moving from place to place. Gases can expand, taking up more space, or compress, taking up less space. Solids have definite textures.

Liquid water flows much more quickly than honey.

Liquids
All liquids flow from one place to another. Different liquids may flow at different rates.

Solids

Although clay and a wooden table are both solids, each one feels different. All solids have a shape, but the shape of some solids can be changed easily.

Gases

A lot of gas has been compressed in this tank. It is under high pressure. Compressed gas from the tank expands, filling many balloons.

▶ **Complete this main-idea-and-details graphic organizer.**

Main Idea
_____

Liquids	Gases	_____
Motor oil and milk _____ at different rates.	When you push on the sides of a balloon, the gas inside is _____.	Glass and sandpaper have different _____.

Sum It Up »

Read the summary statements below. Each one is incorrect. Change the part of the summary in blue to make it correct.

1. A property is a characteristic of matter that is used to determine the state of the matter.

_____

2. A sample of ice has a volume of 1.0 cm³ and a mass of 0.9 g. The density of the ice is 1.1 g/cm³.

_____

3. The particles in a solid are close together, but they can slide past each other.

_____

4. A solid changes to a liquid during a process known as freezing.

_____

5. Solids and liquids can be compressed when put under pressure.

_____

6. The mass of an object can be measured by using a measuring cup.

_____

Read the properties below. Write S for solid, G for gas, and L for liquid. Some properties may have more than one answer.

7. Has a definite texture and shape ____

8. Can melt ____

9. Can freeze ____

10. Can boil ____

11. Takes the volume of its container ___

12. Can condense ____

13. Can flow _____

14. Takes the shape of its container ____

15. Has a definite volume _____

Brain Check

Name _____

Vocabulary Review

1 **Use the clues below to fill in the words in the puzzle.**

1. To squeeze a gas into a smaller space

2. A physical property that describes how something feels

3. The state of matter that keeps its shape and volume when it is placed in a different container

4. The measure of the energy of motion of particles of matter

5. Anything that has mass and volume

6. What happens to a liquid when it releases enough energy

7. Calculated by dividing mass by volume

8. The state of matter that has particles that slide by each other

9. The amount of space something takes up

10. The state of matter that expands to fill its container

Read down the squares with red borders. The word you find will complete the riddle below.

Perry the porcupine's portrait perfectly portrayed his pestering personality and prickly __ __ __ __ __ __ __ __ __ __.

Apply Concepts

2 Tell what property each of the following tools is used to measure.

_____ _____ _____

3 Complete these descriptions of the different states of matter.

_____	_____	Solids
_____	Particles are closer together and move past each other.	Particles are very close and vibrate in place.
_____		
Examples: air; helium in balloons; oxygen in a tank	Examples: _____ _____	Examples: _____ _____

4 Fill in the name of the processes (such as freezing) that are represented.

a _____   b _____

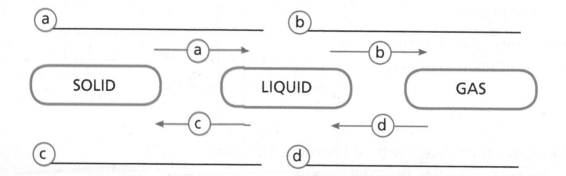

c _____   d _____

See *ScienceSaurus*® for more information about matter.

Take It Home!

SC.5.N.1.3 Recognize and explain the need for repeated experimental trials.

S.T.E.M.

ENGINEERING & TECHNOLOGY

Strong, Light, or Both?

A bicycle wheel has to be strong to be safe. You also want it to be lightweight so it takes less energy for you to pedal the bike. You could easily bend one of these wheel spokes all by itself, but arranged together, they make the wheel strong enough to support your weight and more!

Carbon fiber is used to make this bike wheel strong and lightweight.

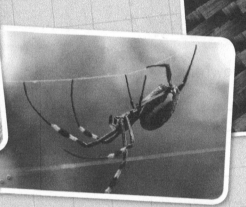

Carbon fiber threads are woven into fabric.

Carbon fiber is smaller and stronger than a human hair!

Spider silk is the strongest, lightest natural material. It is stronger than steel! Carbon fiber is a strong, human-made thread that can be woven into fabric. A single carbon fiber is much finer than a human hair. Carbon fiber is one of the strongest and lightest materials made by people.

CRITICAL THINKING

Circle a natural material. Put an X on a manufactured material. What are two ways these materials are alike?

_____

_____

_____

S.T.E.M. continued

Every design has its upside and its downside. When a design for an object is chosen to meet one purpose, other features may not be as good. A quality that a designer must give up in order to get a desired quality is called a design trade-off. A designer needs to think of both the upside and the downside of a particular design.

Look at these shoes. List two examples of the upside and two of the downside for each shoe. Think of another type of shoe. Draw it in the empty space and explain the trade-offs.

Upside   Downside

_____   _____

_____   _____

_____   _____

Upside   Downside

_____   _____

_____   _____

_____   _____

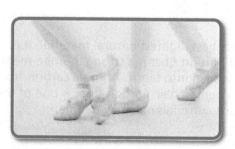

Upside   Downside

_____   _____

_____   _____

_____   _____

Upside   Downside

_____   _____

_____   _____

_____   _____

ENGINEERING DESIGN CHALLENGE

Design It:
Distillation Device

When salt dissolves in water, it spreads out into its tiniest particles. These particles are too small to be seen or to be removed by ordinary filters.

Distillation is a process that separates salt from salt water. When water is boiled, it evaporates, changing into a gas called water vapor. When water vapor comes in contact with a cool surface, it changes back into liquid water. Since salt does not easily evaporate, the water droplets that form don't contain salt.

As distillation continues, all of the water will evaporate from the saltwater solution. The only substance left behind will be pure salt crystals.

Can you develop a way to remove salt from water without boiling it?

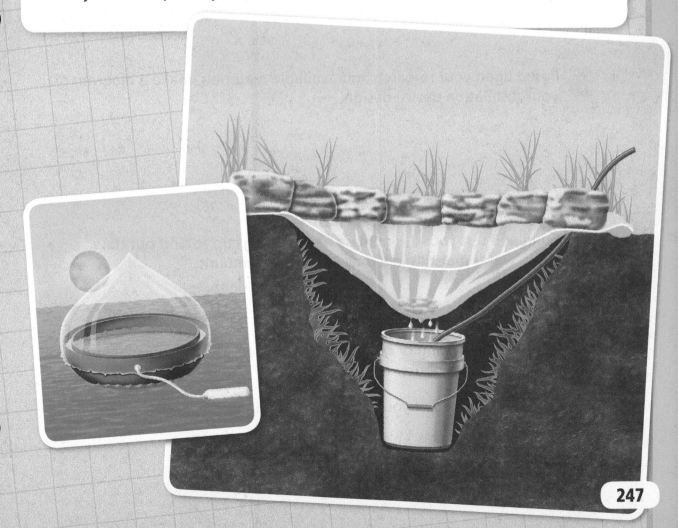

S.T.E.M. continued

DESIGN PROCESS STEPS

1 Find a Problem
2 Plan & Build
3 Test & Improve
4 Redesign
5 Communicate

What to Do:

1. Learn about solutions and dissolving.

2. Find out how distillation separates salt water into salt and pure water.

3. Learn about different distillation devices and how they are used to meet certain needs.

4. Find out what classroom materials you can use to build a distillation device. List them.

5. Based upon your research and available materials, make a diagram of your distillation device design.

6. Build and test your design. Use a measuring cup to find out how much water it distills in a day. Record this amount.

7. Continue improving or redesigning your device until you are satisfied with the final product.

8. Keep a record of your work in your Science Notebook.

© Houghton Mifflin Harcourt Publishing Company

SC.5.P.9.1 Investigate and describe that many physical and chemical changes are affected by temperature.

LESSON 2

ESSENTIAL **QUESTION**

How Does Matter Change?

 Engage Your Brain

As you read the lesson, look for the answer to the following question and record it here.

A piece of iron can change in different ways. How is iron bending different from iron rusting?

_____

_____

_____

ACTIVE **READING**

Lesson Vocabulary
List the terms. As you learn about each one, make notes in the Interactive Glossary.

_____

_____

_____

_____

Main Idea and Details
Detail sentences give information about a topic. The information may be examples, features, characteristics, or facts. Active readers stay focused on the topic when they ask, What fact or information does this sentence add to the topic?

Classifying Change

Slicing apples and cracking eggs are physical changes.

When an apple pie cooks, chemical changes occur. Cooked apples do not have the same properties as a raw apple.

Matter has properties, but matter also undergoes changes. How many different ways does matter change?

ACTIVE **READING** Each visual on these two pages has an empty bubble. Write a C if the visual shows a chemical change. Write a P if it shows a physical change.

Matter has physical properties that can be observed without changing the type of matter. Matter can also change in ways that do not affect the type of matter. These changes are called **physical changes**.

When you sharpen a pencil, the pencil goes through a physical change. The wood shavings and bits of graphite don't look like a pencil any more. But the wood is still wood, and the graphite is still graphite.

Slicing a pie is another physical change.

▲ The properties of the ash and gases that form when wood burns are different from the properties of wood.

▲ When iron rusts, it undergoes a chemical change.

Matter has other properties that cannot be observed without changing the identity of the matter. These properties are chemical properties. For example, you don't know if a type of matter will burn unless you burn it. When matter burns, it changes identity.

In the same way, **chemical changes** result in a change in the identity of matter. When a strawberry rots, it undergoes chemical change. The rotten strawberry's properties are quite different from those of a fresh strawberry. A chemical **reaction** is the process in which new substances are formed during a chemical change.

◄ When you eat apple pie, chemical changes in your body digest the food.

▶ Place a *P* by each physical change and a *C* by each chemical change.

Change	Type
Bacteria decompose leaves.	
A newspaper turns yellow in sunlight.	
Water evaporates.	
Gasoline burns in a car engine.	

Swelling and Shrinking

Why do you think many car owners use one tire pressure in summer and another one in winter? When temperature differs, volume often differs.

ACTIVE **READING** As you read this page, draw two lines under each main idea. Circle an example of matter expanding when it becomes warmer.

Most matter expands when the temperature goes up and contracts when the temperature goes down. Some kinds of matter expand and contract more than others. People may run hot water over the metal lid of a glass jar. This expands the lid so that it's easier to take off the jar.

One exception is water. It expands when it freezes. Because ice takes up more volume than the same amount of liquid water, ice is less dense than water. That's why ice floats in a glass of water. In winter, ice first forms at the surface of a lake.

One of water's unique properties is that it expands when it freezes.

Liquid Water
Volume = 1.00 L

Frozen Water
Volume = 1.09 L

Sometimes water flows into cracks in rocks and freezes. The expanding water makes the cracks in the rock larger and breaks large rocks into smaller pieces.

Expansion Joints

▶ Explain why bridges have expansion joints in them.

_____

_____

_____

_____

◀ This photo shows the same balloon at two different temperatures. The size of a sample of gas depends on its temperature. The gas in a balloon expands when it is warmed. The gas compresses when it is cooled.

Temperature = –80 °C
Volume = 1.9 L

Temperature = 35 °C
Volume = 3.0 L

Tampering with Temperature

When a burner on a stove is really hot, it glows red. A change in color is just one way temperature can affect matter.

ACTIVE READING As you read this page, underline examples of how temperature affects physical changes in matter.

Some physical changes, such as tearing a piece of paper, are not affected by temperature. Other physical changes happen faster or slower at different temperatures. How quickly a change occurs is called the rate of change.

For example, ice on a lake will melt if the air temperature is above 0°C. It will melt even faster if the air temperature is warmer. In the same way, water condenses more quickly on the outside of a very cold soft drink can than it does on a cool can.

Hot! Hot! Hot! As iron is heated, it glows red or yellow.

WOW! This metal rod has been heated to more than 500°C (932°F).

OUCH! The filament of a light bulb is made of a metal called tungsten. It is glowing because it is heated to 2,500°C!

 **DO THE MATH**

Graph Data

The data table shows how long it takes identical ice cubes to melt when placed in equal amounts of water at different temperatures. Make a line graph of these data.

Temperature of water (°C)	Melting time of ice (sec)
14	450
19	300
27	170
42	140
48	90
70	25

When grass and the air around it cool at night, water vapor in the air might condense, forming dew. As morning sunlight warms the air, the dew evaporates. In this photograph, the grass in the shade is wet but the grass in the sun has dried.

Adding it Up!

What happens to the mass of substances during physical or chemical changes?

ACTIVE **READING** As you read these pages, underline examples of conservation of mass.

During physical and chemical changes, matter may change its appearance or its identity. In either type of change, the total mass of the matter before and after the change remains the same. This is called **conservation of mass**. To *conserve* means "to save."

For example, as water boils, it seems to disappear. However, the total mass of the particles of water vapor in the air equals the mass of the water that boiled away. Suppose you tear a 100-gram cardboard box into pieces. The total mass of all the pieces will also be 100 grams. The mass of the cardboard box stays the same. In this example, however, the volume of the cardboard box changes because tearing it into pieces causes it to lose its shape.

The total mass of the mixed salad is the sum of the masses of the vegetables in it.

75 grams

110 grams

90 grams

▶ What is the mass of the salad?
_____

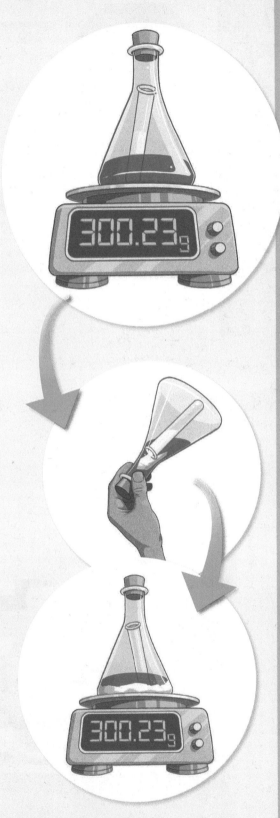

During this chemical reaction, the flask is sealed. Nothing can enter or leave, so the final mass equals the starting mass.

A chemical change turns one kind of matter into another. However, the mass of the matter stays the same. It can be tricky to compare, though. First, you must collect and measure the mass of everything you begin with. Then, you must collect and measure the mass of everything you are left with.

When wood burns, it combines with oxygen from the air. Burning produces ashes, smoke, and other gases. The mass of the wood and oxygen equals the mass of the ashes, smoke, and gases that are produced.

DO THE **MATH**

Solve Problems

In a physical change, sugar is dissolved in water to form sugar water. In a chemical change, iron combines with oxygen to form rust. Fill in the missing values in the table.

Physical Change	Mass (grams)
sugar	125
water	
sugar water	198
Chemical Change	
iron	519
oxygen	23
rust	

Faster or Slower?

Temperature affects the rate at which chemical changes occur, too. Read to find out how.

ACTIVE READING As you read this page, circle two clue words or phrases that signal a detail such as an example or an added fact.

Increasing temperature often speeds up the rate of a chemical change. For example, increasing oven temperature speeds up the chemical changes that occur when a cake bakes or a potato cooks.

Decreasing temperature usually slows down the rate of chemical change. This is why food stays fresh longer when it is kept cool. Also, unused batteries stay charged longer when kept in the refrigerator.

cold water

warm water

An effervescent antacid tablet reacts more quickly with warm water than it does with cold water.

The chemical changes that make food spoil are slowed down by keeping the food in the refrigerator.

258

Fevers

You feel awful. Your head hurts, and you have a fever. Why might having a fever be a good thing?

When you have a fever, your temperature rises above your normal body temperature (about 37 °C). A low fever is between 38 °C and 39 °C. A high fever is greater than 40 °C. Low fevers help the body fight disease. High fevers can cause severe problems.

Temperature can increase for many reasons. For example, certain bacteria have materials that your brain identifies as harmful. The brain sends out signals that cause an increase in the chemical changes that produce energy. Your temperature increases. Bacteria cannot survive at this higher temperature.

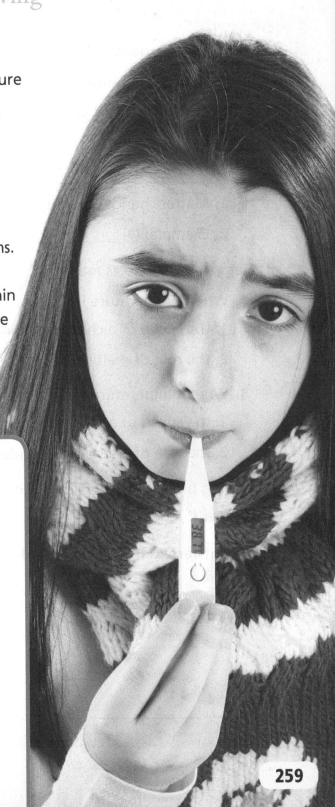

DO THE **MATH**

Use a Number Line

On the number line below, plot the following values in °C.

a. normal body temperature
b. a slight fever
c. a high fever

```
  ┬──┬──┬──┬──┬──┬──
  36 38 40 42 44 46
```

Sum It Up »

The outline below is a summary of the lesson. Complete the outline.

I. Matter undergoes changes.

   A. One type of change is a (1) _____.

     1. Matter does not change identity.

     2. Example: (2) _____

   B. (3) _____

     1. Matter changes identity.

     2. Example: (4) _____

II. Temperature affects matter.

   A. When temperature increases,

     1. the speed of a chemical change (5) _____.

     2. the rate of melting and boiling (6) _____.

   B. When temperature decreases,

     1. the speed of a chemical change (7) _____.

     2. the rate of freezing or condensing (8) _____.

III. During physical or chemical changes, the total mass of matter (9) _____.

Tell whether each change is a physical change or a chemical change.

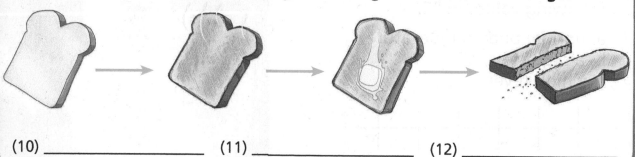

(10) _____ (11) _____ (12) _____

260

© Houghton Mifflin Harcourt Publishing Company

Brain Check

Name _____

Vocabulary Review

1. It's easy to get tongue-tied when talking about how matter changes. Look at the statements below. Switch the red words from one sentence to another until each statement makes sense.

A. In a chemical change, the identity of matter does not change.   _____

B. Water will melt faster on a very cold soft drink can than it will on a cool soft drink can.   _____

C. Another name for a chemical change is a chemical property.   _____

D. Ice will condense more slowly in cold water than in warm water.   _____

E. In a physical change, the identity of the matter changes.   _____

F. When water freezes, its mass decreases.   _____

G. A reaction of matter will stay the same during a physical change.   _____

H. When water freezes, it contracts.   _____

Challenge The words in the boxes below are jumbled. Put them in the correct order to make a meaningful sentence.

changes are rusting and chemical burning	is physical and mass changes in chemical conserved
_____ _____	_____ _____

Apply Concepts

2 Each of the pictures shows a change. Write a *P* by the pictures that show physical changes and a *C* by the pictures that show chemical changes.

3 Make a list of physical changes and chemical changes that you observe or see the effects of in your school.

Physical Changes

_____

_____

_____

_____

_____

_____

_____

_____

Chemical Changes

_____

_____

_____

_____

_____

_____

_____

_____

4 What would make each of the following processes happen faster? On each line, write *increase in temperature* or *decrease in temperature*.

Ice cream melting	Boiling water to cook potatoes
_____	_____

Water condensing on the outside of a glass	Water freezing overnight on a street
_____	_____

5 Explain what is happening in these pictures. Tell whether the changes are physical or chemical.

_____
_____
_____
_____
_____
_____

6 Why is it important to follow the instructions on this jar of food?

_____
_____
_____
_____
_____
_____

7 Draw a picture of a chemical reaction. Then explain what happens and why mass is conserved during the reaction.

_____

_____

_____

_____

_____

_____

8 Explain why most sidewalks have built-in cracks every few feet.

_____

_____

_____

_____

_____

_____

9 Explain what happens in a campfire.

| Wood is made of cellulose, lignin, and other substances. |

↓

| The wood is set on fire, and a _____ change occurs. |

↓

| The cellulose and lignin are changed into other substances, including _____ and _____. |

Take It Home! Ask an adult to help you practice taking the temperature of someone in your family. Determine whether any of your family members have a fever. Explain to family members why people get fevers.

264

© Houghton Mifflin Harcourt Publishing Company

SC.5.P.9.1 Investigate and describe that many physical and chemical changes are affected by temperature. SC.5.N.1.3 Recognize and explain the need for repeated experimental trials. SC.5.N.2.2 Recognize and explain that when scientific investigations are carried out, the evidence produced by those investigations should be.

Name _____

ESSENTIAL QUESTION

How Can Temperature Change Matter?

EXPLORE

Turn the heat up! In this activity, you and your classmates will explore how temperature affects the rate of a chemical change.

Before You Begin—Preview the Steps

① **CAUTION:** Wear safety goggles and an apron. Don't touch the hot water. Use the funnel to add one teaspoon of yeast, a half teaspoon of sugar, and 50 mL of room-temperature water to each balloon.

② Tie the balloons closed. Gently knead each balloon to mix the ingredients. Place one balloon into each tub.

③ Pour ice water into the first tub, and add the same amount of room-temperature water to the second tub.

④ Have your teacher pour the same amount of hot water into the third tub.

⑤ After 30 minutes, remove all three balloons from the water. Use the string and ruler to measure the distance around each balloon.

Materials

safety goggles
lab apron
graduated cylinder
3 balloons
3 plastic tubs
room-temperature water
measuring spoons
funnel
dry yeast
sugar
hot water
ice water
string
ruler

© Houghton Mifflin H
Publishing Company

Set a Purpose

What will you learn from this experiment?

_____

_____

_____

State Your Hypothesis

Write your hypothesis, or testable statement.

_____

_____

_____

_____

Think About the Procedure

Why do you need to add equal amounts of yeast, sugar, and water to each balloon?

_____

_____

_____

_____

How will you be sure that you measure the distance around each balloon in the same way?

_____

_____

_____

_____

Name _____

Record Your Data

In the space below, make a table in which you record your results.

Draw Conclusions

Plot your data on a line graph.

What conclusion can you draw?

_____

_____

Claims • Evidence • Reasoning

1. What are some reasons you might want to repeat this experiment several more times and compare your results to those in other groups?

_____

_____

2. How do the results of this experiment help you understand what happens when bread bakes? Explain your reasoning.

_____

_____

_____

_____

3. Write a claim for why food spoils faster when it is not refrigerated. Support your claim with evidence.

_____

_____

_____

_____

4. Think of other questions you would like to ask about how temperature relates to the rate of a chemical reaction.

_____

_____

_____

SC.5.P.8.2 Investigate and identify materials that will dissolve in water and those that will not and identify the conditions that will speed up or slow down the dissolving process. SC.5.P.8.3 Demonstrate and explain that mixtures of solids can be separated based on observable properties of their parts such as particle size, shape, color, and magnetic attraction.

ESSENTIAL QUESTION

What Are Mixtures and Solutions?

 Engage Your Brain

As you read the lesson, look for the answer to the following question and record it here.

How are a smoothie and a salad alike? How are they different?

_____

_____

_____

_____

 ACTIVE **READING**

Lesson Vocabulary
List each term. As you learn about each one, make notes in the Interactive Glossary.

_____

_____

Problem and Solution
Ideas in this lesson may be connected by a problem-solution relationship. Active readers mark a problem with a *P* to help them stay focused on the way information is organized. When multiple solutions are described, they mark each solution with an *S*.

Matter Mix-Up

A box of colored pencils. A basket of footballs, tennis balls, and hockey pucks. A toy box full of toys. All these things are mixtures. But what is a mixture?

ACTIVE READING As you read the next page, draw two lines under the conclusion. Draw one line under each fact that leads to the conclusion.

This fruit salad is a mixture of different pieces of fruit.

ook at the mixtures on these pages. They have a few things in common. First, two or more substances or objects were combined. The fruit salad has several types of fruit. The laundry pile has several types of clothing. Second, each type of matter in a mixture keeps its own identity. The peach in the fruit salad is the same type of matter as it was before it was mixed into the fruit salad. The jeans in the laundry pile are still jeans.

By now, you've probably figured out that a **mixture** is a combination of two or more substances that keep their identities. The parts of a mixture don't undergo a chemical change. Making a mixture is a physical change.

A carbonated beverage is a mixture of water, gases, and other ingredients.

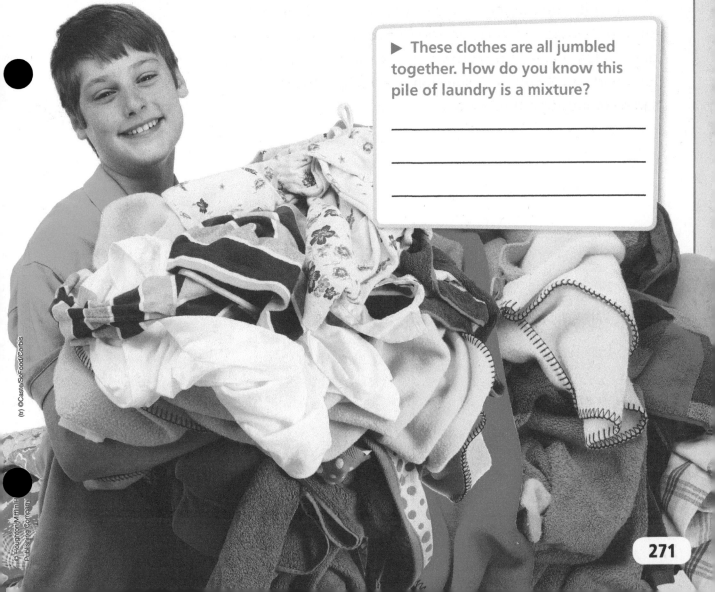

▶ These clothes are all jumbled together. How do you know this pile of laundry is a mixture?

_____

_____

_____

Find a Solution!

In some mixtures, it's easy to see the individual pieces that are mixed together. In other mixtures, small parts are very evenly mixed. What are these special mixtures?

ACTIVE READING As you read these two pages, underline lesson vocabulary words each time they are used.

Each bite of fruit salad contains different combinations of fruit. You can separately taste peaches and different kinds of berries. But what do you notice when you drink a glass of lemonade? Every sip tastes the same. This is because lemonade is a solution. A **solution** is a mixture that has the same composition throughout.

When food coloring is added to water, the two liquids evenly mix, forming a solution.

A solution forms when one substance *dissolves* in another. When something dissolves, it breaks up into particles so tiny they can't be seen even with a microscope. These particles then evenly mix with the other part of the solution. Not everything dissolves. If you put a rock and salt in water, the rock won't dissolve, but the salt will.

Solutions are commonly liquids, such as the mixture of the different liquids that make up gasoline. But not all solutions are liquids. Air is a solution of different gases. Tiny particles of nitrogen, oxygen, and other gases are evenly mixed in air. Brass is an example of a solid solution formed from solid copper and solid zinc.

A mixture of sand and water forms where waves wash over the sand. Such a mixture is not a solution.

Ocean water itself is a solution. It contains several different dissolved substances.

▶ What makes a solution different from other mixtures?

_____

_____

Separating Mixtures

Suppose you really don't like olives. How are you going to get them off that deluxe pizza your friend ordered? Sometimes you need to separate the components of a mixture.

ACTIVE READING As you read this page, put brackets [ ] around the sentence that describes the problem and write *P* next to the sentence. Underline the sentence that describes the solution and write *S* next to it.

Mixtures are not always easy to separate. But since mixing is a physical change, each component in a mixture keeps most of its physical properties. Physical properties such as color, size, melting point, boiling point, density, and ability to dissolve can be used to separate mixtures. Separating a mixture can be very simple. Or it can involve several, complex steps when one method is not enough.

► What property was used to separate the items on this tray?

_____

Density

Every substance has its own density. A less-dense substance will float on a denser substance. Objects will float in water if they are less dense than water. They will sink if they are denser than water.

When One Isn't Enough

A magnet takes away bits of iron.

Water is added. Then the filter removes the soil.

The water is boiled away. Only salt is left behind.

sieve/mesh screen

A sieve or mesh screen has holes that matter can pass through. Matter that is smaller than the holes passes through the mesh screen while matter that is larger than the holes stays above the mesh screen.

magnetic force

A magnet attracts matter that contains iron, separating it from the other parts of the mixture.

filtration

A filter works like a mesh screen with very tiny openings, or pores. Only the smallest bits of matter—like water particles and dissolved particles of salt—can pass through the pores.

evaporation/boiling

Boiling is when a liquid rapidly changes to a gas at the boiling point of the liquid. Evaporation also changes a liquid to a gas, but it occurs at temperatures below the boiling point. During these processes, only the liquid particles leave the solution. Dissolved particles stay behind.

Proportions and Properties

When you make lemonade, it's important to get the amounts of lemon and sugar right. If it's too sweet or too sour, it doesn't taste right. How do proportions affect the properties of a mixture?

Mixtures of metals are called *alloys*. The properties of the alloy depend on how much of each metal is in the mixture. Chemists first decide on the properties they need their alloy to have. Then they decide how much of which metals will give them those properties.

Steel is an alloy. It is made from iron and other substances. Different substances give steel different properties. For example, adding chromium will make steel shiny. Metals such as nickel and titanium can keep it from rusting. Carbon is often added to steel to make it stronger. Other substances help steel used in tools stay sharp or keep from wearing down.

To make an alloy, metals and other elements are melted together and then allowed to harden.

▶ For each steel object on this page, list at least two properties that the steel must have.

_____
_____
_____

Kettle

_____
_____
_____
_____

Sculpture

Steel Building Frame

_____
_____
_____

Use Graphs

Compare and contrast the metals and other substances in stainless steel and tool steel by making two circle graphs.

Substance	Stainless Steel %	Tool Steel %
Iron	74	94
Chromium	18	0
Nickel	8	1
Carbon	0	1
Other	0	4

Sum It Up »

Write _S_ if the photo and caption describe a mixture that is a solution. Write _M_ if they describe a mixture that is NOT a solution.

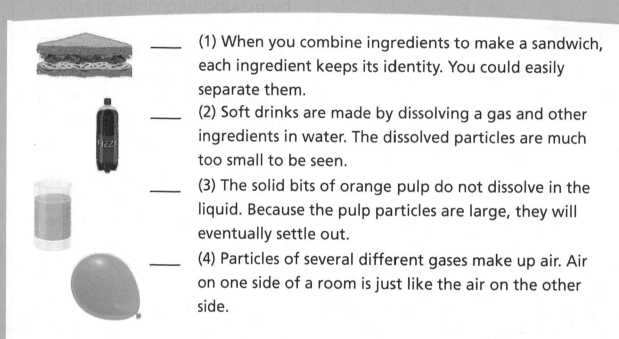

____ (1) When you combine ingredients to make a sandwich, each ingredient keeps its identity. You could easily separate them.

____ (2) Soft drinks are made by dissolving a gas and other ingredients in water. The dissolved particles are much too small to be seen.

____ (3) The solid bits of orange pulp do not dissolve in the liquid. Because the pulp particles are large, they will eventually settle out.

____ (4) Particles of several different gases make up air. Air on one side of a room is just like the air on the other side.

Fill in the missing words to tell how to separate mixtures.

To sort the items in your junk drawer, you'd use observable (5) _____ such as size, color, shape, and (6) _____ attraction. But how would you separate table sugar, sand, and pebbles? Because the pebbles are (7) _____ than the grains of sugar and sand, you could remove them using a sieve, or mesh (8) _____.

You could then add water and shake until the sugar (9) _____.

If you poured this mixture through a coffee (10) _____ into a beaker, the (11) _____ would be left on the filter, but the sugar solution would pass through. Adding heat would cause the water to (12) _____, leaving solid sugar behind.

Brain Check

Name _____

Vocabulary Review

1 Use the words in the box to complete each sentence.

1. Another name for a mesh screen is a _____.

2. During a _____ change, there is no formation of a new kind of matter.

3. A _____ is a tool that attracts objects that contain iron.

4. An object that is less dense than water will _____ when it is placed in water.

5. A _____ is an object used to separate very small particles from a mixture.

6. The amount of matter in a given volume is called _____.

7. _____ is a physical property of an object; for example, round, square, rectangular, or flat.

8. The process by which a liquid changes slowly to a gas is _____.

9. A _____ is a kind of mixture that has the same composition throughout.

10. A combination of two or more substances that keep their individual identities is a _____.

sieve	shape	evaporation	solution*	physical
magnet	mixture*	float	filter	density

* Key Lesson Vocabulary

Apply Concepts

2 Circle the substances below that are solutions.

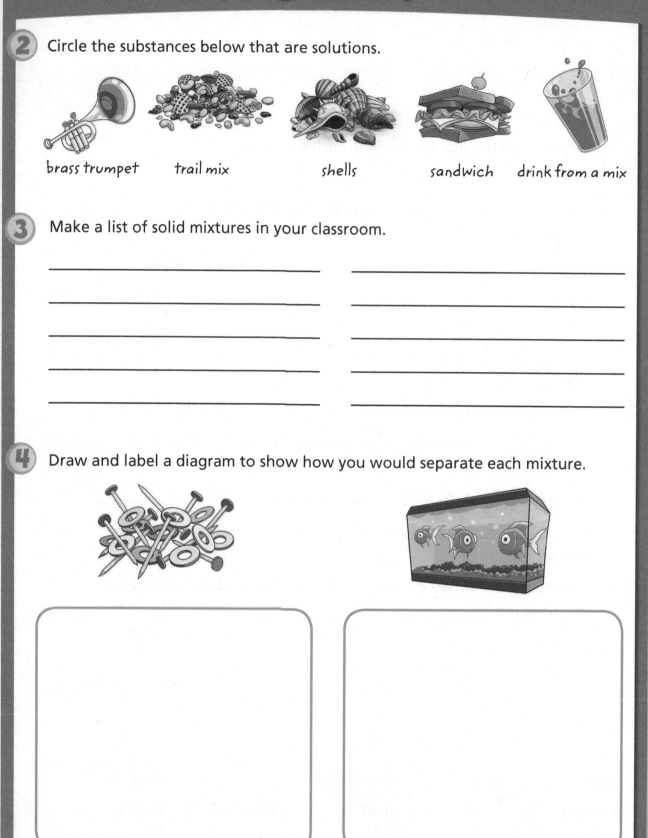

brass trumpet   trail mix   shells   sandwich   drink from a mix

3 Make a list of solid mixtures in your classroom.

_____   _____

_____   _____

_____   _____

_____   _____

_____   _____

4 Draw and label a diagram to show how you would separate each mixture.

5 Answer these questions in terms of what you know about mixtures.

a. How would changing the proportions of substances in an alloy change its properties?

_____

_____

_____

b. Why is it possible to use physical properties to separate a mixture?

_____

_____

c. Recycling help us conserve resources. Draw a line connecting each piece of garbage in a mixed bag with the bin it should be thrown in.

milk jug   soup can   envelope   cardboard box

soda can   water bottle   broken pencil

Garbage   Plastic   Aluminum and Tin   Paper

6 Salt seems to disappear when it is poured into water. Use the terms mixture, solution, and dissolve to explain what happens.

_____

_____

_____

_____

7 Tell how you would use one or more of these tools to separate the mixtures.

Rice from dried soup mix   Salt from saltwater   Nails from gravel

_____   _____   _____

_____   _____   _____

_____   _____   _____

_____   _____   _____

_____   _____   _____

                         _____

8 Tell what would happen if you stirred each of these cups faster.

_____   _____

_____   _____

_____   _____

_____   _____

_____   _____

_____   _____

_____   _____

Water and Sugar

Water and Sand

Take It Home! Share what you have learned about mixtures with your family. With a family member, identify examples of mixtures at mealtime, or in places in your home.

SC.5.P.8.2 Investigate and identify materials that will dissolve in water and those that will not and identify conditions that will speed up or slow down the dissolving process. SC.5.N.1.1 plan and carry out scientific investigations of various types... SC.5.N.1.4 Identify a control group and explain its importance in an experiment.

Name _____

ESSENTIAL **QUESTION**

What Affects the Speed of Dissolving?

Materials

safety goggles
table salt
lab apron
stopwatch
cold tap water
2 spoons
3 clear containers
coarse salt
measuring spoon
warm water

EXPLORE

In this activity, you will explore how to make a solid dissolve in water faster.

Before You Begin—Preview the Steps

① **CAUTION:** Wear goggles and an apron. Use a stopwatch to measure how long it takes for salt to completely dissolve. Stop timing if it has not dissolved after two minutes. Empty and rinse the containers between steps.

② Measure equal amounts of tap water into three containers. Add a spoonful of table salt to each container. Do not stir one container. Stir one at a moderate rate, and the other at a fast rate.

③ Measure equal amounts of tap water into two containers. Add a spoonful of coarse salt to one and a spoonful of table salt to the other. Stir both at the same rate.

④ Pour some cold water into a container, and pour an equal amount of warm water into another. Add a spoonful of table salt to both containers. Stir both at the same rate.

Set a Purpose

What will you learn from this experiment?

_____

_____

State Your Hypothesis

Write your hypothesis, or testable statement.

_____

_____

_____

Think About the Procedure

Why do you need to rinse the containers between steps?

_____

_____

Would it affect the conclusions for this activity if two different groups stirred at different rates? Why?

_____

_____

_____

What is the control group in Step 2 of this investigation? Why is a control important?

_____

_____

_____

Name _____

Record Your Data

Record your results in the data table below.

Time It Takes to Dissolve	
Treatment	Time(sec)
No Stirring	
Stirring Slowly	
Stirring Quickly	
Coarse Salt	
Table Salt	
Cold Water	
Warm Water	

Draw Conclusions

Make a bar graph to display how your test data showed that stirring affects the rate of dissolving.

What conclusion can you draw?

_____

_____

Claims • Evidence • Reasoning

1. You're adding sugar to a glass of iced tea. Cite evidence for how you might speed up how quickly the sugar dissolves.

_____

_____

_____

_____

2. Minerals dissolve in river water. Would you expect minerals to dissolve faster in a fast-moving river or one that moves slowly? Explain your reasoning.

_____

_____

_____

3. A water softener is a device that uses salts to remove certain substances from water. Most home water softeners use salt pellets or rock salt, both of which are chunks of salt. Provide evidence for why you wouldn't want to use table salt in a softener.

_____

_____

_____

4. Think of other questions you would like to ask about the rate of dissolving a solid in water.

_____

_____

_____

SC.5.P.8.4 Explore the scientific theory of atoms (also called atomic theory) by recognizing that all matter is composed of parts that are too small to be seen without magnification.

ESSENTIAL QUESTION

What Is the Atomic Theory?

 Engage Your Brain

As you read the lesson, look for the answer to the following question and record it here.

This building in Brussels, Belgium, is called the Atomium. Why do you think it was given that name?

_____

_____

_____

_____

 ACTIVE **READING**

Lesson Vocabulary
List the terms. As you learn about each one, make notes in the Interactive Glossary.

_____ _____

_____ _____

_____

Visual Aids
A diagram adds information to the text that appears on the page with it. Active readers pause their reading to review the diagram and decide how the information in it adds to what is provided in the text on the pages.

287

More than 2,000 years ago, I stated that all matter is made of tiny, solid balls called atoms. The word atom means "indivisible."

DEMOCRITUS

A Teeny Tiny Theory

From the time of Democritus, scientists have studied matter and proposed theories about it. What do we now think about what makes up matter?

ACTIVE **READING** As you read the next page, draw a line from each part of the atom diagram to the sentences that describe it.

→ **Atoms**

Elements

Compounds

Suppose you could break a silver chain into smaller and smaller pieces. The pieces would become so small that you couldn't see them without a microscope. How small could the pieces get before they were no longer silver? The answer—one silver atom. An **atom** is the smallest unit of an element that maintains the properties of that element.

The **atomic theory** is a scientific explanation of the structure of atoms and how they interact with other atoms. Democritus first suggested that the smallest part of matter is an atom. Over the years, theories that scientists made about atoms have changed as scientists learn more about atoms.

Gold is one type of matter.

Gold brick

Flakes of gold

Atoms are the building blocks of all matter.

Current atomic theory states that an atom is mostly empty space. At its center, there is a small, dense core called the nucleus. The nucleus is surrounded by electrons.

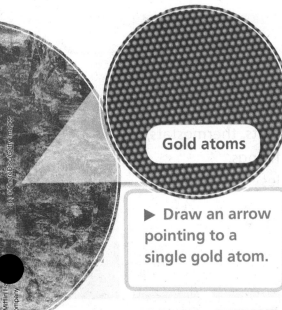

Proton

A *proton* is a positively charged particle found in the nucleus of an atom.

Neutron

Neutrons are also particles found in the nucleus, but a neutron has no charge.

Electron

Electrons are negatively charged particles that speed through an area around the nucleus called the electron cloud.

▶ Use the Venn diagram to compare and contrast electrons and protons.

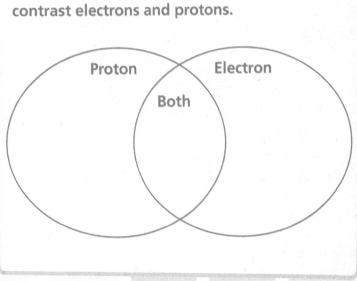

Proton

Electron

Both

Gold atoms

▶ Draw an arrow pointing to a single gold atom.

78	79	80	81	82	83	84	85
Pt	Au	Hg	Tl	Pb	Bi	Po	At

Ir

In the mid-1800s, I organized all known elements by their properties and increasing mass. Scientists still organize elements based on my work.

MENDELEEV

Atoms

→ Elements

Compounds

It's Elementary!

Copper, oxygen, and mercury have one thing in common. They are all elements. Exactly what is an element?

ACTIVE **READING** As you read these two pages, draw a large *E* next to the names of five elements that are described.

There are many kinds of matter. An **element** is the type of matter made of just one kind of atom. All atoms of an element have the same number of protons. For example, boron is an element. Every atom of boron contains exactly five protons. No other element has atoms with exactly five protons.

What's so special about protons? Electrons are far from the nucleus, so they can be gained or lost. Also, different atoms of the same element can contain different numbers of neutrons. Protons stay the same.

Neon

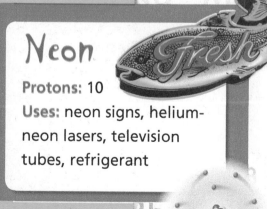

Protons: 10
Uses: neon signs, helium-neon lasers, television tubes, refrigerant

Mercury

Protons: 80
Uses: laboratory instruments, thermostats, dental fillings, pesticides

Chlorine

Protons: 17
Uses: disinfecting water; making paper, paints, plastics, and dyes

Silver

Protons: 47
Uses: jewelry, silverware, photography, welding solder, mirrors

Copper

Protons: 29
Uses: plumbing, coins, electrical wires, making brass and bronze

Draw and Label a Carbon Atom

Use the information provided to draw and label a carbon atom.

Protons: 6
Neutrons: 6
Electrons: 6

Atoms

Elements

→ Compounds

Part of my atomic theory stated that different types of atoms combine to form chemical compounds.

DALTON

Putting It All Together

There are more than 100 elements, but you can see that there are many more types of matter than that. What are these other types?

ACTIVE **READING** As you read this page, draw boxes around the names of the two things that are being compared.

Many atoms go through chemical change with a different type of atom and form molecules. A **molecule** is made up of two or more atoms joined together chemically. A **compound** is a substance formed by atoms from two or more elements.

The properties of a compound are often different from the properties of the elements that form it. For example, atoms of carbon and oxygen will react, forming the compound carbon dioxide. This compound has its own properties that are different than those of carbon and oxygen.

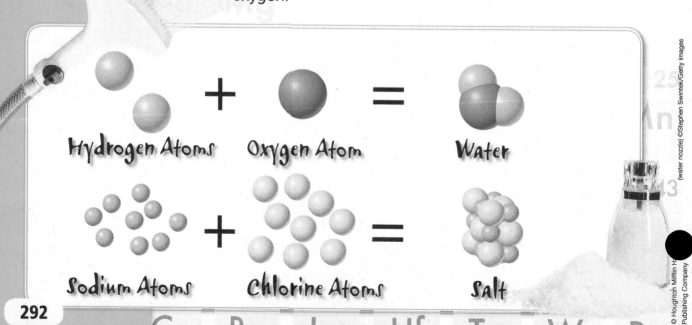

Hydrogen Atoms + Oxygen Atom = Water

Sodium Atoms + Chlorine Atoms = Salt

Cs Ba La Hf Ta W Re

Compounds are made of atoms of at least two different elements.

Firework Colors

Orange	Yellow	Red
calcium chloride	sodium nitrate	lithium carbonate

Orange — calcium chloride
1 calcium
2 chlorine

Yellow — sodium nitrate
1 sodium
1 nitrogen
3 oxygen

Red — lithium carbonate
2 lithium
1 carbon
3 oxygen

Some of the colors in fireworks come from compounds. For example, calcium chloride, which contains one calcium atom for every two chlorine atoms, results in an orange color.

Fructose is often called fruit sugar. For every 6 atoms of carbon in the compound, there are 12 hydrogen atoms and 6 oxygen atoms.

DO THE MATH

Use Fractions

Add the total number of atoms in fructose. In lowest terms, what fraction of fructose consists of:

1. carbon atoms? _____

2. hydrogen atoms? _____

3. oxygen atoms? _____

77	78	79	80	81	82	83	84	85
Ir	Pt	Au	Hg	Tl	Pb	Bi	Po	At

1 Label the parts of this atom.

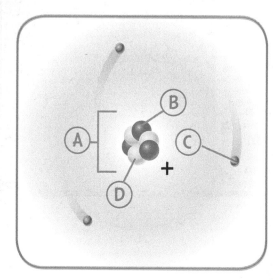

Ⓐ _____

Ⓑ _____

Ⓒ _____

Ⓓ _____

2 Sequence the following from smallest to largest.

____ Ⓐ atom   ____ Ⓑ proton   ____ Ⓒ molecule   ____ Ⓓ nucleus

3 Fill in the blanks.

An atom is the smallest particle of an Ⓐ _____ that has its properties. Our current Ⓑ _____ is the result of the ideas of many scientists over many years. Scientists currently theorize that atoms contain a dense core that is called the Ⓒ _____ . It contains positively charged particles called Ⓓ _____, and Ⓔ _____ , which have no charge. Particles called Ⓕ _____ move around the center of the atom. The identity of an element is determined by the number of Ⓖ _____ in one atom of the element. When two or more atoms are joined together, Ⓗ _____ form.

Brain Check

Name _____

Vocabulary Review

1 For each jumbled term, unscramble the letters to form a term from this lesson. Use the clues to help you.

1. tasmo

＿＿＿＿_◯ The smallest particles of an element

2. ueotnrn

＿_◯＿＿＿＿ The particle in an atom that has no charge

3. retelocn

＿＿＿＿＿_◯＿＿ Moves around the outside of an atom

4. omdocpun

＿＿_◯＿＿＿＿ Formed from at least two types of chemically combined atoms

5. onropt

＿_◯＿＿＿ The positively charged part of the nucleus

6. mitoca rohety

＿＿＿_◯＿＿＿＿＿＿＿ Changed through history as scientists learned more about atoms

7. cnluseu

＿＿＿＿＿＿_◯ The dense, central part of an atom

8. nemtele

◯_＿＿＿＿＿ Contains only one kind of atom

Riddle Put the circled letters into the riddle in the order they are circled.

What did the chemistry teacher get for her birthday?

the element of ＿ ＿ ＿ ＿ ＿ ＿ ＿ ＿ ＿

Apply Concepts

2 Draw and label a diagram of a nitrogen atom. It should have 7 protons, 7 neutrons, and 7 electrons.

3 Use the terms *atom* and *element* to explain what makes silver and gold different.

_____

_____

4 Complete the table.

Compound	Atoms	Fraction of each type of atom
methane	5 total: 1 carbon, 4 hydrogen	
propane	11 total: _____	$\frac{3}{11}$ carbon, $\frac{8}{11}$ hydrogen
hydrogen peroxide	4 total: 2 hydrogen, 2 oxygen	
carbon dioxide	3 total: _____	$\frac{1}{3}$ carbon, $\frac{2}{3}$ oxygen

Take It Home! Check the ingredient lists on labels of several household products. Find the names of two different compounds. Use reference books or the Internet to find out what elements are in the compounds.

Meet the *Atomic All-Stars*

Marie Curie

Marie Curie worked as a scientist in France. She discovered that some elements are radioactive. That means energy radiates, or comes out, of the elements. In 1903, Marie Curie became the first woman ever to win a Nobel Prize. In 1911, she won another. She is one of the most famous female scientists of all time.

In some of Marie Curie's early work on radioactivity, she studied this type of uranium mineral, known as pitchblende.

Inés Triay

Inés Triay is a scientist who works with radioactive materials, too. She works to clean up dangerous wastes that are produced when radioactive elements are used in nuclear power plants. In 2009, President Barack Obama assigned Triay to an important job in the U.S. Department of Energy. She was head of the team that properly disposes of nuclear waste.

The symbol on this sign warns of radioactivity that could be dangerous to your health.

PEOPLE IN SCIENCE

Complete a Timeline

Fill in the boxes with information about Marie Curie and Inés Triay. For each entry you add, draw a line to the correct location on the timeline.

1898 Marie Curie discovers two new radioactive elements, called radium and plutonium.

1896 Marie Curie's teacher, Henri Becquerel, first discovers radioactivity.

1908 Hans Geiger invents a tool now called the "Geiger counter." It measures radioactivity.

_____
_____
_____
_____

1951 For the first time, electricity is generated using radioactive elements.

1934 Marie Curie dies from a disease caused by radiation. No one knew that radioactivity can be very bad for human health.

1979 Two scientists, Godfrey Hounsfield and Allan McLeod Cormack, win the Nobel Prize in Medicine for the C.T. scan machine. It uses small amounts of radiation and takes pictures of the inside of the human body.

_____
_____
_____
_____

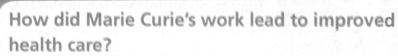

Think About It!

How did Marie Curie's work lead to improved health care?

_____
_____
_____

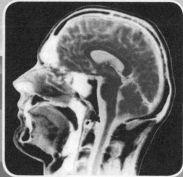

(t) ©Joseph White/Alamy; (b) ©GFC Collection/Alamy; (br) ©BSIP/Photo Researchers, Inc.

Name _____

Vocabulary Review

Use the terms in the box to complete the sentences.

> chemical changes
> compound
> liquid
> physical changes
> solution

1. Matter that has a definite volume but no definite shape is

   a(n) _____.

2. A mixture that has the same composition throughout is

   called a(n) _____.

3. Changes to the identity of matter are called _____.

4. Changes in which the form or shape of a substance changes
   but the substance is still the same type of matter are

   called _____.

5. Matter that cannot be broken into a simpler substance is

   a(n) _____.

Science Concepts

Fill in the letter of the choice that best answers the question.

6. Joseph put water, sugar, and yeast into
   a balloon. Then he put the balloon
   in a warm place for 1 hour. Which of
   the following is most like the change
   happening in Joseph's balloon?

   Ⓐ    Ⓒ

   Ⓑ   Ⓓ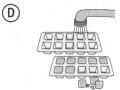

7. Daniel put water, sugar, and yeast into
   a balloon. Then he measured the mass
   of the balloon. He put the balloon
   in a warm place for 2 hours. Then he
   measured the mass again. He repeated
   his experiment three times to get more
   data. Predict how the mass of the balloon
   changed.

   Ⓕ same mass   Ⓗ more mass

   Ⓖ less mass   Ⓘ no more mass

8. Which of these correctly describes a change in the state of water?

    (A) liquid water → melts → solid water

    (B) liquid water → boils → water vapor

    (C) solid water → condenses → liquid water

    (D) water vapor → evaporates → liquid water

9. When an egg is cracked and put in a hot pan, it flows easily. After it cooks for a minute, the egg becomes solid.

    Why does the egg change?

    (F) Breaking the shell is a physical change in the egg that makes it solid.

    (G) Breaking the shell is a chemical change that makes the egg become solid.

    (H) Heating the egg on the stove causes the egg to evaporate and become solid.

    (I) Adding heat causes a chemical change in the particles of the egg that makes it solid.

10. The volume of a given mass of gas is one of its physical properties that can change. Which graph shows how the volume of a gas changes as the temperature of the gas increases?

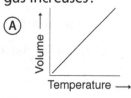
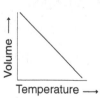
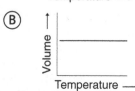
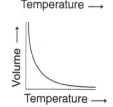

11. Stacey tried to remove a metal lid from a glass jar, but the lid was too tight. Her mother held the jar so that the lid was in hot water for a minute. Then Stacey was able to turn the lid easily. How did the hot water make the lid easier to remove?

    (F) Heating the glass jar made it expand, so the lid turned easily.

    (G) As the metal lid was heated, it expanded so that it was not as tight.

    (H) Water on the metal lid made it easier to hold, so it was easier to turn.

    (I) The water corroded the metal, so it did not hold as tightly to the glass.

12. Which of these statements best describes the effect of temperature on chemical changes?

    (A) Chemical changes generally happen faster at higher temperatures.

    (B) Chemical changes generally happen slower at higher temperatures.

    (C) Chemical changes are not affected by a change in temperature.

    (D) Chemical changes happen only if the temperature is very hot.

13. What does the modern atomic theory state?

    (F) An atom is mostly empty space.

    (G) All atoms are made up of hundreds of smaller particles.

    (H) Atoms of different elements are exactly the same.

    (I) Atoms of different kinds combine to form different elements.

Name _____

14. Claire is studying how quickly sugar dissolves in warm and cold water. First, she dissolves a 4 g sample of raw sugar, as shown in the following figure, in both warm and cold water. Then she dissolves a 4 g sample of white sugar, as shown in the following figure, in both warm and cold water.

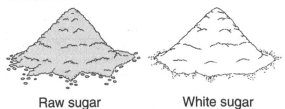

Raw sugar   White sugar

In which of the following solutions would the sugar dissolve the slowest?

(A) raw sugar, cold water

(B) raw sugar, warm water

(C) white sugar, cold water

(D) white sugar, warm water

15. Mrs. Lopez is a chemist who is studying salt crystals. She wants to slow the rate at which the crystals dissolve in a solution of water. What could she do to slow the dissolving rate?

(F) Crush the salt.

(G) Heat the solution.

(H) Cool the solution.

(I) Stir the solution.

16. Nadia has a mixture of oil and water. She wants to separate the mixture. How can she do this?

(A) by using a magnet to attract the oil

(B) by pouring the mixture through a sieve

(C) by evaporating the water from the mixture

(D) by letting the oil float to the top and skimming it off

17. A container holds a mixture of glass shards and iron filings. What is the best way to separate the glass shards from the iron filings?

(F) Use a magnet.

(G) Heat the mixture.

(H) Sort them by size.

(I) Separate them by shape.

18. This diagram shows what happens when water changes state.

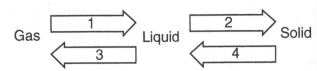

Which statement correctly explains some of the changes shown in the diagram?

(A) Temperature increases in steps 1 and 2.

(B) Energy of water particles decreases in steps 1 and 2.

(C) Energy of water particles decreases in steps 3 and 4.

(D) Motion of water particles decreases in steps 3 and 4.

Apply Inquiry and Review the Big Idea

Write the answer to these questions.

19. Kym tested how quickly 10 g of sugar dissolved in 1 L of water at different temperatures. A graph of her results is shown here. What were Kym's variables? Based on her graph, make a claim about whether she correctly labeled her beakers of water. Use evidence and reasoning to support your claim.

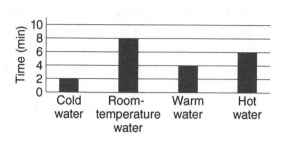

_____

_____

_____

_____

20. Frank was learning about states of matter in science class. He made some drawings but forgot to label them. Describe what each of Frank's drawings shows below.

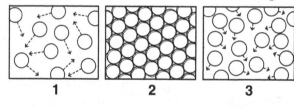

_____

_____

_____

_____

21. Tam was given four equal-sized cubes with different masses, as listed below.

copper: 71.2 g   balsa wood: 1.6 g   brass: 68.0 g   plastic: 9.6 g

What did Tam observe about the volumes of the cubes? Explain.

_____

_____

Tam used these data to order the cubes according to the amount of matter they contain, from least to greatest. What order did she give, and why?

_____

_____

Forms of Energy

A fisherman drives his boat back to shore after a long day at sea.

FLORIDA **BIG IDEA** 10

Forms of Energy

I Wonder Why

In the ocean, fishing boats power through and over the waves. Why do fishing boats need gasoline to run? *Turn the page to find out.*

© Thomas Simone/Alamy

© Houghton Mifflin Publishing Company

Here's Why

Energy is needed to push the boat through the rough waters. This energy comes from gasoline. Without gasoline to burn, the boat's engine wouldn't work.

Essential Questions
and Florida Benchmarks

Science Notebook

Before you begin each lesson, write your thoughts about the Essential Question.

SC.5.P.10.1 Investigate and describe some basic forms of energy, including light, heat, sound, electrical, chemical, and mechanical. **SC.5.P.10.2** Investigate and explain that energy has the ability to cause motion or create change.

LESSON 1

ESSENTIAL **QUESTION**

What Is Energy?

Engage Your Brain

As you read the lesson, figure out the answer to the following question. Write the answer here.

What kinds of energy are represented in this picture?

_____

_____

_____

_____

 ACTIVE **READING**

Lesson Vocabulary
List the terms. As you learn about each one, make notes in the Interactive Glossary.

_____   _____

_____   _____

_____   _____

Compare and Contrast
Many ideas in this lesson are about ways that things are alike or different. Active readers stay focused on comparisons and contrasts by asking how things are alike and how they are different.

Energy
All Around
· · · · ·

What does a melting scoop of ice cream have in common with a kicked soccer ball? The ice cream and the ball both change in some way. What causes these changes?

▶ A soccer ball won't move unless something gives it energy. Energy changes the ball's motion. Circle the thing in the picture that gave the ball energy.

Think about all the ways that you use energy. **Energy** is the ability to cause changes in matter. Energy is involved when matter moves or changes its shape. A change in temperature also involves energy.

Energy can transform, or change, from one form into another. The boy in the picture is using energy to run. The energy came from food that he ate.

When the boy kicks the ball, his foot transfers energy to the ball. The moving ball transfers energy again. Energy moves to particles in the air and on the ground. These tiny particles begin to move faster.

The ball stops moving after it has transferred all its energy. Energy is never used up. It just changes from one form to another.

The tiny particles that make up solid ice cream move slowly. Energy from the sun causes a change in their motion. The particles move faster. The ice cream melts and becomes a liquid.

▶ What caused this ice cream to melt?

_____

_____

_____

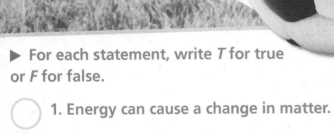

▶ For each statement, write *T* for true or *F* for false.

◯ 1. Energy can cause a change in matter.

◯ 2. Energy can change from one form to another.

◯ 3. Energy can be used up and destroyed.

◯ 4. Energy can be transferred from one object to another.

The Ups and Downs of Energy

Does an object that is not moving have any energy? Let's find out!

ACTIVE **READING** As you read this page, circle the sentences that tell how potential energy and kinetic energy are different.

Does a book sitting on a shelf have energy? Yes! Someone gave it energy by lifting the book to the shelf. The energy is now stored in the book. The energy an object has because of its position or condition is called **potential energy** (PE).

If the book falls off the shelf, it begins moving. Its potential energy changes to the energy of motion. The energy an object has because of its motion is called **kinetic energy** (KE).

_____

When the roller coaster car is at the top of a hill, most of its energy is potential energy due to its position. Gravity will change this *PE* to *KE* as the car starts downhill.

When you compress a spring or stretch a rubber band, your energy is stored in the object as potential energy. The potential energy changes to kinetic energy when you release the spring or rubber band.

The energy of a falling object, a contracting rubber band, or an expanding spring is not all kinetic. As long as these objects are falling, contracting, or expanding they still have potential energy. Look at the image of the roller coaster. The car is somewhere between a high and a low point in the ride. It has both potential and kinetic energy. The sum of all the kinetic and the potential energy an object has is called mechanical energy.

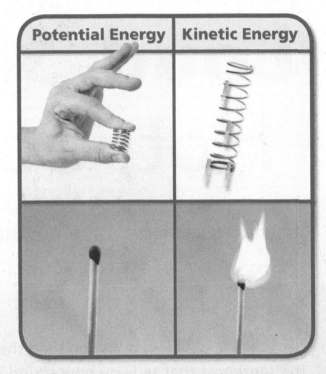

Potential Energy	Kinetic Energy

Position isn't the only way that energy can be stored. A match head has potential energy stored in chemical bonds between its particles. Striking the match releases the stored energy as heat and light. A charged battery also contains potential energy. A battery dies when all of its potential energy has been transformed to electrical energy.

As the car moves downhill, its PE changes to kinetic, or moving, energy. At the bottom of the hill, the car's energy is kinetic. This *KE* becomes *PE* as the roller coaster car travels up the next hill.

▶ Fill in the three bubbles on the roller coaster track. Write *KE* if a coaster car at that position would have mostly kinetic energy. Write *PE* if it would have mostly potential energy.

▶ When does a roller coaster car have the most kinetic energy?

_____

_____

_____

Loud, Soft, Hot, Cold
• • • • •

The kinetic energy of a moving roller coaster car is easy to see. How can you sense energy in tiny particles of matter that are too small to see?

ACTIVE **READING** As you read these two pages, underline the sentences that tell you how sound energy and thermal energy are alike.

When a trumpet makes noise, it vibrates, or moves back and forth. The trumpet transfers energy to tiny particles of air. Each particle of air moves back and forth, bumping into other particles. The sound travels outward.

▶ Draw an arrow to show the direction that sound waves are traveling.

If someone knocks on your door, the particles in the door vibrate. They bump into particles in the air on your side of the door. The sound travels through the door and through the air to you as a sound wave.

Sound energy is —

- a form of energy that is carried as waves in vibrating matter.

- a type of kinetic energy, because particles of matter are moving.

- the cause of all the sounds you hear.

Another type of energy that involves moving particles is thermal energy. *Thermal energy* is the total kinetic energy of the particles that make up a substance.

Thermometers measure thermal energy. You sense thermal energy as temperature. The more thermal energy an object has, the greater its temperature. Thermal energy helps you to stay warm, to cook your food, and to heat water for washing or bathing.

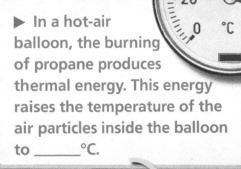

▶ In a hot-air balloon, the burning of propane produces thermal energy. This energy raises the temperature of the air particles inside the balloon to _____ °C.

▶ Rubbing your hands together produces thermal energy.

▶ The air at the top of this icy mountain has very little thermal energy. Its temperature is _____ °C.

⊞ DO THE **MATH**

Use Number Lines

Draw a number line. On the line, place the three temperatures (in °C) shown in the pictures on this page. Then add a point for normal room temperature, 22 °C.

See a Sea of Energy

The sun is the source of the light energy entering the cave.

Your ears use sound energy to hear. What kind of energy allows your eyes to see?

ACTIVE READING As you read, draw boxes around the descriptions of light energy and electrical energy.

Suppose you are using a flashlight in a dark room. You drop the flashlight and it breaks. What can you see? Nothing! Your eyes need light energy to work.

Light energy is a form of energy that can travel through space. Light can also pass through some types of matter, such as air or glass. Light energy travels as waves.

You can see light energy. Some objects give off light. You see all other objects when light reflects, or bounces off, from them and enters your eyes.

▶ List three sources of light.

_____

_____

_____

You see the cave walls when light bounces off them and reaches your eyes.

Electrical energy changes to light energy in a flashlight.

Objects that give off light energy often give off heat. But the two types of energy are different. You can tell them apart by the way you sense the energy. Your skin senses heat, but it cannot sense light energy. Your eyes sense light energy.

Flashlights and television sets produce light. To do this, they use another type of energy, called electrical energy. **Electrical energy** is energy caused by the movement of electric charges. When you use electricity, you are using electrical energy.

Electrical energy can change to other types of energy you can use. Electrical energy changes to thermal energy in a toaster or a stove. Cell phones and stereo speakers use electrical energy to produce sound. In lamps and spotlights, electrical energy changes to light energy.

Computers and other devices that are plugged in use electrical energy.

▶ List three objects that use electrical energy.

_____

_____

_____

Energy in Machines and Food

• • • • •

You have learned about machines that use electrical energy. Some machines don't need to be plugged in. What forms of energy do they use?

ACTIVE READING Draw one line under things that have mechanical energy. Draw two lines under things that have chemical energy.

Many objects, such as a ball thrown in the air, have both kinetic and potential energy. **Mechanical energy** (ME) is the total energy of motion and position of an object. As a ball drops, its potential energy decreases as its kinetic energy increases. Its mechanical energy, though, stays constant. The relationship among these forms of energy is shown by the following equation.

Mechanical Energy = Kinetic Energy + Potential Energy

A machine uses mechanical energy to do work. For example, a fan plugged into the wall uses electrical energy. It changes that energy into the mechanical energy of the spinning fan blades. The spinning fan uses the mechanical energy to do work—moving the air in a room.

▶ Describe how energy in gasoline is transformed in a lawn mower.

_____

_____

_____

_____

_____

_____

314

Have you ever felt as if you were going to "run out of energy"? The energy your body uses comes from the food you eat. Food contains a kind of potential energy called chemical energy. **Chemical energy** is energy that is stored in matter and that can be released by a chemical reaction.

When your body needs energy, it breaks down food and releases potential chemical energy from it. If you use that energy to run or jump, it changes into kinetic energy. Your body also uses chemical energy stored in food to produce thermal energy. This keeps your body at a steady temperature.

Cars use chemical energy in liquid fuel such as gasoline. A flashlight uses the chemical energy stored in a battery to produce light. Some stoves change chemical energy to thermal energy by burning a gas called propane.

▶ Winding the key on the toy increases the toy's _____ energy.

▶ Our bodies use the _____ energy in food to move and stay warm.

▶ The hands on this watch move because the watch has _____ energy.

Spotlight on Energy

A stage production requires different kinds of energy. How many are being used on this stage?

ACTIVE READING As you read these pages, draw a box around each type of energy.

Some stage shows use fire, sparklers, and explosions. These elements turn stored chemical energy into light, heat, and sound energy.

Musicians use mechanical energy to play instruments. The instruments make sound energy that the audience hears as music.

These performers are high above the stage. They have a lot of potential energy due to their position.

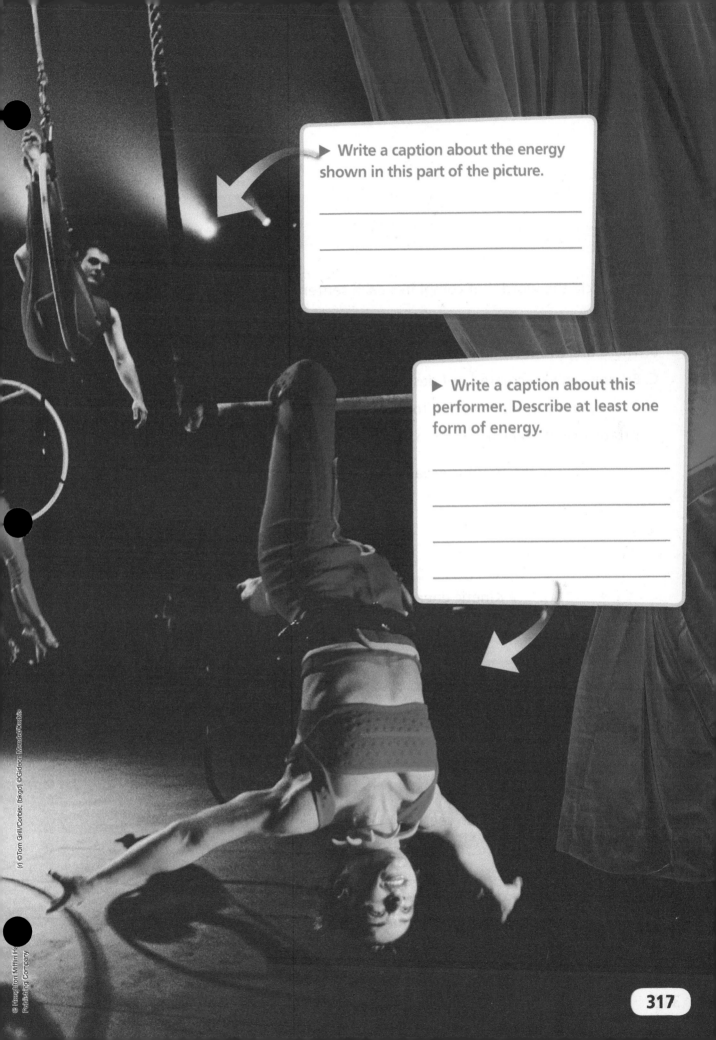

▶ Write a caption about the energy shown in this part of the picture.

_____

_____

_____

▶ Write a caption about this performer. Describe at least one form of energy.

_____

_____

_____

_____

Sum It Up »

Part I: Circle the word that completes each sentence.

A. Energy is the ability to cause motion or create (matter / change).

B. There are two main categories of energy—potential and (thermal / kinetic).

C. Energy can't be created or (destroyed / captured).

D. Energy can change from one form to another, which is called energy
(transformation / conservation).

Part II: Complete the graphic organizer below.

ENERGY

Potential energy is energy stored in an object because of its position or condition.

Kinetic energy is the energy of motion.

A. _____ energy is energy that can be released by a chemical reaction.

B. _____ energy is the total kinetic energy of the particles in matter.

C. _____ energy is the form of energy that you can see.

F. _____ energy is the combination of the potential and kinetic energy an object contains.

D. _____ energy travels as waves through vibrating matter.

E. _____ energy is energy caused by movement of electrical charges.

Name _____

Vocabulary Review

1 Use the clues to fill in the missing letters of the words.

1. __o_____ __a__ e__ ___ __y   stored energy due to position or condition

2. ___o__   a substance that contains useful chemical energy

3. __l_____   energy caused by the movement of electric charges

4. ___n__t___   energy of motion

5. _____a___   to move back and forth

6. __h_____a__   energy of moving particles of matter

7. ___u___   form of energy you can hear

8. ____h__   form of energy you can see

9. ___c_____c___   total potential and kinetic energy of an object

10. _____a__   energy that can be released by a chemical reaction

11. __n___g__   ability to cause changes in matter

12. ___a__   what your body feels thermal energy as

Apply Concepts

2 Complete the matching game. The first one is done for you.

Light Energy ⓔ ③	A. The total kinetic energy of the particles in matter
Thermal Energy ◯◯	B. Energy caused by motion of electric charges
Sound Energy ◯◯	C. Energy that is stored in matter and can be released during a chemical reaction
Electrical Energy ◯◯	D. Energy carried as waves of vibrating matter
Mechanical Energy ◯◯	E. Energy that travels as a wave and that you are able to see
Chemical Energy ◯◯	F. Sum of an object's potential and kinetic energy

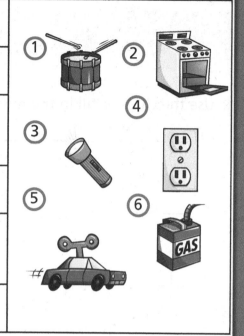

3 Use the terms *potential energy* and *kinetic energy* to tell what is happening to the skier.

_____

_____

_____

_____

_____

4 Identify the types of energy present or produced in each lettered part of the picture.

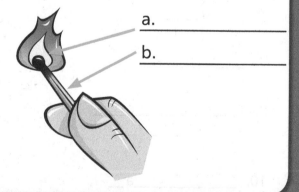

a. _____

b. _____

Take It Home! See *ScienceSaurus®* for more information about energy.

SC.5.P.10.1 Investigate and describe some basic forms of energy... SC.5.P.10.2 Investigate and explain that energy has the ability to cause motion or create change. SC.5.N.1.1 ... plan and carry out scientific investigations of various types... SC.5.N.2.1 Recognize and explain that science is grounded in empirical observations that are testable; explanation must always be linked with evidence.

INQUIRY
LESSON 2

Name _____

ESSENTIAL QUESTION

What Changes Can Energy Cause?

EXPLORE

You use thermal energy produced from electrical or chemical energy to cook food. What other energy source might you use?

Materials

sheet of poster board
2 thermometers
aluminum foil
scissors
tape
string

Before You Begin—Preview the Steps

① Cut a sheet of poster board in half. Cover one side of each half with aluminum foil.

② Make a solar cooker. Bend one half of the poster board, foil side in, into the shape of a U. Tape a piece of string to both edges at the top of the solar cooker so that the cooker holds its shape.

③ Build a second solar cooker that is identical to the first. Place a thermometer in each solar cooker.

④ Place one solar cooker in direct sunlight, and place the other in shade. Predict what will happen to the temperature in each solar cooker.

⑤ Read and record the temperature in each solar cooker every 3 minutes for 15 minutes. CAUTION: Do not touch the foil in your solar cookers when they are in the sun.

Set a Purpose

How will this investigation help you observe changes in matter?

_____

_____

_____

_____

State Your Hypothesis

Write your hypothesis, or testable statement.

_____

_____

_____

_____

Think About the Procedure

How hot do you predict the solar cookers will become?

_____

_____

_____

_____

What variable will you change in this experiment? Why is it important to change only one variable?

_____

_____

_____

Name _____

Record Your Data

Draw a data table, and record your temperature measurements.

Draw Conclusions

Was your hypothesis supported by evidence? Why or why not?

_____

_____

_____

_____

_____

Claims • Evidence • Reasoning

1. What was the purpose of the aluminum foil? How would your results differ if you had made the cooker just from the poster board? Explain your reasoning.

_____

_____

_____

2. Make a claim about how a solar cooker might be useful in places where there is no electricity. Explain your reasoning.

_____

_____

_____

3. How could you improve your solar cooker to make it heat faster?

_____

_____

4. The setup for an experiment is shown below. What problems do you see with the way the experiment is designed? Explain your reasoning.

_____

_____

_____

SC.5.P.10.3 Investigate and explain that an electrically-charged object can attract an uncharged object and can either attract or repel another charged object without any contact between the objects.

LESSON **3**

ESSENTIAL QUESTION

What Is Electricity?

 Engage Your Brain

As you read the lesson, look for the answer to the following question and record it here.

What causes the girl's hair to stand out from her head?

_____

_____

_____

_____

 ACTIVE READING

Lesson Vocabulary

List the terms. As you learn about each one, make notes in the Interactive Glossary.

_____

_____

Main Ideas

The main idea of a paragraph is the most important idea. The main idea may be stated in the first sentence, or it may be stated elsewhere. Active readers look for main ideas by asking themselves, What is this section mostly about?

All Charged Up

You can charge a battery. A football player may charge downfield. How is an electric charge different?

ACTIVE READING As you read these two pages, underline the main idea on each page.

What do you, this book, and your desk have in common? You are all made of atoms. Atoms are the building blocks of all matter. An atom is made of even tinier particles called protons, neutrons, and electrons.

The main difference between protons, electrons, and neutrons is their electric charge. *Electric charge* is a property of a particle that affects how it behaves around other particles.

- Protons have a positive charge (+1).

- Electrons have a negative charge (−1).

- Neutrons are neutral. They have no charge.

When an atom has equal numbers of protons and electrons, the positive charges and negative charges cancel each other. The atom itself has no charge.

Legend

= neutron

= proton

= electron

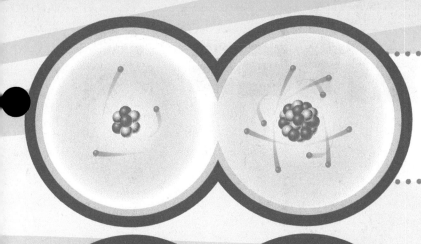

Each of these atoms has equal numbers of protons and electrons. Both atoms are neutral.

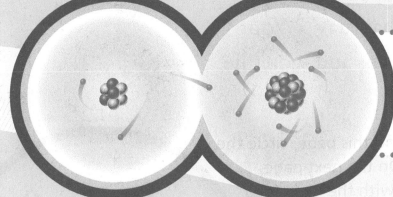

An electron from the atom on the left moves to the atom on the right.

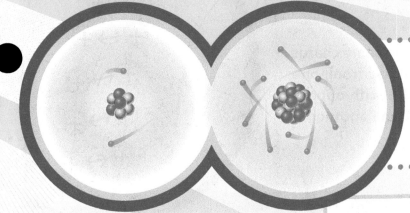

The atom on the left now has a charge of +1. The atom on the right has a charge of −1.

Atoms sometimes gain or lose electrons. Such a gain or loss causes an atom to have an unequal number of positive and negative charges. For example, if an atom with four protons and four electrons gains an electron, the atom will have a charge of −1.

If a neutral atom loses an electron, the number of protons will no longer balance the number of electrons. The atom will have a charge of +1.

▶ Draw an atom with three protons, four neutrons, and four electrons.

What is the charge of the atom?

_____

Opposites Attract

Have you ever had a "bad hair day"? Your hair sticks out in all directions and won't lie flat. What causes that?

ACTIVE **READING** As you read this page, circle the definitions of *attract* and *repel*. On the next page, draw a box around the sentence with the main idea.

Particles with the same charge repel, or push away from, one another. Particles with opposite charges attract one another, or pull together.

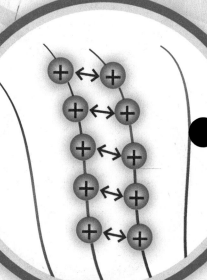

DO THE MATH

Positive and Negative Numbers

Fill in the missing squares.

Original Charge on an Object	Electrons Gained or Lost	Final Charge on the Object
+300	Gains 270	
−300	Loses 525	
−270		−500

In the dryer, atoms in clothing gain and lose electrons. Each piece of clothing becomes charged. The positively charged surfaces attract the negatively charged surfaces. As a result, the clothes stick together.

Electric charges can build up on objects. This buildup of charges is called **static electricity**. Objects with opposite electric charges attract each other. Objects with the same charge repel each other.

When you brush your hair, electrons move from each strand of hair to the brush. Soon all the strands are positively charged. Having the same charge causes the strands to repel one another and stick out.

A charged object can also attract a neutral object. If you rub a balloon on your hair, the balloon picks up extra electrons. They give it a negative charge. When you bring the balloon near a wall, electrons in a small section of the wall are repelled and move away. This leaves a positive charge at the surface of the wall. The balloon sticks to the wall.

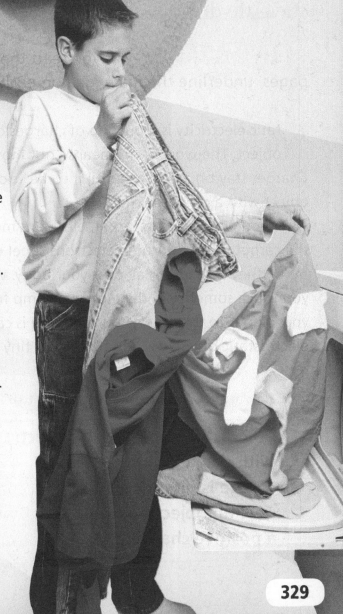

Lightning Strikes

Thunderstorms can be scary. Lightning strikes can be deadly. What is lightning, and how can you stay safe during a thunderstorm?

ACTIVE **READING** As you read these two pages, underline the main idea on each page.

Static electricity is a buildup of charges on an object. The word *static* means "not moving." Charges stay on an object until it comes close to an object with a different charge.

As you walk across a carpet, electrons move from the carpet to you. Because electrons repel each other, they spread out all over your body. When you touch something, the electrons jump from your finger to the object. This jumping is called an electrostatic discharge. You feel it as a tiny shock.

ZAP!
Electrons jump from a person with a negative charge.

▶ Complete this cause-and-effect graphic organizer.

Cause: An object with a negative charge is placed near an object with a positive charge.	→	Effect: _____ _____ _____ _____

Not all electrostatic discharges cause small shocks. Some result in huge shocks. During a thunderstorm, tiny raindrops or ice particles bump into each other. These collisions cause an electric charge to build in the clouds.

Positive charges form at the top of a cloud and on the ground. Negative charges form near the bottom of a cloud.

When the difference in charge between a cloud and the ground is great enough, there is a huge electrostatic discharge that we call lightning.

A lightning spark can jump between two clouds, between a cloud and air, or between a cloud and the ground. The temperature inside a lightning bolt can reach 50,000 °F. That's hotter than the surface of the sun!

Lightning Safety

- Stay inside during thunderstorms.
- Turn off electrical appliances and stay away from windows.
- If you can't get inside a safe structure, wait in a car with a metal top for the storm to pass.
- Know the weather forecast. If you will be outdoors, have a plan in case a thunderstorm develops.

Objects that lightning strikes can catch on fire. A tree struck by lightning may split.

▶ Draw a cloud above the ground. Then draw positive and negative charges to show what causes lightning.

Current Events

You can control electrons by making them flow through a wire in the way water flows in a river.

ACTIVE **READING** As you read these two pages, draw a box around the sentence that contains the main idea.

When electric charges have a path to follow, as they do in the wire below, they move in a steady flow. This flow of charges is called an **electric current**.

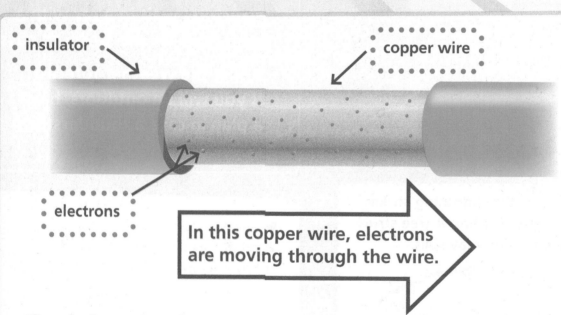

insulator

copper wire

electrons

In this copper wire, electrons are moving through the wire.

Chemical reactions in a battery provide the energy that causes the electrons to flow. An energy station is another source of electric current.

▶ What do the blue dots on this wire represent, and what is it called when they flow?

_____

_____

_____

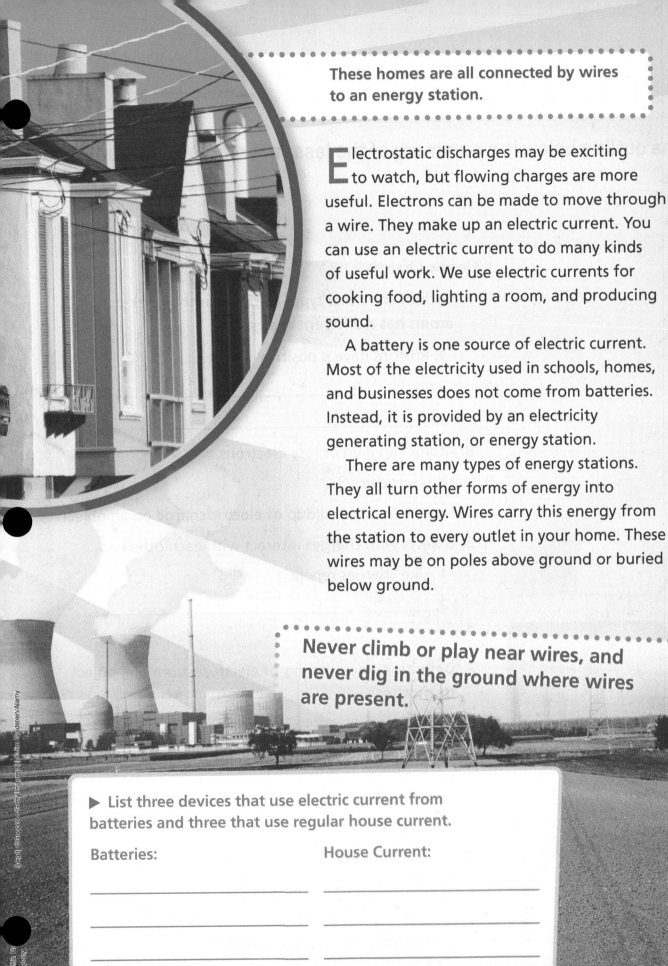

These homes are all connected by wires to an energy station.

Electrostatic discharges may be exciting to watch, but flowing charges are more useful. Electrons can be made to move through a wire. They make up an electric current. You can use an electric current to do many kinds of useful work. We use electric currents for cooking food, lighting a room, and producing sound.

A battery is one source of electric current. Most of the electricity used in schools, homes, and businesses does not come from batteries. Instead, it is provided by an electricity generating station, or energy station.

There are many types of energy stations. They all turn other forms of energy into electrical energy. Wires carry this energy from the station to every outlet in your home. These wires may be on poles above ground or buried below ground.

Never climb or play near wires, and never dig in the ground where wires are present.

▶ List three devices that use electric current from batteries and three that use regular house current.

Batteries:

House Current:

_____   _____

_____   _____

_____   _____

Sum It Up »

The outline below is a summary of the lesson. Complete the outline.

I. Electric Charges

    A. Each of the three types of particles that make up atoms has a different charge.

        1. Protons have a positive charge.

        2. _____

        3. _____

    B. Atoms can gain or lose electrons.

II. Static Electricity

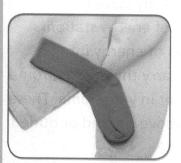

    A. Definition: the buildup of electric charge on an object

    B. Objects with charges interact with each other.

        1. Like charges repel.

        2. _____

III. Electrostatic Discharge

    A. Definition: the jumping of electrons from one object to another

    B. Examples

        1. Getting shocked after walking across a rug

        2. _____

IV. Electric Current

    A. Definition: _____

    B. Sources

        1. _____

        2. Electricity generating stations

Name _____

Vocabulary Review

1 Use the clues to unscramble the words in the box. Use the word bank if you need help.

1. leepr: what two positive charges do to each other

   _____

2. trattac: what a positive charge and a negative charge do to each other

   _____

3. cattis: the type of electricity that results from the buildup of electric charge on an object

   _____

4. ntrruce: The steady flow of electric charges along a path is electric _____.

   _____

5. stipoive: the charge of a proton

   _____

6. ratleun: the charge of a neutron

   _____

7. ateenvig: the charge of an electron

   _____

8. ategenring nattsoi: where electricity is produced

   _____

WORD BANK:

positive	negative	neutral	current
attract	repel	static	generating station

Apply Concepts

2 List the three particles that make up an atom. Describe the charge of each particle.

Parts of an Atom	
Particle	Charge

Where are these particles found in an atom?

_____

_____

_____

3 Draw an atom with 9 protons, 10 neutrons and a charge of −1. Label each part in your drawing.

4 Explain why the balloons are sticking to this cat.

_____

_____

_____

_____

_____

5 Look at the pairs of objects below. The charge of each object is shown. Tell how each pair will interact. Write *attract, repel*, or *nothing*.

+22	−34	_____
0	+130	_____
−40	−81	_____
0	0	_____

6 Complete the sequence graphic organizer.

A wool sock and a cotton shirt _____ against each other in a dryer.

↓

Electrons move from the wool to the _____ .

↓

The two pieces of clothing have _____ charges and they _____ each other.

7 List three ways in which electric current helps you do work, and describe the energy transformation that takes place.

_____

_____

_____

_____

_____

_____

_____

_____

_____

_____

8 Explain why the event in the drawing takes place.

_____

_____

_____

_____

_____

_____

_____

_____

9 Match each drawing with its description. Circle the drawings that show sources of current that people use every day.

| electric current | static electricity | electrostatic discharge | battery |

10 Suppose you are playing soccer at a park and you hear thunder that sounds far away. Describe some things you should and should not do to stay safe.

_____

_____

_____

_____

_____

_____

Take It Home! Do your clothes stick together when they come out of the dryer? If so, how could you prevent this from happening? If not, why don't they stick together? When you put on a sweater, does it ever stick to your hair? Does this happen throughout the year, or only at certain times?

SC.5.P.10.3 Investigate and explain that an electrically-charged object can attract an uncharged object and can either attract or repel another charged object without any contact between the objects. SC.5.N.1.2 Explain the difference between an experiment and other types of scientific investigation. SC.5.N.1.5 Recognize and explain that authentic scientific investigation frequently does not parallel the steps of "the scientific method."

INQUIRY
LESSON 4

Name _____

ESSENTIAL QUESTION

How Do Electric Charges Interact?

Materials

2 balloons
string
tape
wool cloth

EXPLORE

What happens when you give something a charge? In this activity, you will explore how objects with different charges behave.

Before You Begin—Preview the Steps

1. Blow up both balloons and tie a knot in each. Tie a length of string to each knot. Tape both strings to a table so that the balloons hang a few centimeters apart.

2. Hold one balloon by the neck, and rub it with a wool cloth. Gently release the balloon. Observe and record what happens.

3. Run your hand over each balloon. Then rub both balloons with a wool cloth. Release the balloons. Observe and record what happens.

4. Try rubbing the balloons with several other materials. Communicate with your classmates by discussing your observations.

Set a Purpose

What do you think you will observe during this activity?

_____

_____

_____

Think About the Procedure

Why do you rub one balloon, but not the other, in Step 2?

_____

_____

Why do you rub both balloons in Step 3?

_____

_____

Why is this activity not an experiment?

_____

_____

Name _____

Record Your Data

Draw diagrams to show what happened during Steps 2 and 3. Label the diagrams.

Draw Conclusions

What caused the balloons to behave as they did in Steps 2 and 3?

_____
_____
_____
_____

Claims • Evidence • Reasoning

1. What do you think happens when you rub a balloon with a wool cloth?

_____

_____

2. Write a claim about what happens when objects with opposite charges are near each other. Support your claim with an example that you have seen in your everyday activities.

_____

_____

_____

3. Write a claim about what happens when objects with similar charges are near each other. Support your claim with an example.

_____

_____

_____

4. Look at the drawings of balloons to the right. In each pair, the drawing shows the charges on one balloon. Look at the way each pair of balloons is interacting, and draw the charges on the second balloon.

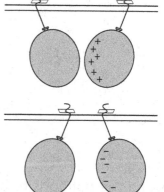

5. What other questions would you like to ask about electric charges?

_____

_____

SC.5.P.10.4 Investigate and explain that electrical energy can be transformed into heat, light, and sound energy, as well as the energy of motion.

ESSENTIAL **QUESTION**

How Do We Use Electricity?

🧠 Engage Your Brain

As you read, figure out the answer to the following question and record it here.

How would this scene have been different in 1910?

_____

_____

_____

📖 ACTIVE **READING**

Lesson Vocabulary

List the terms. As you learn about each one, make notes in the Interactive Glossary.

_____

_____

_____

Signal Words: Sequence

Signal words show connections between ideas. Words that signal sequence include *now*, *before*, *after*, *first*, and *next*. Active readers remember what they read because they look for signal words that identify sequence.

Electricity
Has Many Uses

Suppose you had lived in 1900 rather than today. The pictures show how different your day might have been.

Does a clock radio wake you up in the morning? Do you use an electric toothbrush or hair dryer? How do you cook your breakfast?

Electrical appliances do work. They perform useful tasks by converting electrical energy into other forms of energy, such as sound, thermal, and mechanical energy. Some appliances run on batteries. Others are plugged into a socket, which provides greater electrical energy. Think about the appliances you use each day. How would your day change if there were no electricity?

The only light came from candles or oil-burning lamps. Now we can turn on lamps with the flick of a switch.

Before electricity, food was kept cold in an icebox. Ice was delivered daily to keep food cold.

▶ Draw a picture of the electrical appliance that does the same work as this object.

People used muscles rather than electricity to mix cake batter!

Electricity changed life outside the kitchen, too. The heater in this scene keeps the room warm. Before electricity, a wood stove or fireplace heated the home. Cleaning was harder, too. There were no vacuum cleaners. There was no television to watch or radio to listen to. People entertained themselves by reading or by playing cards.

Many modern appliances, such as mixers and fans, use electric motors. An **electric motor** is a device that converts electrical energy into mechanical energy.

electric heater

There are many devices in this room that use electrical energy. Each device converts electrical energy into other forms of energy.

Then and Now

Match the objects that do the same kind of work. Draw a picture of the missing appliance. Then describe the energy change that takes place in each electrical appliance.

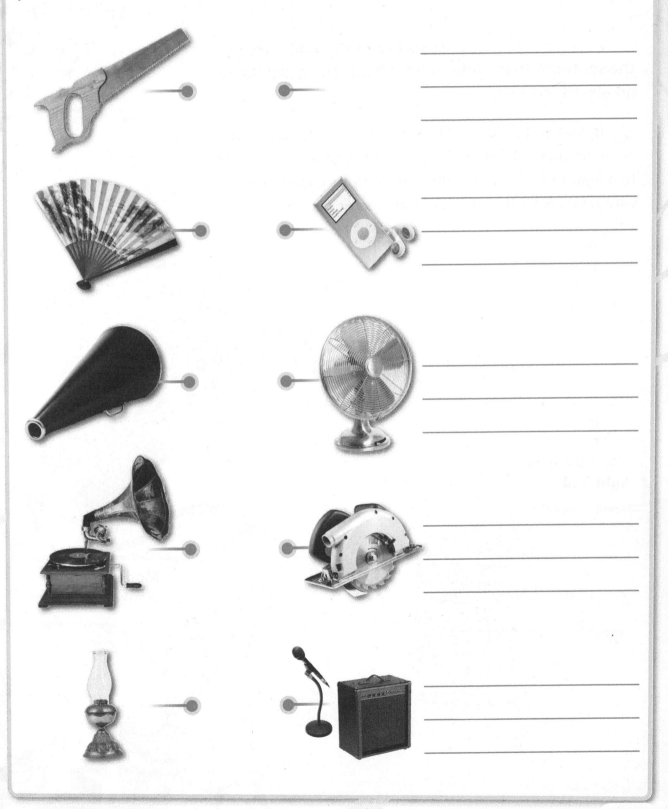

Electromagnets

Electricity and magnetism are related.
One can produce the other.

ACTIVE **READING** As you read this page, circle the sentence that explains how magnetism produces an electric current.

Suppose you slide a coil of wire back and forth around a bar magnet. When the ends of the wire are attached to a light bulb, the bulb lights! Moving a magnet and a wire near each other produces an electric current.

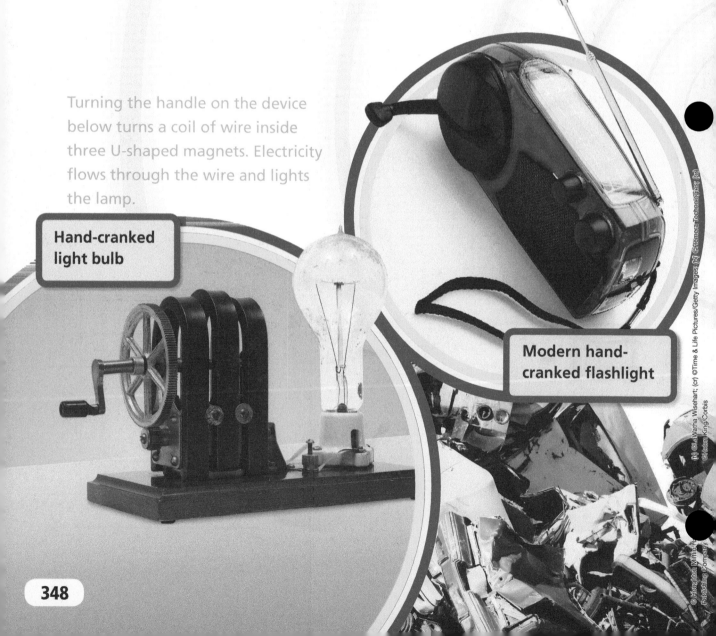

Turning the handle on the device below turns a coil of wire inside three U-shaped magnets. Electricity flows through the wire and lights the lamp.

Hand-cranked light bulb

Modern hand-cranked flashlight

If magnets produce electricity, can electricity make magnets? Yes! Wrapping a coil of current-carrying wire around an iron nail makes the nail a magnet. You can use it to pick up small iron objects such as paper clips. A device in which current produces magnetism is called an **electromagnet**.

Huge electromagnets are used in junk yards. They separate iron and steel objects from other objects. The operator swings the electromagnet over a pile of junk. He turns on the current. All the iron pieces jump to the magnet. The operator then swings the magnet over a container and turns off the current. The magnetism stops, and the iron drops into the container.

Electromagnets have become very important and useful. Every electric motor today contains at least one electromagnet. You can also find electromagnets in telephones, doorbells, speakers, and computers. Doctors can use electromagnets to make pictures of the inside of the body.

▶ In the first box, write the cause of the action in the second box. Then figure out what that effect can cause, and fill in the third box.

_____ _____ _____ _____	An electric current flows through the wire.	_____ _____ _____ _____

Conserving Electricity

You've probably been asked to conserve, or use less, electricity. Why is conserving electricity important?

ACTIVE **READING** As you read, underline a sentence that tells how you can conserve energy.

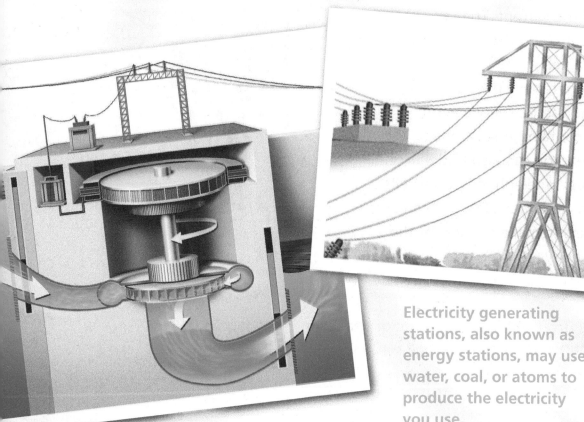

Electricity generating stations, also known as energy stations, may use water, coal, or atoms to produce the electricity you use.

Inside a hydroelectric [hy•droh•ee•LEK•trik] dam, the mechanical energy of falling water is used to turn generators, which change mechanical energy into electrical energy.

The electrical energy is transmitted through a network of substations, high voltage towers, and other components to homes and businesses in the community.

Suppose you spin a magnet inside a coil of wire. A current flows through the wire. You've made a **generator**, a device that converts kinetic energy to electrical energy. Huge generators in energy stations change kinetic energy into electricity. The electricity travels through wires to homes, schools, and businesses.

Some energy stations use falling water or wind to turn generators. Other energy stations convert solar energy to electricity. These resources will never run out. They are called renewable resources.

Most energy stations burn coal or other fuels to heat water. The water rises as steam, which turns the generator. Coal is a limited resource. It will eventually run out. That's why it is important to conserve, or use less, electricity. For example, you can turn off the lights when you leave a room or use a towel instead of a hair dryer.

➗ DO THE **MATH**

Solve a Problem

Sam's electric bill was $200 for the month of June. The air conditioner accounts for $\frac{1}{2}$ of the bill, and the water heater accounts for $\frac{1}{5}$ of the bill. How much did it cost to run each appliance in June?

Sum It Up »

Use information in the summary to complete the graphic organizer.

Electrical appliances use electrical energy to do work and perform useful tasks. Some of these appliances, such as a flashlight or an MP3 player, get electricity from batteries. Others must be plugged into a wall socket. Electrical appliances convert electrical energy into other forms of energy, such as thermal energy, sound energy, and light energy. Many appliances, such as washing machines and fans, contain an electric motor, which converts electricity into the energy of motion. An electric current may also be used to make an electromagnet. Generators in energy stations produce electric current, which travels through wires to homes, schools, and businesses. It is important to conserve electricity because some of the resources energy stations use will eventually run out.

① Main Idea: Electrical appliances use electrical energy to
_____
_____

② Detail: Some appliances work on batteries. Others must be
_____
_____
_____
_____

③ Detail: Electrical appliances convert
_____
_____
_____
_____

④ Detail: Conserving electricity is important because
_____
_____
_____
_____

Brain Check

LESSON **5**

Name _____

Vocabulary Review

1 Unscramble each of the clues to form a word or a phrase from the word bank. Copy each letter in a numbered cell to the cell below with the same number.

TECGARLOETNEM ☐☐☐☐☐☐☐☐☐ 5 ☐☐☐☐

RECLICTE ROOTM ☐☐ 8 ☐☐☐☐☐   ☐☐☐☐☐

TORRAGEEN ☐☐ 4 ☐☐☐☐☐☐

ONECREVS ☐☐☐ 2 ☐☐☐☐

REECUSROS ☐☐☐☐ 1 ☐☐☐☐

GANSEITMM ☐☐☐ 10 7 ☐☐ 3 ☐☐

CICLETERTIY 6 ☐☐☐☐ 9 ☐☐☐☐ 11 ☐

WORD BANK
conserve
electricity
electric motor
electromagnet
generator
magnetism
resources

This lesson is about ☐1 ☐2 ☐3 ☐4 ☐5   ☐6 ☐7 ☐8 ☐9 ☐10 ☐11

Apply Concepts

2 Draw a common electrical appliance. Then explain how it changes electrical energy to other forms of energy and what kind of work it does.

_____
_____
_____
_____
_____

© Houghton Mifflin Harcourt Publishing Company

353

3 Draw an X over each appliance that changes electrical energy to mechanical energy.

Circle each appliance that changes electrical energy to thermal energy.

Draw a square around each appliance that changes electrical energy to sound energy.

Draw a triangle around each appliance that changes electrical energy to light energy.

4 What is the device in this drawing called? What would happen if you put this device near a pile of iron nails? Why?

_____

_____

_____

5 A. What are some resources used to generate electricity in energy stations?

_____

_____

_____

_____

B. Describe three ways that you can conserve electricity.

_____

_____

_____

_____

Discuss with your family some specific ways that you could conserve electricity. You might talk about ways to use less electricity or about things you can do by hand rather than using an electrical appliance.

PEOPLE **IN SCIENCE**

Meet two Scientists Whose Work Shines Bright

Lewis Latimer

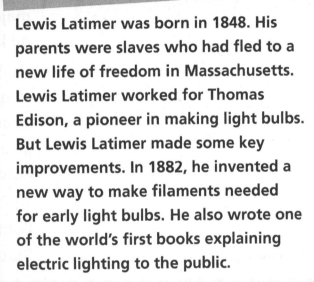

Lewis Latimer was born in 1848. His parents were slaves who had fled to a new life of freedom in Massachusetts. Lewis Latimer worked for Thomas Edison, a pioneer in making light bulbs. But Lewis Latimer made some key improvements. In 1882, he invented a new way to make filaments needed for early light bulbs. He also wrote one of the world's first books explaining electric lighting to the public.

Shuji Nakamura

Shuji Nakamura is a Japanese inventor born in 1954. Working in a small electronics company in 1993, Shuji Nakamura made a discovery. He invented the first successful blue light-emitting diode, or LED. The blue LED made today's bright white LED lights possible. These new LED lights use much less energy than a regular bulb. They can last about 100 times longer, too. Using these lights helps the environment.

Lighting the Way

Fill in the boxes with information about Lewis Latimer and Shuji Nakamura. For each entry you add, draw a line to the correct location on the timeline.

1780 Aimé Argand makes major improvements to the oil lamp.

1879 Thomas Edison's company begins selling incandescent light bulbs, which give off light when a filament inside the bulb heats up.

1923 The first neon lights in the United States are sold.

1960 The first working laser was demonstrated.

_____
_____
_____
_____

1938 The first commercial fluorescent lamps become available for purchase.

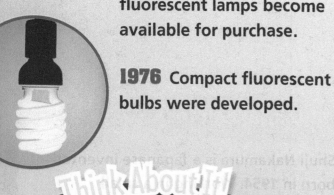

1976 Compact fluorescent bulbs were developed.

_____
_____
_____
_____

Think About It!

Lighting has changed a lot since the days of oil lamps. Why do you think people continue to develop new ways to produce light?

_____
_____
_____
_____

Name _____

Vocabulary Review

Use the terms in the box to complete the sentences.

1. The batteries of a flashlight contain

   _____ energy

2. The ability to cause changes in matter is known

   as _____.

3. Sound energy and thermal energy are both types

   of _____ energy.

Science Concepts

Fill in the letter of the choice that best answers the question.

4. Olivia is combing her hair. After a while, she notices that the comb attracts the hairs on her head as shown below.

Which explanation best describes why the hairs are attracted to the comb?

Ⓐ Combing the hairs caused them to lose their static charge.

Ⓑ Combing the hairs caused the comb to lose its static charge.

Ⓒ Combing the hairs gave them a charge that is opposite the charge on the comb.

Ⓓ Combing the hairs gave them a charge that is the same as the charge on the comb.

5. You rub two balloons on your hair on a dry day. Your hair is attracted to both balloons. Then you bring the balloons near one another. How would you describe what happens to the balloons?

Ⓕ They repel one another.

Ⓖ They attract one another.

Ⓗ They neither attract nor repel one another.

Ⓘ Opposite charges make one balloon become larger and one become smaller.

6. Imagine you bring a negatively charged rod near a piece of metal. What happens within the metal?

Ⓐ Protons in the metal move toward the rod.

Ⓑ Electrons in the metal move toward the rod.

Ⓒ Protons in the metal move away from the rod.

Ⓓ Electrons in the metal move away from the rod.

7. When an electric current runs through a doorbell buzzer, a mechanism inside vibrates back and forth and makes the doorbell work. Which energy transformation occurs when someone pushes the button on a doorbell?

Ⓕ electrical energy into heat energy and sound energy

Ⓖ electrical energy into motion energy and sound energy

Ⓗ motion energy into electrical energy and sound energy

Ⓘ motion energy and sound energy into electrical energy

8. Joe had two toy cars. One car had a spring which he wound up before the car would move. The other car did not have a spring, but it needed a battery to work. How are the two cars different?

Ⓐ The two cars transform different kinds of energy into motion.

Ⓑ One car works only on a level surface, and the other can move up a ramp.

Ⓒ There is no difference between the two cars because they both move forward on a surface.

Ⓓ The two cars both transform electrical energy into motion, but they get the electrical energy in different ways.

9. When Tishana left her bedroom, she flipped the light switch. The light bulb on her lamp stopped giving off light. What caused the light bulb to go out?

Ⓕ The filament in the bulb stopped moving, so it could not make light.

Ⓖ The electric current stopped, so no more electrical energy was converted into light.

Ⓗ The bulb became cooler, so the light bulb stopped converting heat energy into light.

Ⓘ The electric current stopped, so light energy could not be converted into electrical energy.

Name _____

10. Which is **not** something that energy can do?

  (A) be completely used up

  (B) cause an object to move

  (C) change an object's temperature

  (D) change into other forms of energy

11. One type of energy is the result of waves that travel through matter and cause particles in the matter to vibrate. Which type of energy is it?

  (F) chemical

  (G) electrical

  (H) potential

  (I) sound

12. A thermometer shows that the temperature of the air in a room has increased. Which type of energy has increased?

  (A) chemical   (C) electrical

  (B) sound   (D) thermal

13. The picture below shows a burning candle. A candle burns because of energy stored in the particles of wax.

Which type of energy changes take place when the candle burns?

  (F) Chemical energy changes into thermal energy and light energy.

  (G) Electrical energy changes into light energy and chemical energy.

  (H) Kinetic energy changes into potential energy and thermal energy.

  (I) Potential energy changes into kinetic energy and light energy.

Apply Inquiry and Review the Big Idea

Write the answers to these questions.

14. The balloons shown below are part of Eric's investigation into positive and negative charges. He rubbed both balloons with a wool cloth.

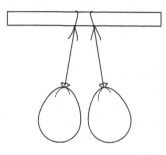

What must be true of the balloons? Explain how you know.

_____

_____

_____

15. The illustration below shows a large dam that is used to produce electricity. Water flows from the lake behind the dam to the river below the dam. It passes through turbines that are connected to generators.

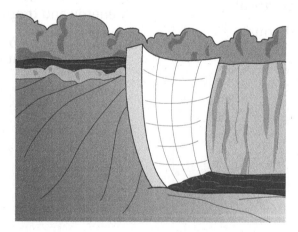

Which energy transformation occurs in this hydroelectric dam? Why is this energy transformation useful?

_____

_____

_____

Working with Electricity

Thomas Edison had a laboratory at his home.

FLORIDA BIG IDEA 11

Energy Transfer and Transformations

I Wonder Why

Thomas Edison had many bright ideas at his winter home in Ft. Myers, FL. Why did Edison want to study electricity? *Turn the page to find out.*

Here's Why

Edison, a great inventor, realized that there were many uses for electricity. He was the first to build an energy station that supplied electricity to homes, schools, and businesses.

Essential Questions and Florida Benchmarks

 Science Notebook

Before you begin each lesson, write your thoughts about the Essential Question.

SC.5.P.11.1 Investigate and illustrate the fact that the flow of electricity requires a closed circuit (a complete loop). SC.5.P.11.2 Identify and classify materials that conduct electricity and materials that do not. SC.5.N.1.1 ... plan and carry out scientific investigations of various types... SC.5.N.2.1 Recognize and explain that science is grounded in empirical observations that are testable...

INQUIRY LESSON 1

Name _____

ESSENTIAL **QUESTION**

What is an Electric Circuit?

Materials

battery (size D) with holder

light bulb with holder

three lengths of wire

switch

paper clip

wooden craft stick

pencil lead

EXPLORE

You flip a switch and a light bulb goes on. What is there between the switch and the bulb that lets this happen? See if you can figure that out by building an electric circuit.

Before You Begin—Preview the Steps

1. Lay out the parts in the order you think will make the bulb light up. Show your plan to your teacher before you connect the parts.

2. Connect the parts to test your plan. Does the bulb light up? Keep working until you "see the light!"

3. Draw a picture of your circuit. Show how the parts are connected.

4. The metal inside a wire allows electricity to pass through the wire. What other materials do that? Replace the switch with an unbent paper clip, a craft stick and then a pencil lead. Record your observations.

Set a Purpose

What will you learn from this investigation?

_____

_____

_____

_____

Think About the Procedure

Did the order in which you arranged the parts make a difference?
Explain.

_____

_____

Was the procedure an experiment? Why or why not?

_____

_____

_____

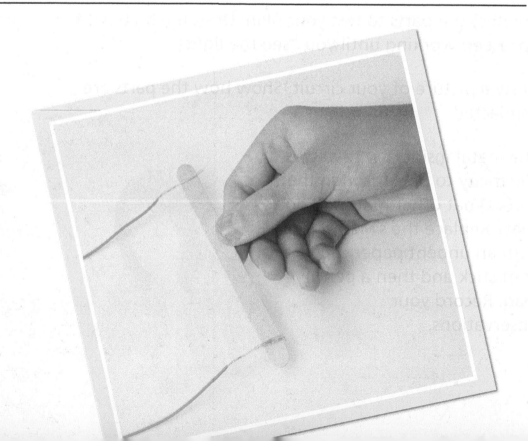

Name _____

Record Your Data

In the space below, draw your circuit that worked. Label each part, and describe how the parts were connected.

Place a check mark next to the materials that enabled the bulb to light up.

Draw Conclusions

How can you build a circuit?

_____

_____

_____

_____

Claims • Evidence • Reasoning

1. Make a claim about why it is helpful to have a switch in a circuit. Explain your reasoning.

_____

_____

_____

2. Make a claim about why a circuit would not work when a wire is replaced with a cotton string. Use evidence to support your claim and explain your reasoning.

_____

_____

3. Look at the first part of the word _circuit_. Why do you think what you built is called a circuit? Explain your reasoning.

_____

_____

4. Look at the picture below. Draw lines to show how three wires could be connected to make the bulbs light up.

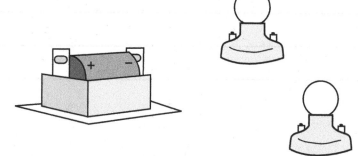

5. Identify the part that performs each of the jobs listed below.

- Source of current   _____

- Carries current   _____

- Turns circuit on and off   _____

- Changes electrical energy _____
  to light

SC.5.P.11.1 Investigate and illustrate the fact that the flow of electricity requires a closed circuit (a complete loop). SC.5.P.11.2 Identify and classify materials that conduct electricity and materials that do not.

LESSON 2

ESSENTIAL **QUESTION**

What Are Electric Circuits, Conductors, and Insulators?

 Engage Your Brain

Find the answer to the following question and record it here.

This picture shows the inside of a robot. What do the dark lines have to do with the robot's operation?

_____

_____

_____

_____

📖 ACTIVE **READING**

Lesson Vocabulary

List the terms. As you learn about each one, make notes in the Interactive Glossary.

_____

_____

_____

Compare and Contrast

When you compare things, you look for ways in which they are alike. When you contrast things, you look for ways in which they are different. Active readers stay focused by asking themselves, How are these things alike? How are these things different?

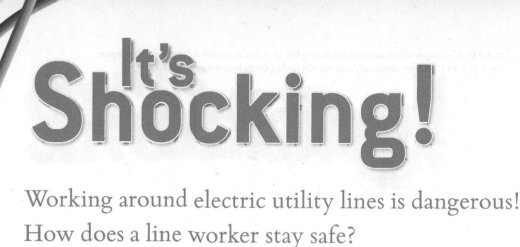

It's Shocking!

Working around electric utility lines is dangerous!
How does a line worker stay safe?

ACTIVE **READING** Draw a box around the sentences that contrast conductors and insulators.

Even on a hot day, a worker who repairs electric utility lines must be bundled up in protective clothing. The thick gloves, the bulky boots, and the hard plastic hat are heavy; however, these clothes protect the worker from an electric shock!

The rubber and plastic used in the protective clothing do not allow electric charges to flow through them. A material that resists the flow of electric charges is called an **insulator**. Electric charges flow easily through metals and some liquids. A material that readily allows electric charges to pass through it is called a **conductor**.

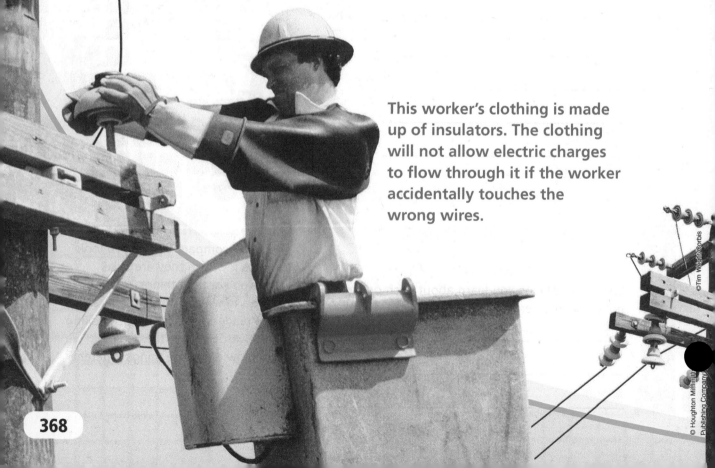

This worker's clothing is made up of insulators. The clothing will not allow electric charges to flow through it if the worker accidentally touches the wrong wires.

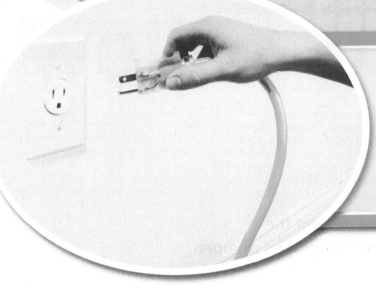

The parts of a plug that you hold and the covering on the wire are insulators. The metal prongs that go into the outlet are good conductors.

Electrical appliances work when electric charges flow through them. The parts that carry electric charges are made from conductors. Insulators are wrapped around the conductors to make appliances safe to handle.

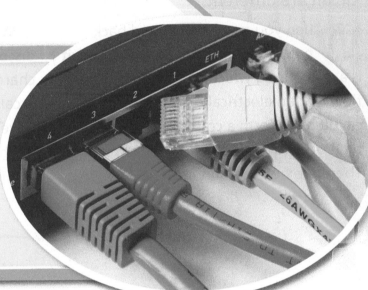

▶ Label the parts of the wire as a conductor or an insulator.

▶ Why are insulators used?

_____

_____

_____

_____

_____

_____

_____

A Path to Follow

If the wiring in a lamp does not change,
why isn't the lamp on all of the time?

ACTIVE **READING** Draw a box around the
sentences that tell you how a closed circuit and an open
circuit are different.

When you go to school and back
home, your path is a loop. A **circuit**
is a path along which electric charges can
flow. For an electrical device to work, the
circuit must form a complete loop. This
type of circuit is called a *closed circuit*.
There are no breaks in its path.

What happens if a loose wire gets
disconnected? The path is broken, and
charges cannot flow. This type of circuit
is called an *open circuit*. Many circuits
have a switch. A switch controls the flow
of charges by opening and closing the
circuit.

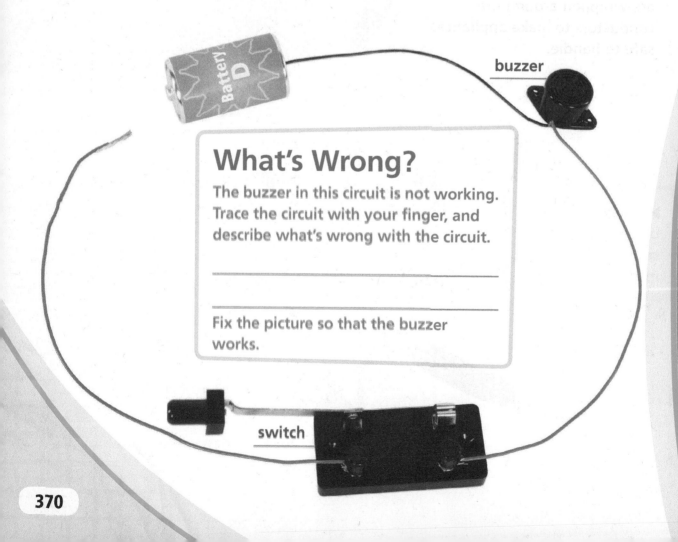

buzzer

What's Wrong?
The buzzer in this circuit is not working.
Trace the circuit with your finger, and
describe what's wrong with the circuit.

_____

_____

Fix the picture so that the buzzer
works.

switch

Open Circuit

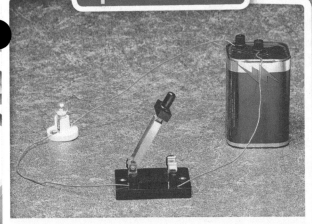

When the switch in a circuit is open, the circuit is not complete. Electric charges cannot flow, so the light stays off.

Closed Circuit

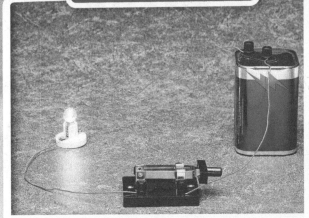

When the switch is closed, the circuit is complete. Electric charges can flow through it to light up the bulb.

▶ The filament in a light bulb is a tiny wire. It is part of the circuit. If the filament breaks, the circuit will be _____.

filament

Who Needs a Map?

To travel from point A to point B, you usually take the shortest route. What if one of the roads on that route is blocked? Simple! You just take another road. What would happen if there were only one road between point A and point B?

ACTIVE **READING** Underline the sentences that compare series circuits and parallel circuits.

Series Circuits

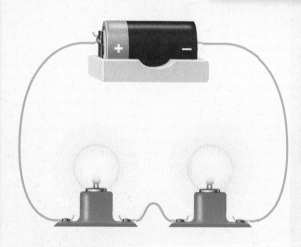

In a series circuit, electric charges must follow a single path. The charged particles move from the battery's positive terminal to its negative terminal.

▶ Draw arrows to show how charges flow in this circuit.

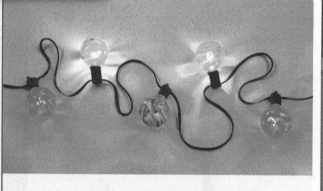

If one light bulb in a series circuit burns out, all of the lights go out, because the circuit is broken.

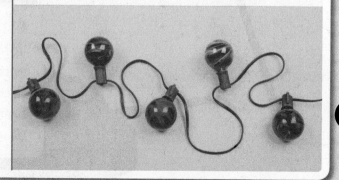

Suppose that the television and all the lights in a room are part of the same circuit. What would happen if one of the light bulbs burned out? It would depend on how the circuit is wired.

A **series circuit** has only one path for electric charges to follow. If any part of the path breaks, the circuit is open. Nothing works!

A circuit with several different paths for the charges to follow is called a **parallel circuit**. If one part of the circuit breaks, the charges can still flow along the other parts.

Color a Complex Circuit

1. Look at the circuit below. Color the bulb or bulbs that should be lit.
2. Draw an X on the switch that is open. Draw an arrow above the closed switch.

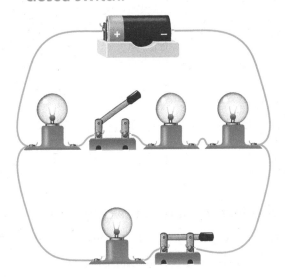

Parallel Circuits

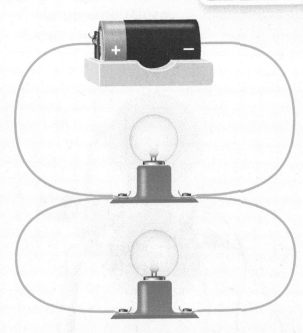

In this parallel circuit, electric charges can flow through both the top loop and the bottom loop.

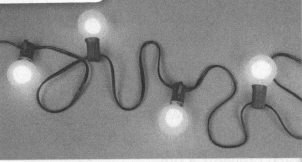

If one part of a parallel circuit breaks, only that part of the circuit stops working.

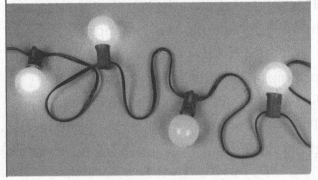

Circuit Overload!

Some house fires are caused by overloaded electrical wiring. How can you use electrical appliances safely?

As electric charges flow through conductors, they produce heat. Insulation protects the materials around these conductors from the heat—up to a point! If the conductor gets too hot, the insulation can melt.

To protect against fires, a fuse or a circuit breaker is added to each circuit. Fuses and circuit breakers are switches that work automatically. They open if charge flows too quickly through a circuit. The flow stops and the wires cool, which prevents a fire.

Circuit overload takes place when too many devices in one circuit are turned on. Each device needs a certain flow of charge. This flow of charge, or current, is measured in units called *amperes*, or amps.

Circuit breakers open when the number of amps is greater than a certain value. Suppose the value for a breaker is 15 amps. The breaker will open if all plugged devices draw more than 15 amps.

television
3 amps

hair dryer
12.5 amps

Wow!

This wire got so hot that it melted the insulation around it. It could have started a fire.

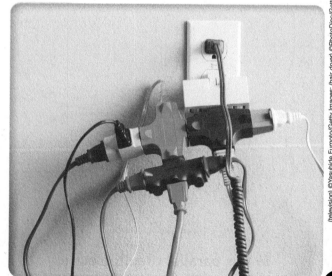

Never plug more appliances into a circuit than it is designed to handle!

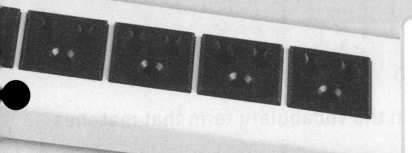

Should You Plug It In?

Draw a line connecting the hair dryer to one of the outlets in the power strip. Then connect the other devices you could use at the same time without overloading a 15-amp circuit breaker.

With power strips like this one, it's possible to plug many devices into a single wall outlet.

That could be a big mistake!

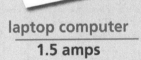

lava lamp
0.5 amp

laptop computer
1.5 amps

clothes dryer
42 amps

This panel contains circuit breakers. Each breaker allows a certain number of amps of electric current to pass through one circuit.

⊞ DO THE **MATH**

Solve Word Problems

1. How many times as much current does a television need than a lava lamp?

_____

2. Circuit breakers are made in increments of 5 amps. What size breaker would you need for a circuit with a television, two laptops, and a lava lamp?

_____

375

Sum It Up »

On each numbered line, fill in the vocabulary term that matches the description.

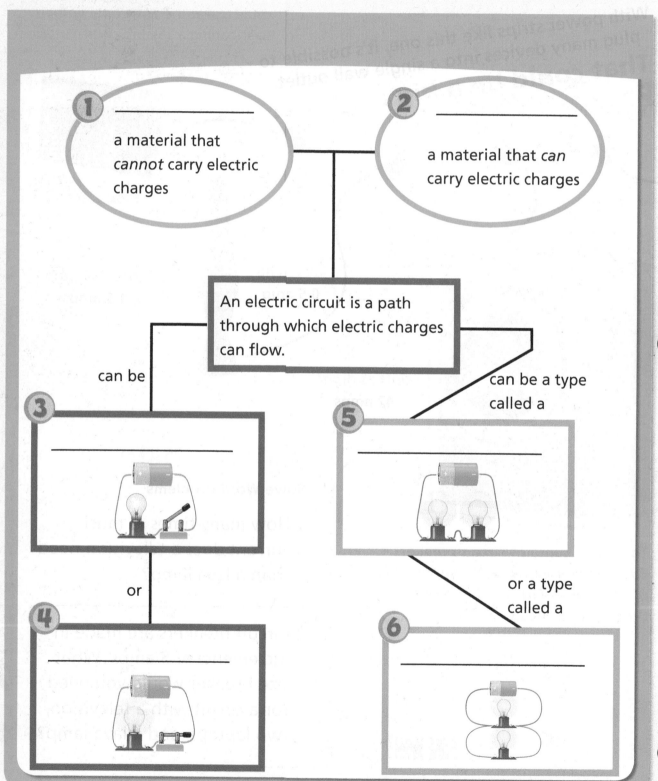

1 _____

a material that *cannot* carry electric charges

2 _____

a material that *can* carry electric charges

An electric circuit is a path through which electric charges can flow.

can be

3 _____

or

4 _____

can be a type called a

5 _____

or a type called a

6 _____

Name _____

Vocabulary Review

① Unscramble the scrambled word in each sentence. Write the unscrambled word after the sentence. The first one is done for you.

A. In some circuits, electrical energy is transformed into light energy by a light lubb.	ⒷU L B 6
B. The wires in a circuit are made of a material that is a doortuccn.	_ _ _ _ _ _ _ _ ◯ 　　　　　　　　　10
C. A path that an electric current can follow is an electric icurict.	_ _ _ _ ◯ _ ◯ 　　　　4　5
D. A circuit in which electric charges can follow several different paths is called a rallpale circuit.	_ ◯ _ _ _ _ _ 　8
E. If a wire is disconnected, the circuit is an enop circuit.	_ _ ◯ _ 　　9
F. The covering on electric plugs and around wires is made of an rainulost.	◯ _ _ _ _ _ _ _ ◯ 2　　　　　　　　7
G. A circuit in which all the devices are connected in a single path is a ressie circuit.	_ _ ◯ _ _ _ 　　3
H. When a light is on, it is part of a scolde circuit.	◯ _ _ _ _ _ 1

Solve the riddle by writing the circled letters above in the correct spaces below.

Riddle: What is another name for a clumsy electrician?

A _ _ _ C _ I _ 　 B _ E _ K _ _
　1 2 3　4　5 　　6 7　8　9 10

Apply Concepts

2 Draw a closed series circuit with two light bulbs, a battery, and a switch. What would happen if one of the light bulbs blows out?

_____

_____

_____

_____

_____

3 Explain what causes an overloaded circuit. How can you prevent an overloaded circuit?

_____

_____

_____

_____

_____

4 Write the word *conductor* or *insulator* on each of the lines. Then infer which type of material is inside the holes in the outlet. Explain your answer.

_____

_____

_____

_____

_____

_____

5 Suppose you are building a series circuit using a small battery and a small light bulb, and you run out of wire. What everyday objects could you use to connect the battery to the light bulb? Explain.

_____

_____

_____

6 Identify each lettered part of the circuit, and explain what each part does.

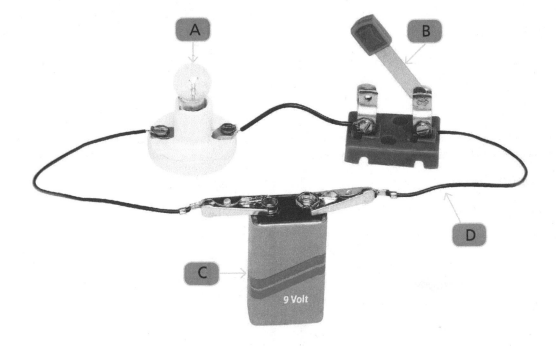

A _____

B _____

C _____

D _____

Study each of the following circuits.

- Make a check mark to show whether the circuit is open or closed.

- Draw the missing parts needed to make the open circuits work.

- Label each circuit as a series circuit or a parallel circuit.

☐ open
☐ closed

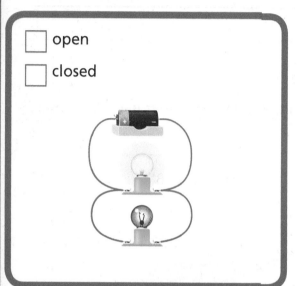

☐ open
☐ closed

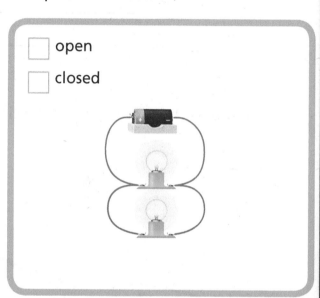

☐ open
☐ closed

_____

☐ open
☐ closed

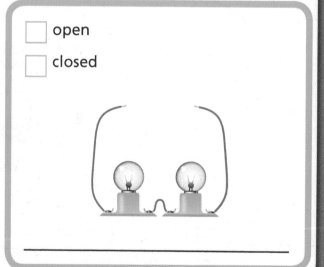

_____

Discuss with your family what you have learned about circuits. Gather some electrical devices and explain how they use electricity. Try flipping some switches in your home, and explain whether they are series circuits or parallel circuits.

SC.5.N.1.2 Explain the difference between an experiment and other types of scientific investigation.

S.T.E.M.

ENGINEERING & TECHNOLOGY

How It Works:

The Electric Grid

At home, you flip a switch and a light comes on. The electricity to power the light comes from generating stations. Generating stations are a part of a larger system know as the *electric grid*. Generators, high voltage steel towers, conductors, insulators, and your home appliances are all parts of this system.

At generating stations, generators transform kinetic energy into electrical energy.

From the generating stations, electrical energy travels over electrical lines on tall steel towers. These lines are made up of a conductor and an insulator.

Coal is a fossil fuel. There is plenty of it in the United States. Most of our electricity comes from burning coal.

Wind turbines are large generators. Turbines use energy from wind to generate electricity.

TROUBLESHOOTING

During prolonged hot weather, many people use air conditioning units to remain cool. How could this affect the electric grid and the environment?

_____

_____

_____

S.T.E.M. continued

Water falling through a turbine can generate electricity. Most hydroelectric generating stations have a dam that blocks a river. A lake forms behind the dam and provides a constant source of falling water. The dam also floods areas that were once dry land. Draw a picture that shows what you think the area behind the dam looked like before the dam was built.

A hydroelectric dam uses energy from moving water to generate electricity.

Research the benefits and risks for each of the first three sources of electrical energy listed below. Fill out the chart. Then identify the energy source described in the last entry.

Electrical energy source	Benefits	Risks
Wind turbines	do not pollute air, land, or water	
Coal-burning generating stations		Coal mines change the landscape; they can cause land, air, and water pollution.
Hydroelectric dams	use water, a renewable resource	
	do not pollute air, land, or water	These produce toxic wastes that must be stored for a very long time.

ENGINEERING DESIGN CHALLENGE

Build in Some Science:
An Attractive Option

Did you know the flow of electric charges through a wire produces magnetism? You can focus this magnetic effect by coiling the wire. Then you can place an iron rod in the middle of the coil to make it even stronger. You've just made an electromagnet.

Unlike a bar magnet or a horseshoe magnet, an electromagnet is not a permanent magnet. Only when electricity flows through the wire does it become a magnet. Once the electricity stops, the device loses its magnetic properties.

Do you think you can turn one or more electromagnets into a useful device? Here's your chance to find out.

Both of these electromagnets work based on the same principles. What makes one magnet stronger than the other? The amount of electricity flowing through its wires! Which electromagnet do you think uses the most electricity?

What to Do:

1 Research electricity and learn about its connection to magnetism.

2 Find out more about electromagnets and their uses. List two uses you learned about.

3 Make an electromagnet from wire, an iron nail, a battery, and a switch. Use paper clips to explore how your electromagnet works.

4 Think about how one or more electromagnets might help make a useful product. What is the use of the product?

5 Draw your design.

6 Discuss your design with others. Improve or redesign it based upon feedback. Explain any improvements you made.

7 Keep a record of your work in your Science Notebook.

Ask an Electrician

Q. Do electricians make electricity?

A. No. Electricity is produced in energy stations and carried to buildings through wires. Electricians work with wires to make sure the electricity moves safely.

Q. Don't electricians worry about electric shocks when they work?

A. Electricians must always turn off electricity to the wires they are working on. Electricity can be dangerous and safety is an important part of the job.

Q. What kind of training do you need to be an electrician?

A. Most electricians learn from experienced electricians while they are attending classes. During this period, they are called an apprentice.

Now It's Your Turn!

What question would you ask an electrician?

_____

_____

_____

_____

Untangle the Wires!

For each circuit, explain what would happen
when the switch at the bottom is closed.

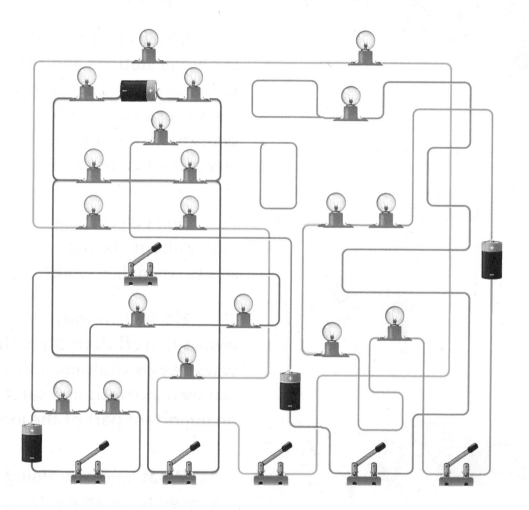

Red: _____

Purple: _____

Green: _____

Orange: _____

Blue: _____

Name _____

Vocabulary Review

Use the terms in the box to complete the sentences.

> circuit
> insulator
> conductor

1. An electrical wire is made of a(n) _____ so that it can carry electricity.

2. A(n) _____ must make a continuous loop or the electricity will not flow.

3. Plastic is a(n) _____ because it does not carry electricity.

Science Concepts

Fill in the letter of the choice that best answers the question.

4. Study the circuit below. When the switch is closed, all three light bulbs are lit.

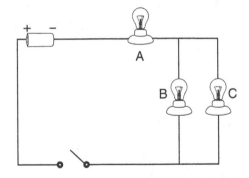

What will happen if Bulb A burns out?

(A) Bulbs B and C will continue to shine.

(B) Bulbs B and C will stop shining.

(C) Bulbs B and C will shine more brightly.

(D) Bulbs B and C will shine less brightly.

5. Jayden uses various objects to complete a circuit. He compares how bright a bulb glows using each object. His results are shown below.

Object	Glow
nail	very bright
crayon	dim
eraser	very dim
pencil lead	bright

Which object is the **best** electrical conductor?

(F) nail   (H) crayon

(G) eraser   (I) pencil lead

Apply Inquiry and Review the Big Idea

Write the answers to these questions.

6. The circuit below consists of a battery, a light bulb, and three switches. All of the switches are open, and the light bulb is off.

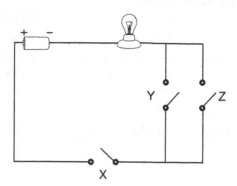

Make a claim about the combination of switches that could be closed and cause the light bulb to remain off. Explain your reasoning.

_____

_____

_____

7. Study the materials in the table below.

Insulators	Conductors
air	gold
cloth	iron
silver	copper
bronze	glass
rubber	aluminum

Which are placed in the wrong column? Explain your reasoning.

_____

_____

_____

Forces
and Motion

FLORIDA BIG IDEA 13

Forces and Changes in Motion

A surfer seems to have found the perfect wave.

I Wonder Why

Why does a surfer need to wax the board before riding the waves? *Turn the page to find out.*

Here's Why

The hard shell of a surf board is smooth and slippery. By waxing the board, the surfer creates bumps, giving the feet something to hold on to.

Essential Questions and Florida Benchmarks

Science Notebook

Before you begin each lesson, write your thoughts about the Essential Question.

SC.5.P.13.1 Identify familiar forces that cause objects to move.... SC.5.P.13.2 ... the greater the force applied to it, the greater the change in motion of a given object. SC.5.P.13.3 ... the more mass an object has, the less effect a given force will have on the object's motion. SC.5.P.13.4 ... when a force is applied to an object but it does not move, ... another opposing force is being applied ... so that the forces are balanced.

ESSENTIAL QUESTION
What Are Forces?

Engage Your Brain

As you read the lesson, figure out the answer to the following question. Write the answer here.

What forces are acting on this cyclist? Are all the forces balanced?

_____

_____

_____

_____

_____

(b) ©George Tiedemann/GT Images/Corbis; (inset) ©George Tiedemann/GT Images/Corbis; (border) ©NDiscAge Fotostock
© Houghton Mifflin H Publishing Company

📖 ACTIVE READING

Lesson Vocabulary
List the terms. As you learn about each one, make notes in the Interactive Glossary.

_____ _____

_____ _____

_____

Cause and Effect
Some ideas in this lesson are connected by a cause-and-effect relationship. Why something happens is a cause. What happens as a result of something else is an effect. Active readers look for effects by asking themselves, What happened? They look for causes by asking, Why did it happen?

PUSHING
and Pulling

You pull on a door to open it. You lift up a backpack. You push on the pedals of a bike to go faster. What is the relationship between force and motion?

The horse and the road it is on both exert a force on the cart.

▶ Draw an arrow that shows the direction of the force applied to the cart by the horse.

Changes in motion all have one thing in common. They require a **force**, which is a push or a pull. Forces can cause an object at rest to move. They can cause a moving object to speed up, slow down, change direction, or stop. Forces can also change an object's shape.

Forces are measured with a spring scale in units called newtons (N). The larger the force, the greater the change it can cause to the motion of an object. Smaller forces cause smaller changes. Sometimes more than one force can act together in a way that does not cause a change in motion.

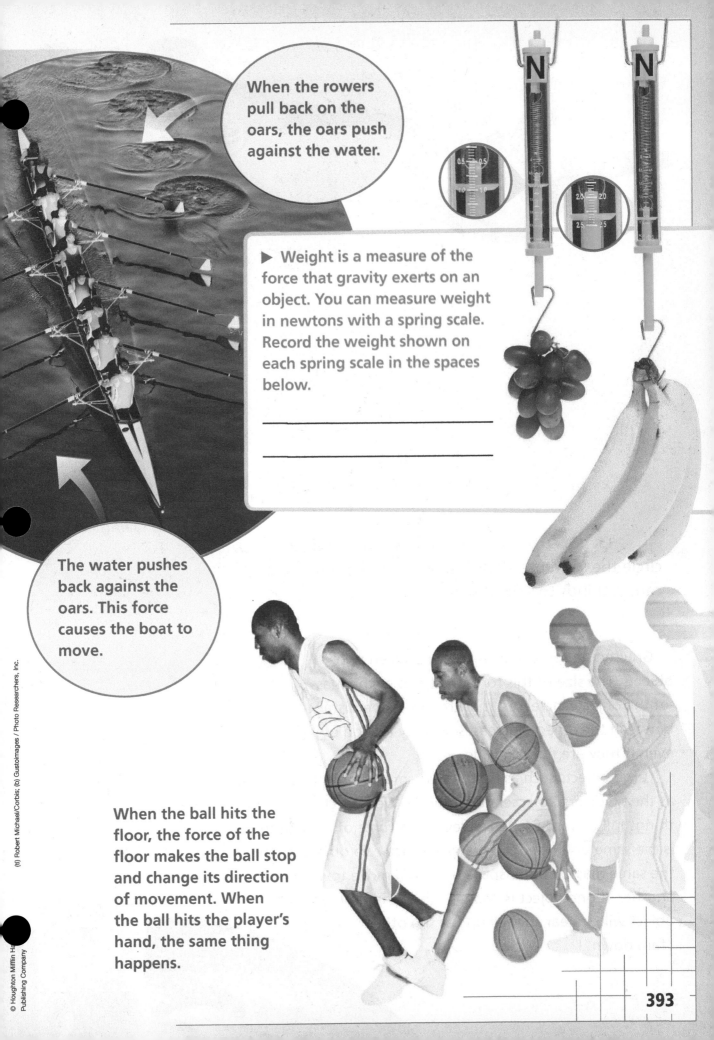

When the rowers pull back on the oars, the oars push against the water.

▶ Weight is a measure of the force that gravity exerts on an object. You can measure weight in newtons with a spring scale. Record the weight shown on each spring scale in the spaces below.

_____

_____

The water pushes back against the oars. This force causes the boat to move.

When the ball hits the floor, the force of the floor makes the ball stop and change its direction of movement. When the ball hits the player's hand, the same thing happens.

TWO COMMON
Forces

What do the skydivers and some of the flower petals have in common? They are both falling! What causes this?

ACTIVE **READING** As you read these pages, circle the sentence that describes a force that causes things to slow down.

→ Gravity

Gravity is a force of attraction between two objects. The size of this force increases as the mass of the objects increases. It decreases as the distance between the objects increases. Gravity acts on objects even if they are not touching.

Large objects such as Earth cause smaller objects, such as the skydivers, to accelerate quickly. We expect to see things fall toward Earth. However, the force of attraction is the same on both objects. If you place two objects with the same mass in outer space, they will move toward one another. If one object is "above" the other, the bottom object will appear to "fall up" as the other "falls down"!

→ Friction

Is it easier to ride your bike on a smooth road or on a muddy trail? Why?

Friction is a force that opposes motion. Friction acts between two objects that are touching, such as the bike tires and the road. Friction can also exist between air and a moving object. This is called air resistance. The skydivers use air resistance to adjust their positions in the air. Their parachutes use this force to slow down their fall.

It is easy to slide across smooth ice because it doesn't have much friction. Pulling something across rough sandpaper is a lot harder because there is lots of friction.

> ▶ In the pictures on this page, circle the places where there is friction between two objects. In the small boxes, write *Inc* if the object is designed to increase friction and *Dec* if the object is designed to decrease friction.

An air hockey table blows air upward. This layer of air reduces the surface friction, so the pieces move quickly.

The tires on this bike are designed to keep the rider from slipping. You have to pedal harder on a rough surface to overcome the force of friction.

BALANCED or Unbalanced?

The tug-of-war teams are both applying forces. So why isn't anyone moving?

ACTIVE **READING** Draw a circle around a sentence that explains why objects don't always move when a force is applied.

When you sit on a chair, the force of gravity pulls you down. The chair pushes you up. You stay in one place because the forces on you are balanced. **Balanced forces** are forces on an object that are equal in size and opposite in direction. They cancel each other out.

The tug-of-war teams in the picture don't move because the forces are balanced. Friction keeps them from sliding. They won't move until one side exerts a larger force. Then, the forces are no longer balanced. **Unbalanced forces** are forces that cause a change in motion. A force must also overcome the force of friction before an object will move.

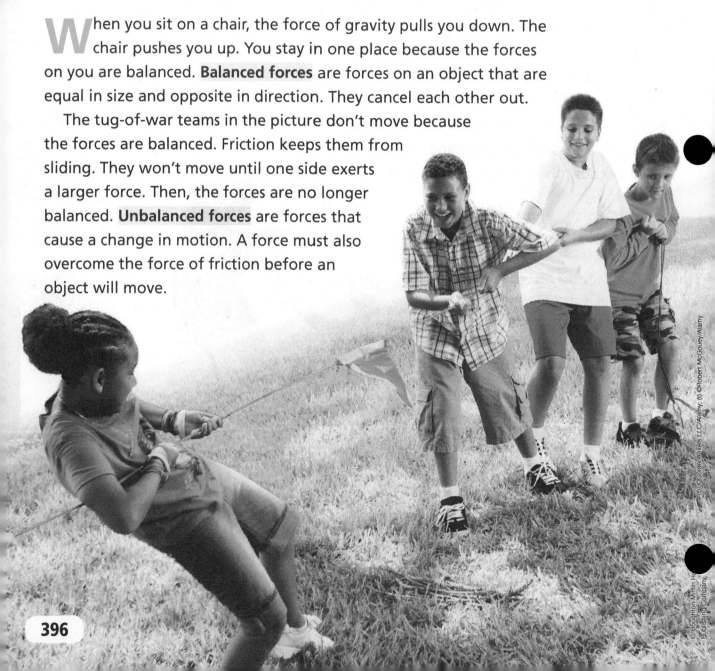

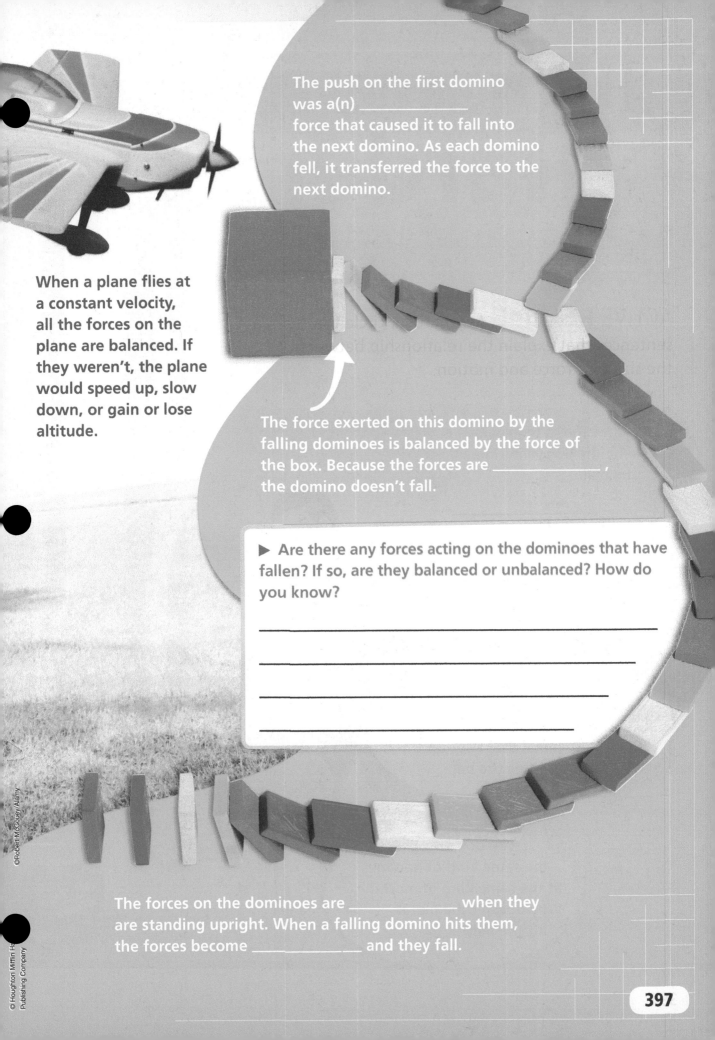

The push on the first domino was a(n) _____ force that caused it to fall into the next domino. As each domino fell, it transferred the force to the next domino.

When a plane flies at a constant velocity, all the forces on the plane are balanced. If they weren't, the plane would speed up, slow down, or gain or lose altitude.

The force exerted on this domino by the falling dominoes is balanced by the force of the box. Because the forces are _____ , the domino doesn't fall.

▶ Are there any forces acting on the dominoes that have fallen? If so, are they balanced or unbalanced? How do you know?

_____

_____

_____

_____

The forces on the dominoes are _____ when they are standing upright. When a falling domino hits them, the forces become _____ and they fall.

PULL (or Push) Harder!

Would you expect a bunt in baseball to go out of the park? Why or why not?

ACTIVE **READING** As you read, circle the sentences that explain the relationship between the size of a force and motion.

▶ Use forces to explain why the boy can't ring the bell.

_____

_____

_____

When the man swings the hammer, he exerts a force on a plate. The plate transfers the force to a piece of metal that rises up the column and rings the bell.

The boy swings the same kind of hammer at the same kind of machine. Why doesn't the metal hit the bell?

If you want to make the bowling ball knock all the pins, you will have to hit them with a lot of force. The greater the force you apply to the ball, the more force it can transfer to the pins. A large force will cause a large change in motion. A small force will cause a small change in motion. The bowling ball's force comes from the mechanical energy you give it when you swing it back and then forward in your hand. This motion changes the ball's velocity. After the ball leaves your hand, its velocity continues to change. A change in an object's velocity is called acceleration. The ball may hit and apply a force to just a few pins, causing them to accelerate in many directions. But if you're lucky, these pins will knock other pins and you will get a strike!

DO THE MATH

Display Data in a Graph

Use the data in the table to make a graph that shows the relationship between the force applied to an object and its acceleration.

Force (N)	Acceleration (m/sec^2)
1	0.5
2	1.0
5	2.5
8	4.0
10	5.0

I'M NOT Moving!

It's easy to lift your empty backpack off the ground. Could you use the same force to lift it when it's full of books?

ACTIVE READING As you read these pages, circle cause-and-effect signal words, such as *because*, *so*, or *therefore*.

The springs in the pictures all exert the same force on the balls, causing them to roll across the page. The ball with the least mass accelerates the fastest. Therefore, it travels the farthest. The same force has a greater effect on an object with a small mass than an object with a larger mass.

▶ Rank the balls by writing *greatest*, *middle*, or *least* in the six blanks.

Foam Ball

mass: _____

acceleration: _____

Baseball

mass: _____

acceleration: _____

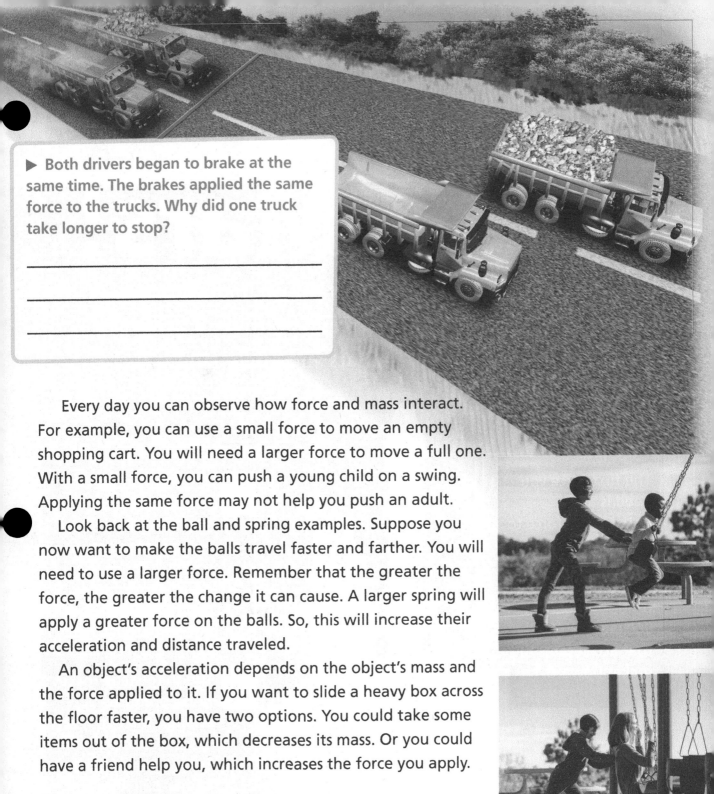

▶ Both drivers began to brake at the same time. The brakes applied the same force to the trucks. Why did one truck take longer to stop?

_____

_____

_____

Every day you can observe how force and mass interact. For example, you can use a small force to move an empty shopping cart. You will need a larger force to move a full one. With a small force, you can push a young child on a swing. Applying the same force may not help you push an adult.

Look back at the ball and spring examples. Suppose you now want to make the balls travel faster and farther. You will need to use a larger force. Remember that the greater the force, the greater the change it can cause. A larger spring will apply a greater force on the balls. So, this will increase their acceleration and distance traveled.

An object's acceleration depends on the object's mass and the force applied to it. If you want to slide a heavy box across the floor faster, you have two options. You could take some items out of the box, which decreases its mass. Or you could have a friend help you, which increases the force you apply.

Steel Ball

mass: _____

acceleration: _____

How did I get to Mars?

LET'S GO to Mars!

How did an understanding of forces help to send a rover to Mars and safely land it there?

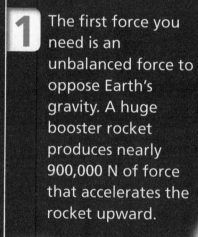

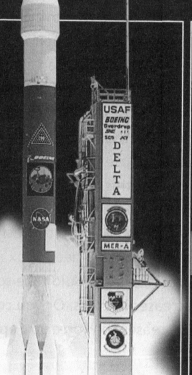

1 The first force you need is an unbalanced force to oppose Earth's gravity. A huge booster rocket produces nearly 900,000 N of force that accelerates the rocket upward.

▶ What forces act on the rocket while it's at rest on Earth's surface? Are they balanced or unbalanced?

_____

_____

_____

_____

_____

2 After the booster rocket falls away, smaller rockets in the second stage fire. The rockets change the direction of the vehicle's motion and put it in orbit around Earth.

3 The third-stage rocket firing produces enough force to reach "escape velocity." Earth's gravity can no longer pull it back down. We're on our way!

Balanced

▶ At what points during the Rover's trip to Mars are the forces on it balanced?

_____

_____

_____

Unbalanced

▶ What unbalanced forces are acting on the Rover as it lands on Mars?

_____

_____

_____

_____

Gravity

▶ Use forces to explain why the Rover required a parachute and "air bags."

_____

_____

_____

During much of the time it takes the spacecraft to travel to Mars, it travels at a constant velocity. The forces acting on the spacecraft are balanced, so its motion does not change.

Tiny rockets occasionally fire to keep the spacecraft on course. During these times, the forces are unbalanced.

As the spacecraft approaches Mars, gravitational attraction begins to accelerate it toward the surface. Like a person jumping from a plane, the Rover detaches from the spacecraft. Parachutes open to slow its fall. Then a big ball inflates around the Rover. When the Rover hits the surface of Mars, it bounces around until it comes safely to rest.

Mars Rover air bag testing

Sum It Up »

Change the part of the summary in blue to make it correct.

1. Forces are pushes and pulls that increase the speed of objects.

   _____
   _____

2. Gravity is the force of attraction between a planet and another object.

   _____
   _____

3. An object moving through the air slows down because it is affected by the force of gravity.

   _____
   _____

4. When balanced forces act on an object, the object falls.

   _____
   _____

5. In order for an object to change its speed or direction, someone has to push it.

   _____
   _____

Brain Check

Name _____

Vocabulary Review

1 A foreign-language teacher placed words from other languages into the following sentences. For each sentence, write the English word that means the same as the foreign word. Then use the circled letters to complete the riddle.

1. **Italian** — A push is an example of a forza. Another example is a pull.

   _ ⃝ _ ⃝ _
      11   3

2. **French** — The force of attraction between Earth and objects on its surface is pesanteur.

   _ ⃝ _ _ _ _ _
      8

3. **Russian** — The force between two moving objects that are touching is Трение.

   ⃝ _ _ _ _ ⃝ _
   4   7

4. **German** — Two forces that are equal in size but opposite in direction are ausgeglichene Kräfte.

   _ _ _ _ _ ⃝ _ _ _ _ ⃝ _ _ ⃝
                10   5   9

5. **Portuguese** — Two forces that are not equal in size are Forças desequilibradas.

   ⃝ _ _ _ _ _ _ _ _ _ _ _ _ _ _ _ ⃝ _
   2   6

6. **Chinese** — A 彈簧秤 is a tool that can be used to measure the size of a force.

   ⃝ _ _ _ _ _ ⃝ _ _ _ ⃝
   1   12   13

Riddle: What conclusion did the student draw?

The _ o _ r _ e of the _ o _ c _ is the h _ _ _ _ e, of _ _ _ ur _ _ _.
   1   2   3   4   5   6   7 8 9   10 11   12 13

Try saying that five times fast!

2 Draw pictures of two activities that you might do. In the first, draw a pushing force. In the second, draw a pulling force.

pushing force

pulling force

3 The golfer applied a force when he hit the ball. Describe at least two forces acting on the ball as it rolls. Draw arrows to show the forces.

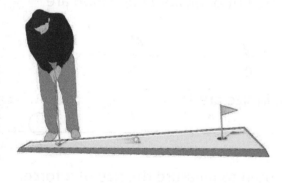

_____

_____

_____

_____

_____

4 Two students are using a catapult to try and hit a target. The catapult has only one setting. The first time they tried, they used Rock B. Which of the remaining rocks is likely to come closer to the target? Why?

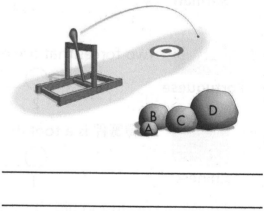

_____

_____

_____

_____

_____

5 Use the words *balanced* and *unbalanced* as you name and describe the forces acting in each of these pictures.

a. accelerating

b.

c.

_____   _____   _____
_____   _____   _____
_____   _____   _____
_____   _____   _____
_____   _____   _____

6 Draw what will happen to a ball that you throw straight up into the air. Explain why this happens.

7 Explain why it is easy to slip on a floor that is wet.

SLIPPERY
WHEN WET

_____   _____
_____   _____
_____   _____
_____   _____
_____   _____

8 Look at the drawings to the right. Mary measured the distance each ball traveled. Draw lines to match the ball with the distance it traveled.

Explain why each ball traveled a different distance.

25 cm

15 cm

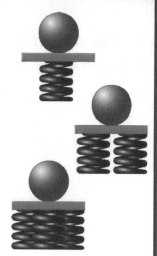

20 cm

_____

_____

_____

9 Give an example of each of the following.

a. A force is applied but nothing happens.

_____

b. A force causes an object to change shape.

_____

c. A force causes an object to change position.

_____

d. A force causes an object to stop moving.

_____

10 Circle the object(s) whose velocities are not changing. Draw an up arrow next to the object(s) whose speeds are increasing. Draw a down arrow next to the object(s) whose speeds are decreasing.

A car travels 35 miles per hour around a bend in the road.

A car comes to a stop when a traffic light turns red.

A race car accelerates when a race begins.

A car is driving 45 miles per hour down a straight road.

 See *ScienceSaurus*® for more information about force and motion.

SC.5.N.1.5 Recognize and explain that authentic scientific investigation frequently does not parallel the steps of "the scientific method."

S.T.E.M.

ENGINEERING & TECHNOLOGY

Football Safety Gear

Football is a rough sport. In order to protect players from injury, designers have developed protective gear.

The first helmets were custom made out of leather by horse harness makers. Later, ear holes and padding were added. These helmets had little padding and no face guards.

Hard plastic shells, fitted foam linings, and metal facemasks now make helmets more protective. Some helmets even contain sensors that transmit signals to warn if a player's head has been hit hard enough to cause a serious injury.

CRITICAL THINKING

How do modern materials make it possible to build a better helmet than one made of just leather?

_____

_____

_____

When engineers develop new materials, it can spark new and improved designs of all sorts of familiar objects.

Choose two pieces of safety gear from your favorite sport or activity. Draw each piece of gear. Do research to find out what material makes up each piece. Label the materials. Explain how one material's properties made it a good design choice.

_____

_____

List three features of this bicycle helmet. Draw arrows to the features that are for safety. Circle the features that are for comfort.

_____

_____

_____

_____

ENGINEERING DESIGN CHALLENGE

Design It:
Balloon Racer

Have you ever inflated a balloon, then released it? If so, you've observed jet propulsion.

The blast of air that shot out of the balloon's nozzle produced an opposite and equal reaction. This opposite reaction causes the balloon to fly off in the opposite direction of the escaping air.

Now, it's time to apply your understanding of forces to the design of a balloon car racer.

1 Find a Problem

2 Plan & Build

DESIGN PROCESS STEPS

5 Communicate

3 Test & Improve

4 Redesign

What to Do:

1 Find out about jet propulsion and how it is used by racing cars.

2 Find out what materials are available to build a balloon racer. List the materials.

3 Based upon your research and available materials, make a diagram of the design for your balloon car racer.

4 Build your design.

5 Think about how you will test your design's speed. What additional tools and materials will you need to test it? Speed is calculated using the formula $s = d/t$.

6 Measure the distance traveled and the time the racer took to travel the distance. Calculate the model's speed.

7 Continue improving or redesigning and testing your racer until you are satisfied with the final product.

8 Compare its performance in a classroom race with balloon racers designed by other students.

9 📔 Keep a record of your work in your Science Notebook.

SC.5.P.13.1 Identify familiar forces that cause objects to move... SC5.P.13.2 Investigate and describe that the greater the force applied to it, the greater the change in motion of a given object. SC5.P.13.3 Investigate and describe that the more mass an object has, the less effect a given force will have on the object's motion. SC.5.N.1 plan and carry out scientific investigations... SC.5.N.1.3 Recognize and explain the need for repeated experimental trials.

Name _____

ESSENTIAL QUESTION

How Do Forces Affect Motion?

EXPLORE

What can you do to make a toy truck move faster or travel farther?

Before You Begin—Preview the Steps

① **CAUTION:** wear goggles. Cut a rubber band in half, and tie the ends around the legs of a chair.

② Place a piece of tape on the floor. Mark lines that are 1 cm, 2 cm, and 5 cm behind the rubber band.

③ Place a toy truck against the rubber band. Pull the truck back to the 1-cm mark, and release it. Measure the distance the truck travels, and record the data. Repeat this step two more times.

④ Repeat Step 3 using the 3-cm and 5-cm marks.

⑤ Place four bolts in the toy truck. Launch the truck from the 3-cm mark, and record the distance it travels. Repeat this step two more times.

⑥ Add four more bolts to the truck. Repeat Step 5.

Materials

safety goggles
giant rubber band
chair
tape
ruler
toy truck
meterstick
metal bolts

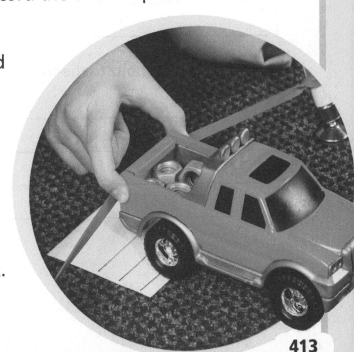

Set a Purpose
What will you learn from this experiment?

_____

_____

_____

State Your Hypothesis
Write your hypothesis, or testable statement.

_____

_____

_____

_____

Think About the Procedure
Why do you use a rubber band to start the cars, rather than your hand?

_____

_____

_____

_____

Why do you add bolts to the truck?

_____

_____

_____

_____

Name _____

Record Your Data

In the table below, record the data you gathered.

How Forces Affect Motion

Part 1	Distance rubber band was streched								
	1 cm			3 cm			5 cm		
Distance traveled (cm)									

Part ii: Rubber band streched to 3 cm	Empty Car	Car with 4 bolts	Car with 8 bolts
Distance traveled (cm) Trial 1			
Distance traveled (cm) Trial 2			
Distance traveled (cm) Trial 3			

Draw Conclusions

Each time you changed a variable and launched the truck, you ran three trials. Calculate the average distance traveled by the truck in each experimental setting.

Experimental settings	Average distance traveled (cm)
Rubber band at 1 cm	
Rubber band at 3 cm	
Rubber band at 5 cm	

Experimental settings	Average distance traveled (cm)
truck with 0 bolts	
truck with 4 bolts	
truck with 8 bolts	

Draw two bar graphs to display your data.

Claims • Evidence • Reasoning

1. Interpret your data. Write a claim about how an object's mass is related to its change in motion when acted on by a force.

_____

_____

_____

2. Cite evidence that supports your claim and explain why the evidence supports the claim.

_____

_____

_____

3. Write a claim about how the size of the force applied to an object affects its motion.

_____

_____

4. Cite evidence that supports your claim and explain why the evidence supports the claim.

_____

_____

_____

5. Why is it important to repeat an experiment several times or to have several people perform the same experiment? Explain your reasoning.

_____

_____

_____

SC.5.P.13.1 Identify familiar forces that cause objects to move, such as pushes or pulls...
SC.5.P.13.4 Investigate and explain that when a force is applied to an object but it does not move,
it is because another opposing force is being applied ... so that the forces are balanced. SC.5.N.1.1
... carry out scientific investigations... SC.5.N.2.2 ... evidence ... should be replicable by others.

INQUIRY
LESSON 3

Name _____

ESSENTIAL QUESTION

What are Balanced and Unbalanced Forces?

Materials

spring scale
3 wood blocks with hooks
sandpaper
waxed paper
oil

EXPLORE

Think about an object that is not moving. What do you need to do to make it move? Does the mass of the object make a difference?

Before You Begin—Preview the Steps

1. Use the spring scale to lift a block. Observe and record the force needed to overcome the force of gravity.

2. Repeat Step 1 with two blocks and then again with three blocks.

3. Place one block on its side on a piece of sandpaper. Attach the spring scale, and pull it gently. Record the scale reading just as the block begins to move. Repeat this measurement two more times.

4. Repeat Step 3 with the block on other surfaces, such as waxed paper and waxed paper that has been coated with vegetable oil.

Set a Purpose

What will you learn from this experiment?

_____

_____

Think About the Procedure

What forces are acting on the blocks when they are sitting on the table?

_____

_____

Why will you pull the block across several different surfaces?

_____

_____

Name _____

Record Your Data

Record your measurements in this table.

Forces Investigation	
Action	**Force(N)**
Lift one block	
Lift two blocks	
Lift three blocks	
Pull block on sandpaper	
Pull block on waxed paper	
Pull block on oiled paper	

Draw Conclusions

What is required to start an object moving?

_____

_____

_____

Claims • Evidence • Reasoning

1. The block below is being pulled to the right. Draw arrows to show the forces acting on the object. Label each arrow.

2. At what points during this activity were the forces on the block balanced? Draw the block, and show the forces as arrows.

3. Write a claim about how an object's mass is related to the upward force needed to overcome the pull of gravity. Cite evidence to support your claim.

_____

_____

_____

_____

4. Write a claim about why the blocks required a different force to begin moving on the three different surfaces. Cite evidence to support your claim.

_____

_____

_____

_____

420

① A safety engineer helps design and test devices to make them safer.

② Safety engineers make changes to designs to avoid possible dangers.

③ I'm a crash test dummy. Some safety engineers use me as a model.

THINGS TO KNOW ABOUT
Safety Engineers

④ Safety engineers can make machines, such as cars, safer to use.

⑤ Safety engineers make cars safer with inventions such as seat belts and air bags.

⑥ Some safety engineers focus on stopping specific dangers, such as fires.

⑦ Safety engineers help society have fewer injuries and illnesses.

⑧ Some keep germs from spreading into our food and making us sick.

⑨ They may focus on protecting workers from getting hurt on the job.

⑩ To do their jobs, safety engineers need to study physics, chemistry, math, and human behavior.

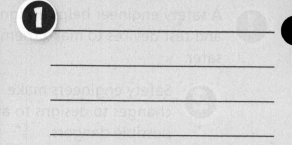

CAREERS IN SCIENCE

Now You Be the Engineer!

1 What do you think is the best thing about being a safety engineer?

2 How do safety engineers help society?

3 What safety features in cars have safety engineers helped to develop?

4 What question would you like to ask a safety engineer?

1 _____
_____
_____
_____
_____

2 _____
_____
_____
_____
_____
_____
_____

3 _____
_____
_____

4 _____
_____
_____
_____

Name _____

Vocabulary Review

Use the terms in the box to complete the sentences.

> balanced forces
> force
> friction
> gravity
> unbalanced
> forces

1. Forces that cause a change in motion are _____.

2. A force of attraction between two objects, even if they are not touching, is _____.

3. A push or a pull, which causes movement or change in an object's movement or shape, is a(n) _____.

4. Forces on an object that are equal in size and opposite in direction are _____.

5. A force that opposes motion and acts between two objects that are touching is _____.

Science Concepts

Fill in the letter of the choice that best answers the question.

6. Suri places magnets on three identical toy cars, as shown below. Then Suri measures how far each car rolls when she launches it from the same starting point using the same stretched rubber band.

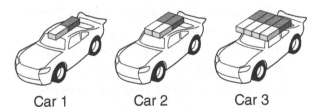

Car 1   Car 2   Car 3

Which statement is true?

(A) Car 3 will travel the longest distance.

(B) Car 1 will travel the shortest distance.

(C) Car 1 will be the least affected by the force acting upon it.

(D) Car 3 will be the least affected by the force acting upon it.

7. When you coast down a hill on a bicycle, you move faster and faster. Then when you keep coasting on a level surface, you eventually stop moving. What causes you to stop?

(F) No force is acting on your bike on the level surface, so it stops moving.

(G) After you reach the bottom of the hill, you run out of energy, so you stop moving.

(H) Friction between the tires and the ground is an unbalanced force that changes your motion.

(I) Gravity affects you when you move downhill, but there is no gravity when you move on a level surface.

8. Katie uses all her force to roll a bowling ball away from her body. Then Katie repeats the same procedure with a soccer ball. How does the movement of the two balls contrast?

(A) The soccer ball moves a greater distance because more force is acting on it.

(B) The soccer ball moves a greater distance because it has less mass.

(C) The bowling ball moves a greater distance because it has more mass.

(D) The bowling ball moves a shorter distance because less force is acting on it.

9. An object is traveling in a straight line in space. No forces are affecting it. What will happen to the object's motion?

(F) It will move faster and faster because there is no force to stop it.

(G) It gradually will stop because there is no force to keep it moving.

(H) It will stop immediately when the force that started its motion goes away.

(I) It will not change. It will continue in the same direction at the same speed.

10. Four forces are acting on the block shown in the following illustration:

- F is the applied force.
- F_f is friction.
- F_g is the gravitational force.
- F_n is the upward force of the table on the block.

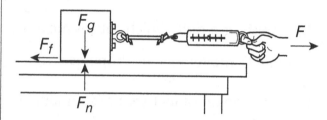

If a force F is applied to the block and it does not move, which statement is true?

(A) F and F_f are equal.

(B) F and F_g are equal.

(C) F_f is greater than F.

(D) F_g is greater than F.

11. A group of students measured the amount of force needed to move a weight across a dry plastic tabletop. Then they poured some water on the table and repeated the experiment on the wet surface. The students found that less force was needed to make the weight start moving on the wet surface than the dry surface. What caused the difference in the results of the two experiments?

(F) change in the amount of gravitational force on the weight

(G) change in the mass of the weight used in the experiment

(H) change in the friction between the weight and the surface

(I) change in the friction between the weight and the scale used to measure force

Name _____

12. Jean held a spring scale with a weight hanging on its hook. She observed that the force on the scale was 3 N. Why was the force greater than 0 N even though the weight was not moving?

Ⓐ The 3-N force was balancing the force of gravity.

Ⓑ The weight was not moving, but the forces on it were constantly changing.

Ⓒ The spring scale was broken, so it showed 3 N even though the real force was zero.

Ⓓ The 3-N force was the amount of unbalanced force on the weight.

13. A crane raises and lowers objects and also moves them back and forth. The following illustration shows a crane lifting a heavy box.

What must the crane work against in order to lift the box upward?

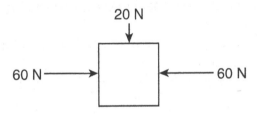

Ⓕ wind

Ⓖ friction

Ⓗ gravity

Ⓘ cable tension

14. The following table shows the masses of several different objects. You want to toss each object a distance of 2 meters.

Object	Metal washer	Plastic disk	Rock	Wooden block
Mass (g)	1.5	34	16	22

Which object will require the most force to toss it 2 meters?

Ⓐ metal washer

Ⓑ rock

Ⓒ plastic disk

Ⓓ wooden block

15. The following table shows the masses of four blocks and the forces that are being applied to them.

Block color	Mass (g)	Pushing force (N)	Friction (N)
Red	50	24	6
Green	100	24	6
Blue	40	24	6
Yellow	75	24	6

Which block will have the greatest change in motion?

Ⓕ red

Ⓖ blue

Ⓗ green

Ⓘ yellow

16. The following illustration shows the forces that are acting on a box.

20 N

60 N ———→ ←——— 60 N

What type of motion will the forces cause?

Ⓐ The box will remain in its current position.

Ⓑ The box will move downward in a straight line.

Ⓒ The box will move to the right in a straight line.

Ⓓ The box will move back and forth from the left to the right.

Apply Inquiry and Review the Big Idea

Write the answers to these questions.

17. Jermaine wondered if a heavy ball rolls down a ramp faster than a light ball. Use the space below to describe an investigation he could conduct in order to find out.

_____

_____

_____

_____

_____

_____

18. This worker is pushing a box with a force, which is shown by the arrow. The box does not move.

    Make a claim about what keeps the box from moving even though the worker is pushing on it?

    _____

    _____

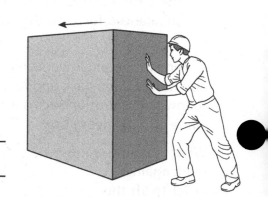

19. Explain how forces can apply to objects in space, even though objects in space can look and feel weightless.

_____

_____

_____

_____

_____

20. The spring scale shown has a weight attached to it. When the weight was attached, the pointer on the scale moved downward.

    Make a claim about what will happen if a second weight is added to the spring scale? Support your claim with evidence and explain your reasoning.

    _____

    _____

The Structure of Living Things

FLORIDA BIG IDEA 14

Organization and Development of Living Organisms

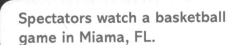

Spectators watch a basketball game in Miama, FL.

I Wonder Why

These basketball players are working hard and sweating. Why do athletes use sports drinks instead of just water? *Turn the page to find out.*

Here's Why

When the body gets hot, sweat helps cool it down. Sweat is made up of water and salts. Salts are important to keep the body working. Sports drinks replace water and salts that are lost by sweating.

Essential Questions and Florida Benchmarks

Science Notebook

Before you begin each lesson, write your thoughts about the Essential Question.

SC.5.L.14.1 Identify the organs in the human body and describe their functions, including the skin, brain ... and sensory organs. SC.5.L.14.2 Compare and contrast the function of organs and other physical structures of plants and animals, including humans....

ESSENTIAL QUESTION

What Are Organs and Body Systems?

Engage Your Brain

Find the answer to the following question in this lesson and record it here.

What part of your body serves the same function as the part of the octopus shown here?

_____

_____

_____

_____

_____

ACTIVE READING

Lesson Vocabulary

List the terms. As you learn about each one, make notes in the Interactive Glossary.

_____   _____

_____   _____

_____

Main Ideas and Details

Detail sentences give information about a main idea. The information may include examples, features, characteristics, or facts. Active readers look for details that support the main idea.

Building a BODY

Your body has hundreds of different parts! These parts work together to keep you healthy.

ACTIVE **READING** As you read these two pages, circle each lesson vocabulary term and underline its definition.

Every living thing needs certain things to survive. An **organism** is a living thing. It is made of parts that work together to meet its needs. Some parts are extremely small. Others are large.

An **organ** is a body part that is made up of smaller parts that work together to do a certain job. For example, your eye is an organ. It is made of a clear lens, a colored iris, and other parts that work together to enable you to see.

Groups of organs work together. An **organ system** is a group of organs that work together to do one type of job. Your mouth and stomach are part of one organ system. They work together to supply your body with energy from food. You have many organ systems in your body.

Eyes

Eyes are organs that help you _____. They send information about the world around you to another organ, your brain.

Teeth

Your teeth are bones, and bones are organs. What do teeth do?

_____

Muscles

Muscles are organs that help you _____. Messages from your brain tell your muscles what to do.

Animals are organisms. Plants are organisms, too. Did you know that plants have organs? Roots absorb nutrients and water for the plant. Leaves use sunlight to make food for the plant. Stems support the leaves. Stems also transport water from the roots and food from the leaves. A protective layer covers the plant and keeps the plant from drying out.

Like plants, humans have organs that work together to help us stand. We have an organ that protects us from drying out. We have organs that supply us with food. Plant and animal organs are different, but they are all alike in one way: They all help an organism meet its needs so it can live.

Match It!

▶ Draw a line to connect the plant part to an animal part that does a similar job.

Bones

Bones support your body. They enable you to stand. Each bone in your body is an organ.

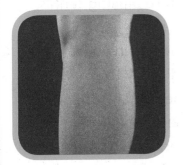

Mouth

Your mouth brings food into your body. Your lips, teeth, and tongue work together to help you chew and swallow food.

Skin

What's the largest organ in your body? Your skin is. It protects your body from germs and keeps your body from drying out.

Bark

Stems

Leaves

The Information HIGHWAY

Keep your eye on the ball! In just seconds you can see a ball, run toward it, and swing a racket! How does the body relay all of the information needed to do this? Read on to find out.

ACTIVE **READING** As you read this page, underline the names of parts of the nervous system.

Sensing your surroundings and communicating information within the body are the main jobs of your *nervous system*. Your nervous system is made of tiny structures called *nerve cells*. Chains of long nerve cells make up nerves. Nerves carry information to and from the **brain**. The brain is the organ that processes information. It's like a computer made of millions of nerve cells working together.

A rope-like bundle of nerves, called the *spinal cord*, runs along your backbone. Your spinal cord is the main pathway for information traveling to and from the brain. Nerves connect to your spinal cord from all over your body.

Some of these nerves send information to the brain. Others receive signals from the brain.

Imagine that you're playing tennis. Nerves in your eyes sense light. These nerves, like other nerves in your head, send information directly to your brain without routing the signal through your spinal cord. You see the ball coming toward you. Your brain decides on an action. It sends instructions through your spinal cord to nerves in your body. The messages from your brain "tell" your legs to run across the court and your arms to swing the racket and hit the ball. All of this communication takes place in seconds!

Information Relay

Fill in the blanks to describe the path that a nerve signal might take in this tennis player.

1. The boy's _____ sense the ball coming toward him.

2. His _____ processes this information.

3. Messages from the _____ travel down the _____ _____.

4. _____ in his arms deliver the message from his brain to swing the racket.

SENSING Surroundings

A carnival is a feast of sights, sounds, tastes, and smells! How do you sense all of that information?

ACTIVE **READING** As you read this page, draw a box around phrases that describe sensory structures.

Senses are your body's way of gathering information about the world around you. Special structures in certain parts of your body can detect light, sound, and chemicals in the air and in the food you eat.

A Sight: The part of the eye that gives us our eye color is a muscle called the *iris.* Light enters the eye through a hole in the iris called the *pupil,* passes through the lens, and hits the back of the eye, called the *retina.* Inside the retina are special nerve cells that detect light. They send signals that travel along nerve pathways to the brain. The brain interprets this information and we see.

B Hearing: The part of your ear that you see is called your outer ear. The outer ear funnels sound into the middle ear. In the middle ear, sound causes the eardrum to vibrate. The vibrations are passed to tiny bones called the hammer, anvil, and stirrup. These bones pass vibrations to the inner ear. There, a fluid-filled structure called the cochlea [KOH•klee•uh] passes vibrations to tiny hairs attached to nerves. The nerves send messages about the vibrations to the brain, and you sense sound.

C Smell: When you breathe, air travels through your nose. Inside your nose are structures that sense chemicals in the air. They are attached to nerve cells in the olfactory bulb that send messages to the brain about the chemicals they sensed. This makes up your sense of smell.

D Taste: Have you ever noticed small bumps all over your tongue? These bumps are called *taste buds.* They sense the chemicals in food. Taste buds are attached to nerves that send messages to the brain about the chemicals they sense. The brain interprets this information as the sense of taste.

A Eyes

Light enters the eye through the _____, passes through the _____, and hits the _____, where special structures detect _____.

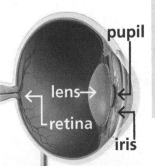

pupil

lens→

←lens

retina

iris

B Ears

Sound enters the ear. Vibrations pass from the _____ to tiny bones, through the _____, to tiny hairs attached to nerves.

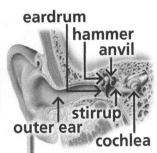

eardrum

hammer

anvil

outer ear

stirrup

cochlea

C Nose

When you breathe, structures in the nose detect _____ that are carried in the air.

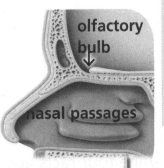

olfactory bulb

nasal passages

D Tongue

When food enters the mouth, special structures on the tongue sense _____ in food. These structures are called _____.

taste buds

FAZOLET

Sensory OVERLOAD

All organisms have sensory structures that help them survive. Flies have compound eyes. Instead of 1 lens, they have over 5,000!

ACTIVE **READING** As you read these two pages, find and underline four facts about plant and animal senses.

Animal Senses

Draw an animal that you are familiar with. Label its sensory organs, and describe how it uses them.

Sight

Snails have their eyes on the ends of stalks. The eyespots can sense light and dark. You can see eyespots on the tip of each eyestalk shown here.

Sound

Bats "see" with their ears! They make squeaking noises and listen for the sounds to echo back to them. The way the sound bounces and the amount of time it takes for the sound to return let the bat know what is in its path. Dolphins use a very similar system under water.

Smell

Moths have "noses" on the tops of their heads. The moth's antennae [an•TEN•ee] have structures that sense chemicals in the air.

Touch

The Venus' flytrap has special leaves that are sensitive to touch. When a fly lands on them, the fly touches trigger hairs. The hairs send a message to the leaves of the plant, and the leaves snap shut. The fly is trapped!

The SKIN You're In

Some people don't think of skin as an organ, but it is. Our bodies couldn't survive without it.

ACTIVE READING As you read, circle the different parts of the integumentary system described below.

Covering your body is a protective layer called **skin**. Skin is part of the *integumentary* [in•teg•yoo•**MEN**•ter•ee] *system.* Fingernails, toenails, and hair are, too. This system helps to protect the inside of your body.

Skin keeps germs out. If you've ever had a cut that got infected, you know how important it is to keep germs from entering your body. At the same time, skin keeps water in. Your waterproof skin keeps you from becoming dehydrated.

What happens when you get too hot? Sweat helps cool your body. Also, tiny blood vessels near the surface of the skin help to cool your blood.

But what if you get cold? Hair helps to keep your head warm in cold weather. Hair also helps to protect your scalp from injury and shades your scalp from the sun's harmful rays.

Fingerprinting

Draw your own friction ridges in the circles at the tips of these fingers.

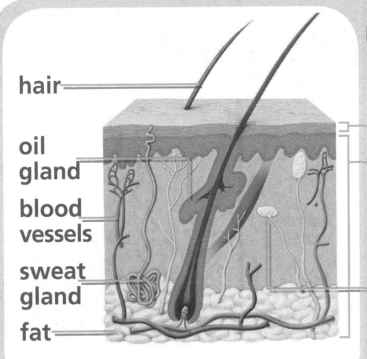

Epidermis

This is the outer layer of the skin. It is thin in some places, like your eyelids, and thick in others.

Dermis

This is the inner layer of the skin. It contains hair follicles, sweat glands, blood vessels, and nerve endings.

Nerve endings

These are special structures that sense touch, heat, cold, pain, pressure, and vibration.

hair

oil gland

blood vessels

sweat gland

fat

Look at your fingers. Do you see swirls, loops and waves? These are friction ridges, which form your fingerprints. They allow your fingers to be more sensitive to touch.

Plant and Animal COVERINGS

Would you want to pet a cactus? There are many different kinds of plant and animal coverings. They all protect the plant or animal.

ACTIVE **READING** Circle the different types of plant and animal coverings that are listed below.

Take a look at the examples of animal coverings on these pages. Can you identify them? Animals such as monkeys, horses, and rabbits are covered in soft fur. Birds are covered with feathers. Fish and snakes are covered in scales. Some animals, such as lobsters and turtles, have hard shells.

Plants do not have skin, but they do have special coverings. Many trees are covered with a thick, hard bark to protect the inner plant. Plant leaves have a waxy coating that keeps the plant from drying out.

Even though plant and animal coverings may look different, they still protect the organisms from predators, disease, injury, and drying out.

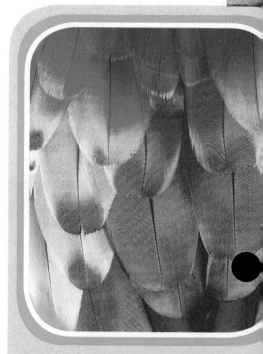

These colorful feathers cover the bird's skin. They keep the bird warm and keep water out. Feathers on the wing help the bird fly.

tree bark

440

Plant leaves have a waxy coating that helps keep the plant from drying out when the weather is hot and dry.

Ouch! This cactus has sharp spines that keep predators away.

DO THE **MATH**

Use a Scale

scale = 1 centimeter

Look at these magnified scales from a banded rainbow fish. The black line on the picture is a scale showing how many scales are in 1 centimeter. If the body of the fish is 12 cm long, how many scales long would the fish's body be?

_____

_____

_____

This monkey has thick fur. Fur helps to keep the monkey warm in cold weather.

Sum It Up >>

Fill in the blanks in the following sentences.

1. All living things are called (a)_____ .
   An (b)_____ is a body part that does a certain job in the body.
   Several of these parts work together to make up an (c)_____ _____.

Read the summary statements. Match each statement with the correct image.

2. The brain, spinal cord, and nerves form the nervous system. The nervous system senses the environment, sends information to the brain, processes information, and sends instructions to the body.
_____

3. The eyes, ears, nose, and tongue are sense organs. They have special parts that sense the environment.
_____

4. Skin, hair, and nails are part of the human integumentary system. It protects internal organs, helps maintain body temperature, and provides waterproofing.
_____

5. Plants and animals have specialized organs for sensing the environment, like compound eyes, antennae, and trigger hairs.
_____

6. Plants and animals have special body coverings such as bark, fur, feathers, quills, scales, and shells.

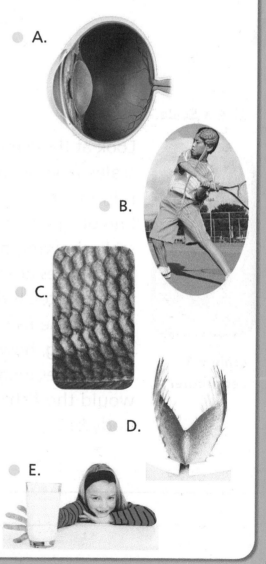

A.

B.

C.

D.

E.

Brain Check

Name _____

Vocabulary Review

① Unscramble the words on the right to fill in the blanks in each sentence.

1. The _ _ _ _ _ _ _ system sends messages throughout your body.	s r n u o e v
2. The _ _ _ _ _ _ _ _ _ _ _ _ __ system protects the body's organs.	n e n i g e m t t a y r u
3. An _ _ _ _ _ _ _ _ is a living thing. It is made up of parts that work together.	s n g m a r o i
4. The _ _ _ _ is the largest organ in the body. It covers and protects the other organs.	i n k s
5. The _ _ _ _ _ receives messages from the body, processes the information, and sends instructions to the body.	r b i n a
6. An _ _ _ _ _ system is a group of organs that work together to do a job.	o g n r a
7. _ _ _ _ _ _ _ _ _ are used by moths to "smell" the world around them.	e t n n n e a a
8. The _ _ _ _ _ _ include sight, taste, smell, hearing, and touch.	s s s e e n

Bonus: How many body parts can you think of that have only three letters?

_____   _____   _____

_____   _____   _____

_____   _____   _____

Apply Concepts

2 Some areas of the body have more sensory structures than others. Which do you think would have more? For each pair of body parts, circle the one you think would have more sensory structures. Then state your reason.

Why? _____

_____

_____

_____

Why? _____

_____

_____

_____

3 Draw a line to connect the animal to the description of its senses.

Have "noses" on their antennae to "smell" the air

Has compound eyes on moveable eyestalks

Uses an echo system to find objects in water

4 How are the senses of taste and smell alike?

_____

_____

_____

_____

5 Which of the following structures is used to sense touch?

a. eyestalk

b. antenna

c. trigger hair

d. compound eye

See *ScienceSaurus*® for more information about living things.

444

SC.5.L.14.1 Identify the organs in the human body and describe their functions, including the skin... SC.5.N.1.4 Identify a control group and explain its importance in an experiment. SC.5.N.1.6 Recognize and explain the difference between personal opinion/interpretation and verified observation.

INQUIRY LESSON 2

Name _____

ESSENTIAL **QUESTION**

How Does the Body Stay Cool?

Materials

3 paper towels
3 thermometers
3 paper plates
marker
graduated cylinder
water
rubbing alcohol
fan

EXPLORE

When you are hot, you sweat. This allows your body to cool off. In this activity, you will explore what happens as three towels cool. Think about how this relates to your body's cooling system.

Before You Begin—Preview the Steps

CAUTION: Be sure to protect your eyes from splashing liquids. Keep alcohol away from flames.

1. Wrap a paper towel around the bottom of each thermometer. Place each thermometer on a plate.

2. Label the plates *Dry*, *Water*, and *Alcohol*. Record the starting temperature of each thermometer.

3. Make sure the water is at room temperature. Measure 50 mL of water. Pour the water on the paper towel on the plate labeled *Water*.

4. Obtain 50 mL of rubbing alcohol from your teacher. Pour it on the paper towel on the plate labeled *Alcohol*.

5. Place all three plates in front of the fan. Record the temperature on each thermometer every minute for five minutes.

Set a Purpose

What will you learn from this experiment?

_____

_____

_____

_____

State Your Hypothesis

Write your hypothesis, or testable statement.

_____

_____

_____

_____

Think About the Procedure

Which sample is the control? What is its purpose? Why is it important to have a control in an experiment?

_____

_____

_____

Name _____

Record Your Data

Record your observations in a data table.

Draw Conclusions

How did your results compare with your hypothesis?

_____

_____

_____

_____

Claims • Evidence • Reasoning

1. What was the difference between the starting temperature and the ending temperature for each of your experimental groups? Show your work in the space below.

_____

_____

2. Make a bar graph in the space below to display your data.

3. Write a claim for how this activity relates to the role of sweating. Explain your reasoning.

_____

_____

4. A swamp cooler is a type of air conditioner that blows air over a wet surface. Use your data to make a claim about whether you think this would be an effective way to cool a building.

_____

_____

_____

5. Why is it important that your body be able to cool itself?

_____

_____

SC.5.L.14.1 Identify the organs in the human body and describe their functions, including the ... brain, heart, lungs ... muscles and skeleton.... SC.5.L.14.2 Compare and contrast the function of organs and other ... structures of plants and animals, including humans, for example: some animals have skeletons for support—some with internal skeletons others with exoskeletons—while some plants have stems for support.

LESSON 3

ESSENTIAL QUESTION

What Body Parts Enable Movement, Support, Respiration, and Circulation?

Engage Your Brain

Find the answer to the following question in this lesson and record it here.

What is the difference between you and an animal that can breathe underwater?

_____

_____

_____

ACTIVE READING

Lesson Vocabulary

List the terms. As you learn about each one, make notes in the Interactive Glossary.

_____   _____

_____   _____

_____

Main Ideas

The main idea of a paragraph is the most important idea. The main idea may be stated in the first sentence, or it may be stated elsewhere. Active readers look for main ideas by asking themselves, What is this section mostly about?

Strong Bones and Mighty Muscles

What would your body be like without bones and muscles? Your body would be a shapeless blob!

ACTIVE **READING** As you read these two pages, draw two lines under each main idea.

Organs that support and protect the body and store minerals are called **bones**. The ribs and skull are bones that protect internal organs. Bones attached to muscles help move the body. Bones have a hard outer layer that contains calcium. Inside bones is a spongy layer where blood cells are made.

The place where two or more bones meet is called a joint. Some joints, like the joints in your skull, don't allow the bones to move. Others joints, like the joint in your shoulder or knee, allow different types of movement. *Ligaments* [LIG•uh•muhntz] connect the bones of a joint.

Feel the tip of your nose. This is cartilage. Cartilage cushions the ends of bones and forms flexible parts like your ears and nose. Bones, ligaments, and cartilage form the *skeletal system*.

What Do Bones Do?

- support the body
- anchor muscles
- protect internal organs
- store minerals like calcium
- make blood cells

©Photodisc

Muscles often work in pairs. When one muscle contracts, the other muscle in the pair relaxes. Cooperation allows the contracting muscle to move the bone that it's attached to. When the opposite muscle contracts, the first muscle relaxes. What happens if both muscles contract at the same time?

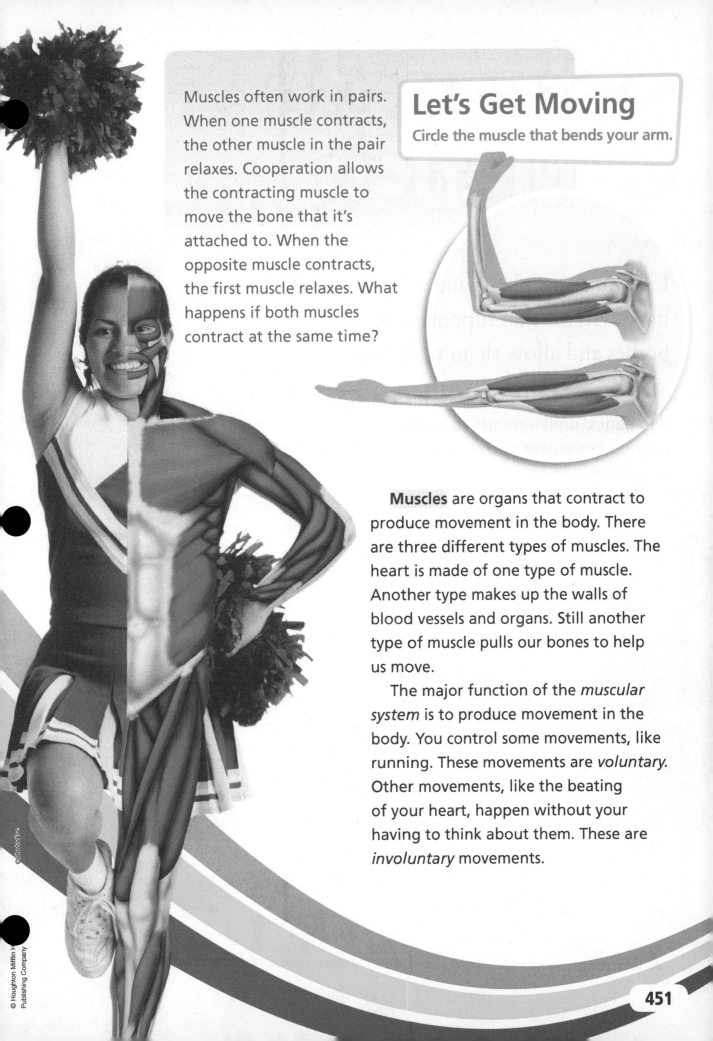

Let's Get Moving

Circle the muscle that bends your arm.

Muscles are organs that contract to produce movement in the body. There are three different types of muscles. The heart is made of one type of muscle. Another type makes up the walls of blood vessels and organs. Still another type of muscle pulls our bones to help us move.

The major function of the *muscular system* is to produce movement in the body. You control some movements, like running. These movements are *voluntary*. Other movements, like the beating of your heart, happen without your having to think about them. These are *involuntary* movements.

Strength and Motion

Like humans, plants and animals have systems that support their bodies and allow them to move.

ACTIVE **READING** As you read these two pages, underline structures that provide movement and support in plants and animals.

Sunflower blooms can be over two feet wide! The thick stem helps to support the heavy flower at the top. The flower and leaves slowly turn throughout the day to follow the movement of the sun across the sky.

Cicadas [si•**KAY**•duhz] have a hard outer layer, called an **exoskeleton**. It's like having bones outside their bodies. Exoskeletons help protect them from being eaten. Their muscles are attached to their exoskeletons and move their bodies by pulling from the inside. As cicadas grow, they shed the old exoskeleton. Underneath is a new one.

A Hardened Life

How would your life be different if you had an exoskeleton?

_____

_____

_____

The seal's flexible body lets it glide through water. Its flippers help it swim.

Sea stars use water in tiny tubes, called tube feet, to move. Muscles squeeze water into and out of the tubes, causing the tube feet to move. Suction cups on the ends of the feet help the sea star grip surfaces.

This sensitive plant responds to touch by closing its leaves.

Breathe In, Breathe Out

Take a deep breath. Do you feel "inspired"? You should. *Inspire* is another word for breathing in. Breathing out is called *expiring*.

ACTIVE **READING** As you read the text below, draw boxes around the five parts of the respiratory system that are described.

Organs in the *respiratory system* bring in oxygen that the body needs and release carbon dioxide, the body's waste gas. The main organs of the respiratory system are the **lungs**. Lungs are spongy organs that expand to fill with air.

Air enters your body through your nose or mouth. It flows through a tube in your throat called the *trachea* [TRAY•kee•uh]. The trachea branches into two smaller tubes called bronchi [BRAHNG•ky]. Where the bronchi enter the lungs, they branch into many bronchioles [BRAHNG•kee•ohlz]. At the end of each bronchiole are tiny sacs called alveoli [al•VEE•uh•ly]. Alveoli make up most of the lungs. When you inhale (breathe in), air flows into the lungs and the alveoli inflate like tiny balloons. When you exhale (breathe out) air flows back out of the alveoli and out of the lungs.

DO THE **MATH**

Solve Word Problems

On average, a person breathes about 20 times per minute.

There are 60 minutes in an hour. How many times does a person breathe in one hour?

_____

_____

There are 24 hours in a day. How many times does a person breathe every day?

_____

If you take in about 1 liter of air with each breath, how much air passes through your lungs every day?

_____

You have two bronchi, one for each lung. These bronchi branch into smaller tubes called bronchioles.

Airflow

Draw arrows to show the path that air takes into and out of the alveoli.

Tiny blood vessels surround the alveoli. Red blood cells in the vessels absorb oxygen. At the same time, carbon dioxide is released from the blood into the alveoli.

Asthma Attack

Asthma is an illness that makes it hard for a person to breathe. During an attack, some kids say it feels like breathing through a straw.

ACTIVE **READING** As you read these two pages, draw a star next to what you consider to be the most important sentence, and be ready to explain why.

Constricted Airways

When people are having an asthma attack, their bronchi become swollen. The swelling makes their airways smaller. It is much harder to get air in and out of the lungs. People having an asthma attack may cough, wheeze, or feel like a weight is sitting on their chest. They struggle to breathe. Medication can help end an asthma attack. After the attack, a person's airways return to normal.

▶ Fill in the sequence of events that lead to an asthma attack.

Asthma trigger enters airway	→	Airway becomes irritated	→	Bronchi become _____

Airways become smaller	→	It becomes difficult to _____

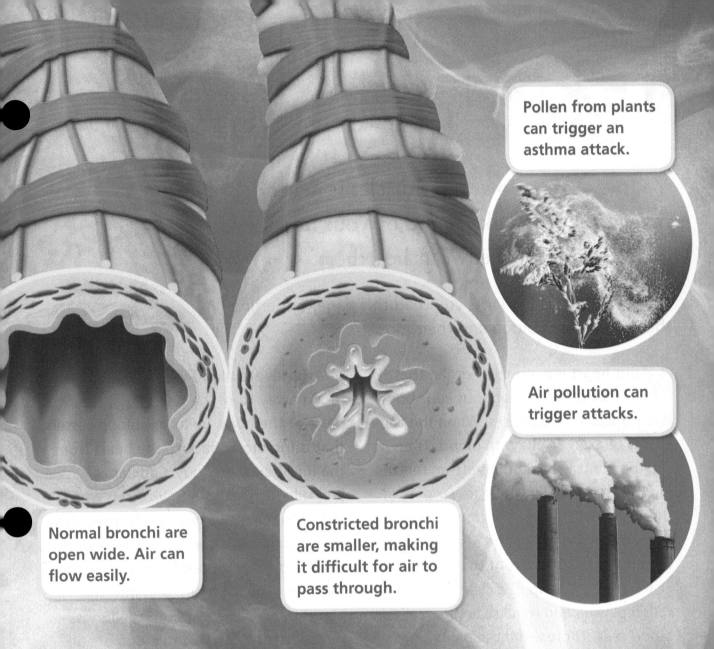

Pollen from plants can trigger an asthma attack.

Air pollution can trigger attacks.

Normal bronchi are open wide. Air can flow easily.

Constricted bronchi are smaller, making it difficult for air to pass through.

Triggers

The exact causes of asthma aren't known. Many people are born with it, but people sometimes develop asthma as they get older. Doctors do know that there are things that can cause an asthma attack. These things are called asthma triggers. Smoke, air pollution, and allergies are all possible triggers that start the process of an asthma attack.

Management

People who have asthma try to avoid things in the air that trigger attacks. However, a person can't always avoid triggers such as pollen or air pollution. A doctor can give people who suffer from asthma a device called an inhaler. An inhaler releases a mist of medicine that a person breathes in. This medicine can help open up airways during an attack. Other types of medicine help to prevent asthma attacks.

Beat It

Your heart is a powerful muscle. It never rests! The drum-like sound of your heart's contractions is called your heartbeat.

ACTIVE **READING** As you read this page, underline the four parts of blood and their jobs.

Your **heart** is a muscular organ that pumps blood throughout your body. It contracts in two phases. When the top part is relaxed, it fills with blood. Then the top contracts and the bottom relaxes. Blood is squeezed into the lower part of the heart. The lower part contracts and squeezes blood out of the heart, into vessels, and to all parts of the body.

Blood is made up of a clear liquid called plasma and small structures called blood cells. There are three main types of blood cells—red cells, white cells, and platelets.

Arteries are blood vessels that carry blood away from the heart to different parts of the body. Veins are blood vessels that bring blood back to the heart from the lungs and the body. Capillaries [KAP•uh•lair•eez] are tiny vessels with very thin walls. Oxygen and nutrients can pass through capillary walls to the body. Carbon dioxide passes from the body, through capillary walls, and into the blood to be carried back to the lungs.

The heart, vessels, and blood are all part of the *circulatory system.*

Red blood cells carry oxygen throughout your body.

White blood cells help fight disease.

Platelets stop bleeding by sticking together and forming clots.

Plasma carries nutrients and blood cells throughout the body.

458

Arteries are thick vessels that move blood carrying oxygen away from the heart and to the body.

Veins move blood carrying waste material back to the heart and lungs so the process can begin again.

Capillaries connect arteries and veins. Capillaries have extremely thin walls that allow gases and nutrients to pass through.

Heartbeat Rate

How many times does your heart beat in a minute while you are sitting?

_____

Now, do 25 jumping jacks. How many times does your heart beat in a minute?

_____

Got Lungs?

Respiration and circulation may look very different in plants and animals, but these systems still have the same purposes.

ACTIVE **READING** As you read these two pages, circle lesson vocabulary each time it is used.

Circulation or Respiration?

Write a *C* or an *R* in the circle next to each picture to tell whether circulation or respiration is being described.

Fish cannot breathe in air. Instead, they have special structures called gills that can take oxygen from water.

Spiders have structures called book lungs that look like tiny books whose pages can fill with air. Book lungs bring oxygen to the spider's blood.

Our hearts have four parts, or chambers. Fish hearts have only two chambers. Blood goes from the heart to the gills, then to the body, and then back to the heart.

lungs

air sacs

Birds use huge amounts of energy to fly. They also use a lot of oxygen. To keep air flowing through their lungs constantly, birds have special sacs that store air. With these sacs, even when a bird is breathing out, air is moving into the lungs.

Plants take in air through special openings in leaves called *stomata*. The word *stoma* means "mouth," which is what these tiny structures look like.

Most plants have a transport system that moves fluid throughout a plant's body. This cross-section of a stem shows bundles of plant vessels.

Sum It Up »

Read the summary statements below. Each one is incorrect. Change the part of the summary in blue to make it correct.

1. The circulatory system consists of bone, cartilage, and ligaments. Your lungs work in pairs to move your body.

   _____
   _____

2. The respiratory system brings in carbon dioxide for the body to use and releases oxygen as a waste product.

   _____
   _____

3. The muscular system carries blood through your body. It consists of the heart, blood vessels, and blood.

   _____

4. Plants bring air into their bodies using structures called mouths.

   _____
   _____

5. Fish take in air through hearts, and spiders take in air through exoskeletons.

   _____
   _____
   _____

Brain Check

Name _____

Vocabulary Review

1 Draw a line from each term to its definition or description.

1. tube

2. bronchi

3. circulatory

4. muscles

5. heart

6. respiratory

7. lungs

8. exoskeleton

9. bones

10. skeletal

A. body parts that work in pairs to help your body move

B. the organ system that moves air into, around, and out of your body

C. the organ system that supports your body

D. hard body parts that support your body

E. hard covering on the outside of some animals' bodies

F. pumps blood throughout the body

G. the organ system that moves blood around the body

H. organs that expand to fill with air

I. type of feet used by sea stars to move

J. two tubes that connect to the trachea and to bronchioles

Apply Concepts

2 For each action on the left, write the opposite action in the blank to the right.

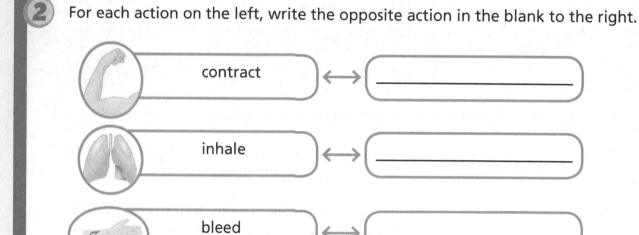

contract ⟷ _____

inhale ⟷ _____

bleed ⟷ _____

3 What are two structures in animals that serve the same purpose as lungs?

_____   _____

4 Think about how different types of animals move, breathe, and circulate blood. Place the words from the bank below under the picture of the organism that has that structure. You may not use all the words.

tube feet	stem	muscles	gills
book lungs	bones	exoskeleton	lungs

sea star

dog

spider

_____   _____   _____

_____   _____   _____

_____   _____   _____

© Houghton Mifflin Harcourt Publishing Company

5 Fill in the process chart below to describe the path that air takes through the respiratory system.

Air enters through the mouth or nose, and travels through the _____ .

Then it flows through the large tubes called _____ and the smaller tubes called _____ until it reaches the _____ .

There, oxygen enters the blood and _____ _____ leaves the blood and enters the _____ .

The air flows back out through the _____ and then through the larger _____ .

Then it passes through the _____ and finally leaves the body through the mouth or nose.

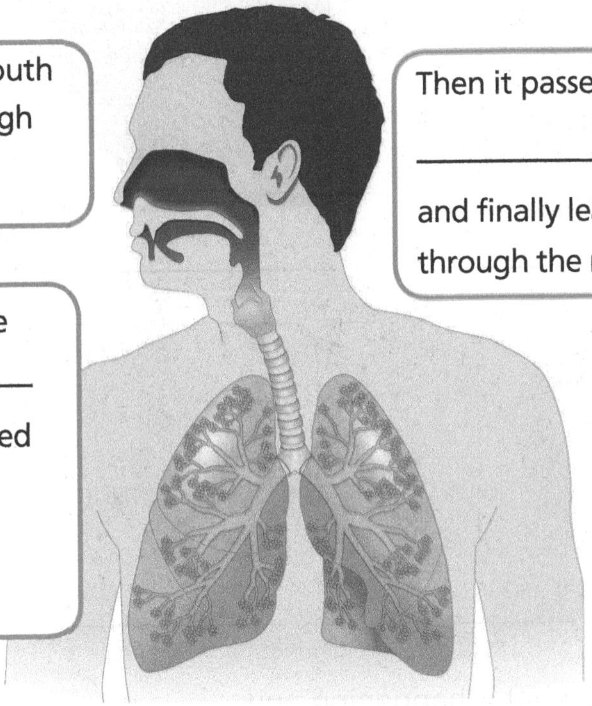

6 _____ is a disease that causes the bronchioles to _____ which makes _____ difficult.

7 How is the function of muscles and bones related?

_____

_____

_____

_____

_____

8 Label each of the following as an example of respiration or circulation.

_____   _____   _____

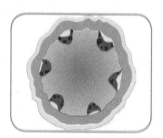

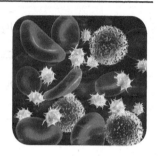

_____   _____   _____

9 Think about what is happening and identify the part of blood that is being used.

1. You get a cut. The _____ help to close the cut.

2. The _____ _____ _____ help to fight infection and get rid of germs.

3. The _____ helps carry all of these blood cells to the wound area.

10 Which part of the body has thin walls that allow oxygen to pass through?

a. arteries

b. veins

c. capillaries

d. bronchioles

 **Take It Home!** Make a model of a skeleton using different types of pasta. You can model a human skeleton or the skeleton of another animal. Talk with your family about the different bones and what purpose they serve.

SC.5.N.2.1 Recognize and explain that science is grounded in empirical observations that are testable; explanation must always be linked with evidence.

S.T.E.M.

ENGINEERING & TECHNOLOGY

Pumping Blood

1950s Early Machines

The first device to artificially keep blood flowing through the body was the heart-lung machine. It was used to keep a patient alive when the patient's heart was being operated on. These machines are still used in surgeries today. They remove blood from the body, transfer gases, and put the blood back in.

1964 Artificial Heart Program
The National Institutes of Health began a program to develop an artificial heart that could replace a defective human heart.

1982 First Artificial Heart
The first artificial heart was implanted into a person. This heart was designed to be temporary until the patient could receive a donor heart for a transplant.

1990s Heart Assist Devices
An LVAD (left ventricular assist device) is an implanted device that keeps a patient alive while waiting for a donor heart. A natural heart transplant is still the longest-term solution for patients.

2010s Artificial Hearts Today
This is the first self-contained artificial heart. It is designed as an alternative to a heart transplant.

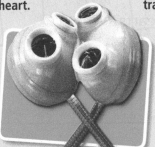

TROUBLESHOOTING

How have mechanical devices that circulate blood improved over time?

_____

_____

Artificial hearts are the last resort for patients who cannot survive without them, even just to wait long enough for a transplant of a donor heart.

Do research on how real human hearts work and on the most modern artificial heart. Draw and label a diagram of the human heart and a replacement heart. Describe how each heart pumps blood.

_____

_____

You Decide

What are the advantages and disadvantages of artificial hearts? What improvements would reduce the disadvantages?

_____

_____

_____

_____

_____

_____

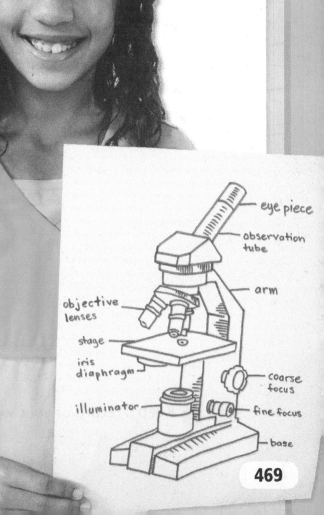

Owner's Manual: Using a Microscope

Communication is an important part of the engineering process. Once you have a subject, you need to find out what others already know about it. Then, as you work on your project, you'll share your ideas with team members. Lastly, you'll need to explain your final design. This explanation can include instructions in the form of an owner's manual that tells how to properly use your device.

Have you ever used a microscope before? If so, you know that there are certain steps that you must follow in order to use this tool correctly. Suppose you had to compose a five-page manual that explained how to use a microscope to a fourth grader. Could you do it? Let's find out.

- eye piece
- observation tube
- arm
- objective lenses
- stage
- iris diaphragm
- coarse focus
- fine focus
- illuminator
- base

S.T.E.M. continued

DESIGN PROCESS STEPS

1 Find a Problem
2 Plan & Build
3 Test & Improve
4 Redesign
5 Communicate

What to Do:

1. Learn more about different types of microscopes and how they help us observe objects close up.

2. Using two hands, carefully transport a classroom microscope to your table.

3. Make a drawing of this observation tool. Label the microscope parts.

4. As a team, discuss the directions for using and caring for this microscope. Write step-by-step instructions that explain how to properly use and care for this tool in the classroom.

5. Keep a record of your work in your Science Notebook.

© Houghton Mifflin Ha Publishing Company

SC.5.L.14.1 Identify the organs in the human body and describe their functions, including ... lungs, stomach, liver, intestines, pancreas ... reproductive organs, kidneys, bladder.... SC.5.L.14.2 Compare and contrast the function of organs and other physical structures of plants and animals, including humans....

ESSENTIAL **QUESTION**

What Body Parts Enable Digestion, Waste Removal, and Reproduction?

Engage Your Brain

Find the answer to the following question in this lesson and record it here.

If you could see through your body, this might be what you'd see when you look in the mirror. What is the coiled tube inside your belly, and what does it do?

_____

_____

_____

ACTIVE **READING**

Lesson Vocabulary

List the terms. As you learn about each one, make notes in the Interactive Glossary.

_____ _____

_____ _____

_____

Using Charts

A chart adds information to the text that appears on the page with it. Active readers pause their reading to review the chart and decide how the information in it adds to what they are reading.

Down the Hatch

When you swallow food, it passes through a long tube in your body. As it travels, it is broken down into smaller pieces, and all of the useful parts are absorbed by the body. All that is left over is waste.

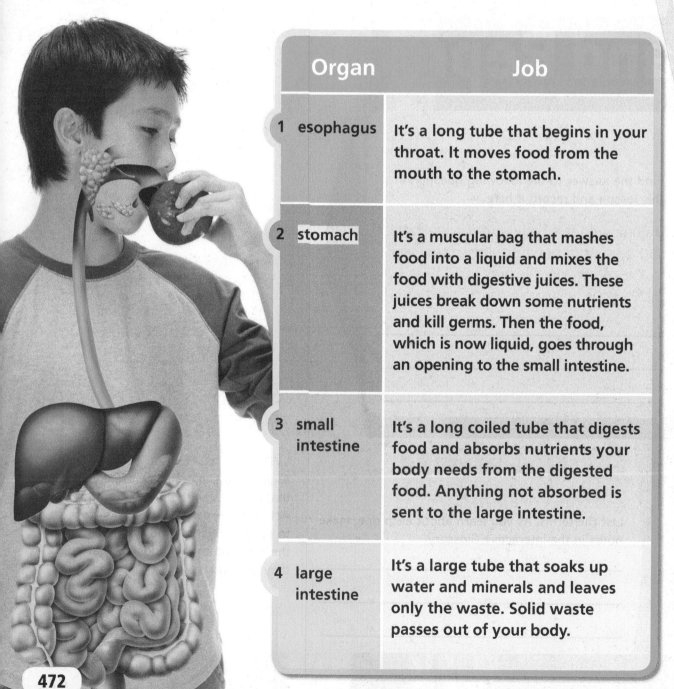

Organ	Job
1 esophagus	It's a long tube that begins in your throat. It moves food from the mouth to the stomach.
2 stomach	It's a muscular bag that mashes food into a liquid and mixes the food with digestive juices. These juices break down some nutrients and kill germs. Then the food, which is now liquid, goes through an opening to the small intestine.
3 small intestine	It's a long coiled tube that digests food and absorbs nutrients your body needs from the digested food. Anything not absorbed is sent to the large intestine.
4 large intestine	It's a large tube that soaks up water and minerals and leaves only the waste. Solid waste passes out of your body.

472

▶ In each box below, write the name and function of the organ that is shown.

_____
_____
_____

_____
_____
_____

The **liver** makes a juice called *bile* that helps break large blobs of fat into tiny droplets so that the fats can be broken down more easily.

The gallbladder stores bile from the liver and sends it to the small intestine only when food passes through.

The **pancreas** makes juices that are released into the small intestine. These juices break down fats and proteins into small pieces that can be absorbed.

_____
_____
_____

_____
_____
_____

Food for Thought

You have two boxes of cereal in your hand. How do you know which is the healthier choice? You can read their food labels to help you decide.

ACTIVE READING As you read these two pages, draw a star next to what you consider to be the most important sentence, and be ready to explain why.

Packaged foods must have a label that gives you information about what is inside the package. This is called nutrition information. Learning how to use nutrition information can help you make healthy food choices.

Each part of a nutrition label has different information. For example, you can learn how many servings are in the box. You can also learn how many Calories [KAL•uh•reez] each serving has. Calories are a way to measure how much energy your body will get from your food. Carbohydrates, proteins and fats are used by the body for energy.

The nutrition label has information about more than just energy. It also lists the amounts of important nutrients that the food contains. Bones need calcium for strength. Sodium is used by the nerves to send signals. Vitamin A helps with your eyesight. Protein is used to build muscle. Fats are used to make important chemical signals and to store energy. As you can see, reading food labels can help you make choices that fulfill all of your body's nutrition needs.

 DO THE **MATH**

Solve Word Problems

One serving of this cereal provides you with 160 mg of sodium. This is 7% of your body's daily needs. How many milligrams of sodium equal 100%?

_____

_____

_____

Nutrition Facts

Serving Size ¾ cup (30g)
Servings Per Container About 14

Amount Per Serving	Corn Crunch	with ½ cup skim milk
Calories	120	160
Calories from Fat	15	20
	% Daily Value**	
Total Fat 2g*	**3**%	**3**%
Saturated Fat 0g	**0**%	**0**%
Cholesterol 0mg	**0**%	**1**%
Sodium 160mg	**7**%	**9**%
Potassium 65mg	**2**%	**8**%
Total Carbohydrate 25g	**8**%	**10**%
Dietary Fiber 3g		
Sugars 3g		
Other Carbohydrate 11g		
Protein 2g		

*Amount in Cereal. A serving of cereal plus skim milk provides 2g fat, less 5mg cholesterol, 220mg sodium, 270mg potassium, 31g carbohydrate (19g sugars) and 6g protein.

Percent Daily Values are based on a 2,000 calorie diet. Your daily values may be higher or lower depending on your calorie needs:

	Calories	2,000	2,500
Fat	Less than	65g	80g
Fat	Less than	20g	25g
terol	Less than	300mg	300mg
	Less than	2,400mg	2,400mg
m		3,500mg	3,500mg
ydrate		300g	375g
ber		25g	30g

The serving size will help you make smart decisions about how much of a food you should eat to get the right amount of nutrients in your diet.

The "% Daily Value" tells you what percent of this nutrient a serving of this food will provide compared to how much you should get in a full day.

This section shows how many grams (g) or milligrams (mg) of each type of nutrient you should get each day, depending on how many Calories you need.

▶ How many Calories are in 1 serving, with $\frac{1}{2}$ cup skim milk?

_____

Waste Removal

Digesting food produces one kind of waste. Using the nutrients produces another. The *excretory system* rids the body of this waste and keeps your body's water and salt levels in balance.

ACTIVE READING As you read this page, underline the different types of waste that are described.

Your body "burns" nutrients much like a fire burns wood. Your body doesn't produce ash, but the "burned" nutrients do make waste products. For example, as protein is broken down, ammonia is made. Ammonia is very toxic! The liver converts ammonia to urea [yoo•REE•uh], which is less toxic. But if urea builds up it makes you sick, so your body gets rid of it as urine. A small amount of urea is also released in sweat.

Like a fire, your body uses oxygen and produces a waste gas called carbon dioxide. Carbon dioxide is released by your lungs when you breathe out.

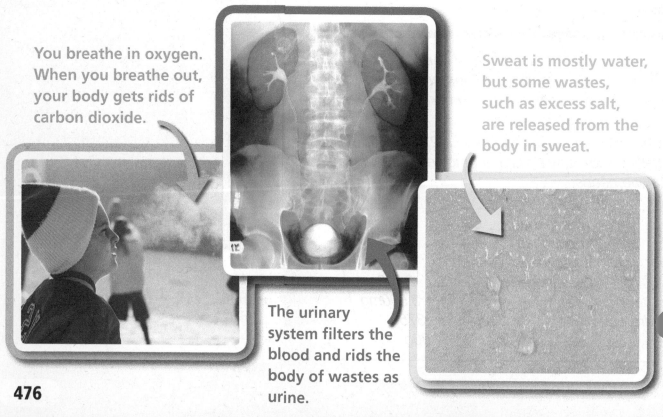

You breathe in oxygen. When you breathe out, your body gets rids of carbon dioxide.

The urinary system filters the blood and rids the body of wastes as urine.

Sweat is mostly water, but some wastes, such as excess salt, are released from the body in sweat.

(bl) ©David R. Frazier Photolibrary, Inc./Alamy; (c) ©Medical Body Scans/Photo Researchers, Inc.; (br) ©Jason Hetherington

© Houghton Mifflin H
Publishing Company

The Urinary System

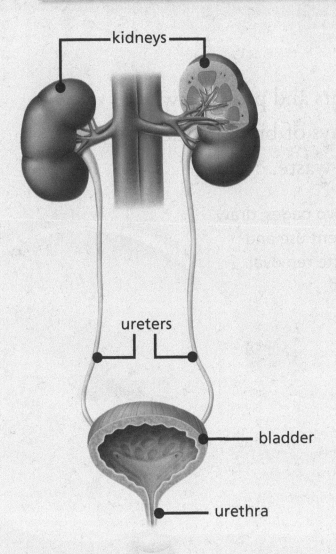

kidneys

ureters

bladder

urethra

1 The **kidneys** are organs that remove waste from the blood. They also help to conserve water and to make sure the blood does not have too much or too little salt.

2 After the kidneys filter the blood, the waste, *urine*, collects in tubes called *ureters* [YUR•ih•tuhrz]. These take the urine to the bladder.

3 The **bladder** stores urine and then releases it from the body. The bladder can stretch like a balloon. It can hold up to a pint at a time!

4 The urethra [yu•REE•thruh] is a small tube that takes urine from the bladder to outside of the body.

Organize It—Sequence

Write the organs in order to show the path of urine through the urinary system.

Eating and Excreting

All living things use nutrients and produce waste. Living things have many ways of breaking down nutrients and getting rid of waste.

ACTIVE **READING** On these two pages, draw circles around descriptions of nutrient use and squares around descriptions of waste removal.

Flies spit out acids onto food. Food is partly digested outside the fly's body! Then the fly sucks up the nutrients through a straw-like mouthpart.

Bird droppings aren't made of urine. Instead, they are made of uric acid and digestive waste. Uric acid is a very powerful acid that damages statues.

No Stomach? No Problem!

Which two organisms below have no digestive system?

_____

Jellyfish bring food into their mouths to digest it. Then they get rid of the waste by sending it back out of their mouths!

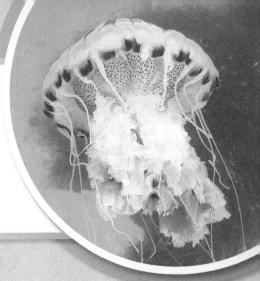

Marsh grasses live in salty areas where most plants could not survive. The leaves of marsh grasses get rid of excess salt.

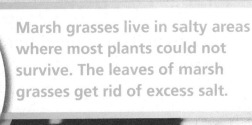

Grass is tough to digest! To get nutrients from grass, cows must chew their food twice and have four sections of stomach! The arrows show the path of food through a cow's digestive system.

Tapeworms have no digestive system. Instead they live inside other animals' digestive systems. As digested food flows past, a tapeworm soaks up nutrients through its skin.

Cycles of Life

What do babies, plantlets, tadpoles, and larvae have in common? They're all organisms that came from other organisms.

ACTIVE **READING** As you read these two pages, find and underline the different names for young organisms.

Animals and plants all have *reproductive systems*. This system has one very important job: to make new organisms.

Human males and females have reproductive organs that make special cells. The male reproductive cells are made in the testes [TES•teez]. Female reproductive cells are made in the ovaries [OH•vuh•reez]. These reproductive cells join to form an embryo [EM•bree•oh]. The embryo develops in the mother's body for nine months. It grows and changes until it can survive outside the mother's body. At this time, a baby is born.

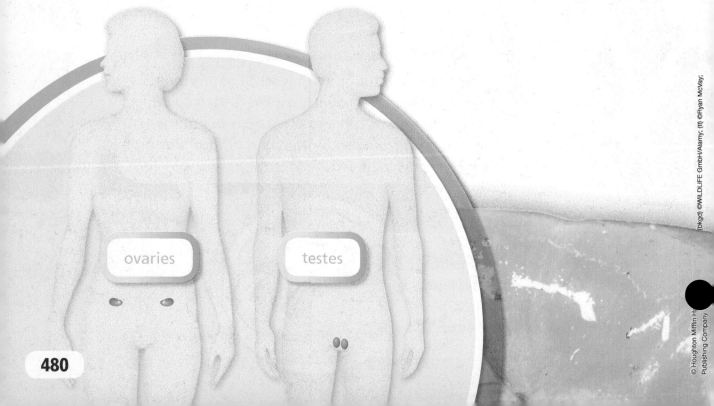

ovaries

testes

A spider plants grows little "plantlets" at the end of some stems. These plant buds can be broken off to grow new plants.

Insects lay eggs that hatch into larvae [LAR•vee], like the ones shown here. Insects go through several stages before they reach adult form.

Many plants make seeds. Male plant reproductive cells join with female reproductive cells and develop into a seed. Dandelion seeds are carried by wind. If they land in soil, they begin to grow and develop into a new plant.

Many frogs lay their eggs in a jelly-like pile. The eggs must stay wet, or they will die. Tadpoles hatch from the eggs. Tadpoles start out looking like fish with large heads. Slowly they grow legs and their tails become smaller and smaller. Little by little they turn into adult frogs.

Sum It Up »

Complete the summary paragraph by filling in the blanks. Then place the words in the list below the summary paragraph with the correct system at the bottom of the page.

Your body is made up of many 1._____ that work together in systems. The 2._____ system is a long tube that travels through your body. It takes the nutrients out of food for your body to use. The 3._____ system is responsible for removing waste from your body. The 4._____ system makes special cells that produce new organisms. Plants and animals also have ways to get energy, remove waste, and reproduce.

testes	small intestine	esophagus
kidneys	ovaries	ureters
stomach	large intestine	
urethra	bladder	

Digestive System	**Urinary System**	**Reproductive System**
5. _____	9. _____	13. _____
6. _____	10. _____	14. _____
7. _____	11. _____	
8. _____	12. _____	

Brain Check

Vocabulary Review

Name _____

1 Use the words in the box to complete each sentence.

1. The _____ are bean-shaped organs filter the blood and remove wastes.

2. The long tube that connects the mouth to the stomach is the _____.

3. The _____ expands and fills up with urine until it is ready to be released.

4. The _____ makes juices that break down protein in the small intestine.

5. The _____ system moves food through your body and absorbs the nutrients.

6. The _____ makes a juice that breaks large blobs of fat into smaller blobs.

7. The _____ system helps an organism make new organisms.

8. The _____ mashes food and mixes food with digestive juices.

| bladder | digestive | esophagus | kidneys |
| liver | pancreas | reproductive | stomach |

Apply Concepts

2 Think about how organs depend on other organs to do their work. Complete each sentence.

1. Food couldn't reach the stomach without the _____ and the _____ .

2. Kidneys couldn't work without the _____ because _____ couldn't leave the body.

3. The small intestine couldn't work without the _____ because fats couldn't be broken down.

3 Describe the life cycle of the tadpole shown here.

_____
_____
_____
_____
_____

4 Explain how each of the items shown below are alike.

stomach and blender

_____
_____
_____

kidney and coffee filter

_____
_____
_____

bladder and water balloon

_____
_____
_____

5 Scientists have discovered a new animal. Is it possible for it to have no digestive system? Why or why not? _____

_____

_____

Take It Home Write the words *small intestine, pancreas, esophagus, liver, large intestine, gall bladder,* and *stomach* on index cards. Eat a snack. Ask your family to explain how each organ helps to digest your food.

SC.5.L.14.2 Compare and contrast the function of organs and other physical structures of plants and animals, including humans....

◯ PEOPLE IN SCIENCE

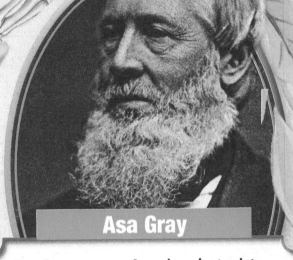

Meet the *Grays* of Biology

Henry Gray

Henry Gray was a surgeon in London. He was fascinated by the science of anatomy. Anatomy is the study of the parts of the body. In 1858, when he was only 31 years old, Henry Gray published a book on anatomy. It became one of the most famous scientific books of all time: *Gray's Anatomy*. The book included drawings of all of the organs and systems of the human body. Henry Gray died three years later from smallpox, but his work lives on. In 2009, the 40th edition of *Gray's Anatomy* was published. It is still used today by doctors, students, and other scientists.

Asa Gray

Asa Gray was an American botanist. He studied plants. He lived around the same time as Henry Gray, but the two men were not related. They never even met. Still, their work had some things in common. Asa Gray wrote a book known as *Gray's Manual*. Working with a scientific illustrator named Isaac Sprague, Asa Gray published a book that had information about almost every plant in the Northern United States. It was written more than a century ago. But *Gray's Manual* is still used by botanists today. Asa Gray is considered to be one of history's most important botanists.

Be a Scientific Illustrator

Try your hand at scientific illustrations! See how well you can produce an anatomical drawing of the bones of the human hand. Then try making a botanical illustration of the raspberry branch.

Bones of the Human Hand

Raspberry Branch

Name _____

Vocabulary Review

Use the terms in the box to complete the sentences.

> brain
> skin
> lungs

1. The _____ forms a protective

   covering of the body.

2. Fish gills take in oxygen from water and release
   carbon dioxide. This is similar to the function of the

   human _____.

3. The _____ is the organ that processes

   information in the body.

Science Concepts

Fill in the letter of the choice that best answers the question.

4. During recess, Renee scraped her knee,
   so the nurse put a bandage on it. Which
   of the functions below that are normally
   provided by skin is now being provided by
   the bandage?

   Ⓐ preventing dehydration

   Ⓑ regulating body temperature

   Ⓒ keeping bacteria out of the body

   Ⓓ sensing when it is being touched

5. Latoya knows that skin produces oil,
   water, and salt. She wants to find out
   which of these causes cooling. She creates
   the following table to record data.

	Towel soaked in oil	Towel covered in salt	Towel soaked in water	Towel that is clean and dry
Starting temperature				
Temperature after 1 min				
Temperature after 10 min				

   Which towel is the control?

   Ⓕ towel soaked in oil

   Ⓖ towel covered in salt

   Ⓗ towel soaked in water

   Ⓘ towel that is clean and dry

6. In the early days of telephone use, there were no computers. To make a phone call, a person had to call an operator. The operator would connect two callers. The operator performed a function that is most similar to which human body part?

(A) brain

(C) eyes

(B) nose

(D) skin

7. Animals have body coverings, such as skin, that protect them. This protective layer can be used to protect the animal from extreme temperatures and to help it blend in with its environment to avoid predators. Look at the body coverings of these animals. Which animal has a body covering that will best protect it from bites and scratches during an attack by a predator?

(F)

(H)

(G)

(I)

8. The following picture shows some muscles and bones of the arm.

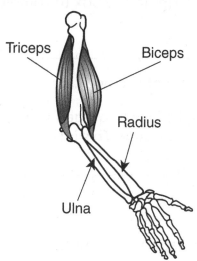

As this arm bends, which word describes what the biceps muscle is doing?

(A) relaxing

(C) contracting

(B) retracting

(D) constricting

9. How do nutrients in digested food reach the bloodstream?

(F) They are absorbed by the large intestine.

(G) They pass from the esophagus into the blood.

(H) They are absorbed into the bloodstream by the small intestine.

(I) They are absorbed into the bloodstream through the pancreas wall.

Name _____

10. Digestion takes place in the digestive tract, shown here.

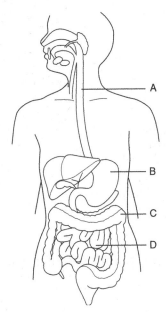

In what order does food move through the organs of the digestive tract?

Ⓐ A, B, C, D

Ⓒ A, B, D, C

Ⓑ A, C, B, D

Ⓓ A, D, B, C

11. The following picture shows the flow of blood through the human circulatory and respiratory systems.

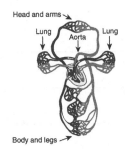

Which statement is true of the large blood vessel called the aorta?

Ⓕ It carries blood to the heart.

Ⓖ It carries blood to the lungs.

Ⓗ It carries blood that is high in oxygen.

Ⓘ It carries blood that is high in carbon dioxide.

12. Cells in the body use nutrients and oxygen for energy. Which body system transports oxygen and nutrients throughout the body?

Ⓐ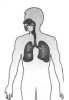

Ⓒ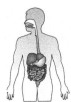

Ⓑ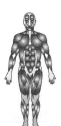

Ⓓ

Apply Inquiry and Review the Big Idea

Write the answers to these questions.

13. The following picture shows how plant tissues carry water and nutrients throughout a plant.

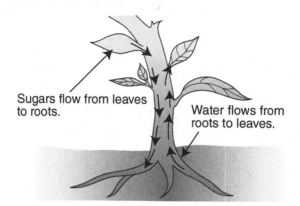

Sugars flow from leaves to roots.

Water flows from roots to leaves.

Make a claim about which human body system is similar to this plant's vascular system. Explain your reasoning.

_____

_____

_____

_____

14. Insects have a hard outer covering called an exoskeleton. How do an insect's exoskeleton and a human's skeletal system compare?

_____

_____

_____

_____

Changes in Environments

FLORIDA BIG IDEA 15

Diversity and Evolution of Living Organisms

Sea turtles lay their eggs on Florida beaches.

I Wonder Why

Sea turtles hatch in the sand and make their way to the ocean. Why do sea turtles need to be protected? *Turn the page to find out.*

Here's Why

Human activities, such as walking on nests, can accidentally harm turtle eggs. Turtle nests are protected so that the young turtles can safely hatch and reach the ocean.

Essential Questions and Florida Benchmarks

Science Notebook

Before you begin each lesson, write your thoughts about the Essential Question.

SC.5.L.15.1 Describe how, when the environment changes, differences between individuals allow some plants and animals to survive and reproduce while others die or move to new locations.

LESSON **1**

ESSENTIAL **QUESTION**

How Do Environmental Changes Affect Organisms?

 Engage Your Brain

Find the answer to the following question in this lesson and record it here.

A forest fire can change a landscape in a matter of minutes! Trees are burned, and animals run for shelter. How could a forest fire be a good thing?

_____

_____

_____

_____

📖 ACTIVE **READING**

Lesson Vocabulary
List the terms. As you learn about each one, make notes in the Interactive Glossary.

_____   _____

_____   _____

_____

Compare and Contrast
Many ideas in this lesson are connected because they explain comparisons and contrasts—how things are alike and different. Active readers stay focused on comparisons and contrasts when they ask themselves, How are these things alike? How are they different?

It's All
Around You

As far as we know, Earth is the only planet that we can live on. Water and air are two important reasons why life is possible on Earth.

ACTIVE READING As you read this page, circle things that make up environments on Earth.

water

What do oceans, clouds, fish, and birds all have in common? These things are all part of the environment. The **environment** is all of the living and nonliving things in nature. We depend on the environment for our food, air, and water and for a safe place to live. We share the environment with all other life on Earth. Every other living thing also depends on the environment to meet its needs for food, air, water, and a place to live. In this way, every living thing on Earth is connected.

You and the other living things around you interact with each other and with the nonliving parts of the environment. For example, think about the ways that honeybees interact with the living and nonliving things around them. Bees get nectar from a field of flowers, drink water from puddles, and sting animals if they get too close to the hive. Living things that interact with each other form a community. A community of living things and the nonliving things around them are called an **ecosystem**. Bees, birds, flowers, soil, water, and sunlight are all part of an ecosystem.

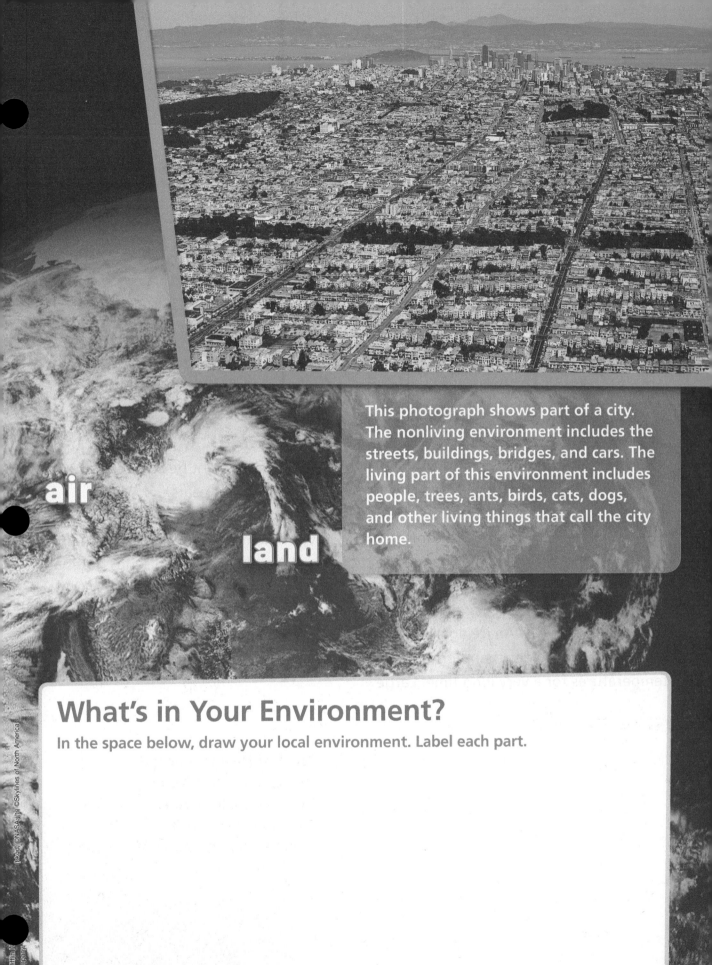

air

land

This photograph shows part of a city. The nonliving environment includes the streets, buildings, bridges, and cars. The living part of this environment includes people, trees, ants, birds, cats, dogs, and other living things that call the city home.

What's in Your Environment?

In the space below, draw your local environment. Label each part.

Change Comes Naturally

The environment can change in response to natural events. Some of these events occur quickly. Others take place more slowly.

Storms can bring heavy rains and flood the land, which changes the environment. Natural events, such as floods, earthquakes, volcanic eruptions, and droughts, can change the environment very quickly.

In contrast, events such as an ice age happen more slowly. An ice age happens when Earth has colder-than-normal temperatures for a very long time. Large areas of land might be covered with ice for thousands of years.

Volcanic eruptions can also change the environment over a long period of time. How? A violent eruption sends gases and dust high into the air. The materials block sunlight from reaching Earth's surface. This can cause temperatures to drop for months or years.

PACIFIC OCEAN

ATLANTIC OCEAN

The last ice age reached its peak about 18,000 years ago. Ice nearly 4 kilometers thick covered large parts of North America.

© Houghton Mifflin Harcourt Publishing Company

Is It Cold Enough For You?

Think about the environment during an ice age. How do you think the ice age affected living things?

_____

_____

_____

_____

_____

_____

Volcanoes can cause rapid change as hot flowing lava scorches the surrounding ecosystem. Volcanoes can also cause long-term change as dust and gases block out the sun's rays.

A forest fire is a natural cause of environmental change. Forest fires destroy vegetation. But many ecosystems need fire to stay healthy. Some trees even make seeds that cannot grow unless they have been burned!

Animal Architects

Living things are affected by their environment. Living things, in turn, can cause changes to their environment. These changes can be both helpful and harmful, depending on the point of view.

ACTIVE **READING** As you read this page, draw boxes around clue words that signal examples.

Beavers are only about 1 meter long, but they have a very large effect on their environment. For example, beavers use their teeth to cut trees. They use the trees to build dams across streams. Beaver dams cause ponds and wetlands to form.

The trees that beavers cut down to build their dam are harmed. In addition, organisms that lived in the flowing water of the stream and on the dry land around the stream must move.

But beaver dams provide a home for organisms that rely on ponds and wetlands. Ponds made by beaver dams increase the number of different kinds of organisms that can live in the area.

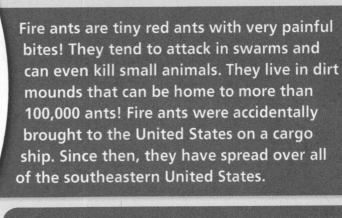

Fire ants are tiny red ants with very painful bites! They tend to attack in swarms and can even kill small animals. They live in dirt mounds that can be home to more than 100,000 ants! Fire ants were accidentally brought to the United States on a cargo ship. Since then, they have spread over all of the southeastern United States.

Harvester ants are large ants that eat seeds. As fire ants spread, they wipe out colonies of native harvester ants. Fire ants are an invasive animal. This means that they are invading an ecosystem that was not their original home. In their new home, they affect the native plants and animals.

Harvester ants are a favorite food of the horned lizard. Because there are fewer harvester ants, horned lizards have less food to eat. Now very few horned lizards remain. If they are not protected, in time there may be no horned lizards left!

Cause and Effect

Fill in the graphic organizer below to show a cause-and-effect relationship between fire ants and their ecosystem.

Cause ⟶ **Effect**

_____   _____

_____   _____

Humans Change the Environment

Humans are part of the environment and we have a large impact on our ecosystems. The effects of humans on the environment are both harmful and beneficial.

ACTIVE **READING** As you read these two pages, draw brackets around phrases that describe ways people harm the environment. Underline phrases that describe ways people help the environment.

Many human activities are harmful to an ecosystem. For example, people mine coal to get energy to power homes and businesses. Open-pit mining, like the mine shown here, kills all the plants living in that area. Other organisms must move to find food.

People cut down forests to use the wood or to clear space for homes. When the trees in an area are cut down, as they were in the bottom photograph, organisms that usually live in the forest must move or die. This effect is called habitat destruction. A *habitat* is a place where an organism usually lives.

Humans produce a large amount of waste that is disposed of as trash. Most trash ends up in landfills. If landfills are not built properly, wastes can pollute soil and water. **Pollution** is any harmful substance that gets into the environment. Pollution can kill organisms or cause diseases.

Not all changes caused by humans are harmful. People work to protect their environment and to protect organisms from harm as a result of ecosystem change. Protecting ecosystems and the organisms living in them is called **conservation.**

People try to restore habitats and repair damaged ecosystems by replanting trees and cleaning up pollution. People also remove invasive plants and animals so native organisms can survive.

In addition, people try to help organisms affected by natural disasters. People care for animals injured or orphaned by these disasters.

What Can You Do To Help?

In the space below, list things that you can do to help the environment. Include things you already do and things you would like to do in the future.

_____

_____

Living Things Change

Look at the snakes slithering down this page. Each snake looks different, but they are all the same kind of snake. Why don't they look the same?

ACTIVE **READING** As you read these two pages, circle the clue word or phrase that signals a detail such as an example or an added fact.

You don't look exactly like your parents. You have many similarities, but there are also small differences that make you unique. Every organism is slightly different from every other organism. Sometimes these differences can be very important.

Corn snakes, like the ones shown here, come in many colors and patterns. Some are very light colored, some are golden brown, and some are bright orange. Suppose a hawk is flying over a wheat field, looking for a snack. Which of these snakes is least likely to become lunch? If you guessed the golden brown snake, you are correct. Why? Its color would blend in with the wheat. The hawk would not see it, and the snake would survive. The snake would reproduce and pass on its coloring to its offspring. Its golden brown offspring would have a better chance of surviving in the wheat field and would also produce more offspring. Eventually, most of the snakes living in the wheat field would be golden brown.

DO THE MATH

Find Median and Mean

Length of Corn Snakes	
Snake 1	3.5 m
Snake 2	5.5 m
Snake 3	4.6 m
Snake 4	5.1 m
Snake 5	4.8 m
Snake 6	3.9 m
Snake 7	5.3 m

Adult corn snakes vary not only in color, but also in length. The table shows the lengths of several adult corn snakes. Study the data, and then answer the questions.

1. The median is the middle number of a data set when the numbers are placed in numerical order. Find the median of the data set. _____

2. The mean is the average of a data set. Find the mean of the data set. _____

Sometimes living things change because their environment changes. For example, bacteria have changed as a result of their changing environment. Since the discovery of antibiotics, people have learned how to kill bacteria. The first antibiotic, penicillin, saved many lives by killing bacteria that cause disease.

But in a very large population of bacteria, a few are not affected by penicillin. These bacteria survive and multiply. Over time, they produce large populations of bacteria that are not affected by penicillin.

Researchers have had to find new antibiotics to kill these bacteria. But, again, some bacteria are not killed. These bacteria continue to multiply.

Many types of antibiotics have been developed. And bacteria have become resistant to many of them. Now there are bacteria that are resistant to almost all known types of antibiotics. These bacteria are extremely difficult to kill.

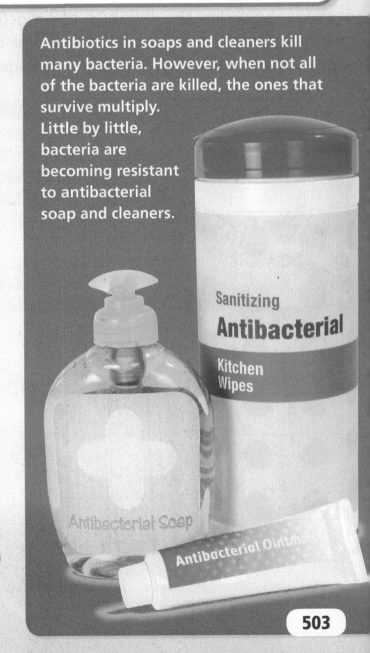

Antibiotics in soaps and cleaners kill many bacteria. However, when not all of the bacteria are killed, the ones that survive multiply. Little by little, bacteria are becoming resistant to antibacterial soap and cleaners.

Gone!

Some living things change when their environment changes. Some living things move to new places. Others simply do not survive.

ACTIVE **READING** As you read these two pages, underline the definition of *extinction*. Circle pictures of organisms that became extinct because of natural environmental change.

Millions of years ago, Earth was covered with giant reptiles! Now, most of those reptiles are extinct. Extinction happens when all the members of a certain kind of living thing die. Giant reptiles, such as the *Tyrannosaurus rex* shown here, lived in a time in which Earth was warm. Over time, the environment cooled, and many of the reptiles could not survive.

These dinosaurs, *Diplodocus* and *Triceratops* (from left to right), were large plant-eaters. They became extinct about 65 million years ago.

504

The Tasmanian wolf lived in Australia and New Guinea. Ranchers believed the wolves killed sheep and cattle, but this was never proven. The Tasmanian wolf was hunted to extinction by the 1930s.

The dodo bird lived on an island in the Indian Ocean. Around 1600, people came to the island. People hunted the birds for food. They cut down the island's forests to make room for houses. Nonnative animals, such as cats and pigs brought by people, destroyed the dodo birds' nests. Within 80 years after they were discovered, the dodo birds were extinct.

Time Traveler

If you could go back to the island of the dodo birds in 1600, what advice would you give to people to help conserve the dodo birds?

_____

_____

_____

_____

Today, people work to conserve habitats and protect organisms from extinction. Even so, many organisms are in danger of becoming extinct. As these organisms' environments continue to change, some will adapt, some will move, and some will not survive.

Sum It Up »

Read the summary statements below. Each one is incorrect. Change the part of the summary in blue to make it correct.

1

1. Pollution is all the living and nonliving things that affect an organism's life.

_____

2. Some natural events that cause the environment to change slowly include earthquakes and floods. _____

3. People can help conserve habitats by mining, building landfills, and cutting down forests. _____

_____

4. Protecting ecosystems is an example of extinction. _____

2 The idea web below summarizes the lesson. Complete the web.

If the environment changes, living things change, 6. _____, or do not survive.

A community of living things and their environment are an 7. _____.

Living things rely on their environment for 5. _____, air, _____, and a place to live.

In a city, the buildings, streets, air, and water are all 8. _____ parts of the environment.

Fast environmental change can be caused by 9. _____ and _____.

Brain Check

Name _____

Vocabulary Review

① Use the clues to unscramble the words below.

1. iavinvse
   _ _ _ _ _ _ _ _ _ : A nonnative animal that moves into a new place

2. ecnntavosroi
   _ _ _ _ _ _ _ _ _ _ _ _ : Protecting ecosystems and the organisms living in them

3. nlpituloo
   _ _ _ _ _ _ _ _ _ : Litter on the ground or harmful chemicals in the water

4. tsymeeocs
   _ _ _ _ _ _ _ _ _ : A group of organisms and their environment

5. radonsiu
   _ _ _ _ _ _ _ _ : A type of giant extinct animal

6. eeautrtpmer
   _ _ _ _ _ _ _ _ _ _ _ : How hot or cold something is

7. vebera
   _ _ _ _ _ _ : Can be helpful or harmful, depending on point of view

8. aaicbter
   _ _ _ _ _ _ _ _ : Have adapted to antibiotics

9. vmetneonrin
   _ _ _ _ _ _ _ _ _ _ _ : Everything around a living thing, including air, water, land, and sunlight

10. txoniecnit
    _ _ _ _ _ _ _ _ _ _ : Happened to dodo birds and Tasmanian wolves

11. navoolc
    _ _ _ _ _ _ _ : Can cause long-term environmental change by blowing dust and gases into the sky

Bonus: What kind of dinosaur accidentally smashes everything in its path?

_____ _____

Apply Concepts

2 Label each of the following pictures as a change caused by people, by animals, or by a natural event.

_____

_____

_____

_____

_____

_____

_____

_____

_____

_____

_____

_____

3 List some nonliving things found in Earth's environment. Give an example of how you use each thing.

_____

_____

_____

_____

_____

_____

4 Draw one circle around animals that became extinct because of natural events. Draw two circles around animals that became extinct because of human activities.

© Houghton Mifflin Harcourt Publishing Company

5 In the first box below, draw a landscape that includes a river. In the second box, draw how the same landscape might look after a flood. Include captions explaining how the environment changed.

6 Fill in the graphic organizer below to describe how beavers change the environment. The first box is already completed.

Beavers build a dam in a stream.

↓

↓

Describe a way that people might be able to solve each environmental problem listed below.

7 Coal mining can harm habitats and cause pollution.

_____

_____

_____

8 Cutting a forest destroys habitats and can lead to soil erosion.

_____

_____

_____

9 Waste from garbage in landfills can enter the ground and pollute soil and water.

_____

_____

10 Imagine that an orange tree frog eats only a certain type of small blue fly. A giant red fly starts moving into the tree frog's ecosystem. The red fly eats all the blue fly's food. In the space below, draw and illustrate a flow chart that shows what might happen to the frog.

Bonus: How might orange frogs change because of the red fly?

_____

_____

Take It Home!   See *ScienceSaurus*® for more information about organisms.

Quest for the Serpent Eagle

Jane Juniper is a wildlife surveyor. She is deep in the forest of Madagascar, an island off the coast of Africa, observing birds.

What's that sound? Jane hears a loud, screeching bird call that she never expected to hear. It sounds like... But could it be?

Jane tiptoes quietly through the forest, searching the trees for movement. There!

Jane stands perfectly still. The bird has a dark back and a striped chest. It has yellow eyes, and sharp talons. But it's not supposed to exist!

Jane Juniper has studied all about African birds. It takes her just a moment to be sure. But she is still amazed! With her camera she collects evidence of her find.

Jane Juniper, wildlife surveyor, found a bird that was thought to be extinct—a Madagascar Serpent Eagle!

Now You Be the Surveyor

Imagine you're a wildlife surveyor. Survey the forest below. Write the kinds of animals you find and the number of each kind.

SC.5.L.15.1 Describe how, when the environment changes, differences between individuals allow some plants and animals to survive and reproduce while others die or move to new locations. SC.5.N.1.1 ... plan and carry out scientific investigations of various types... SC.5.N.1.4 Identify a control group and explain its importance in an experiment.

Name _____

ESSENTIAL **QUESTION**

How Does Drought Affect Plants?

Materials

5 plastic cups
black marker
125 seeds
potting soil
water
measuring cup

EXPLORE

A drought happens when a place gets much less rainfall than normal. What happens to plants when their environment changes and they do not get the usual amount of water?

Before You Begin—Preview the Steps

(1) Label the cups A through E.

(2) Fill each cup with moist potting soil. Plant 25 seeds in each cup.

(3) Water the cups according to the following schedule:

- Cup A—50 mL of water each day

- Cup B—25 mL of water each day

- Cup C—50 mL of water every other day

- Cup D—50 mL of water once a week

- Cup E—no water

(4) Make a hypothesis about how the seeds in the different cups will grow.

(5) Place the cups on a sunny windowsill. Observe the cups for two weeks.

SC.5.L.17.1 ... Compare how the environment ... ; (interactions between individuals who share ...
source and strategic to survey and reproduce ...) leaves life events in the habitat.
SC.5.N.1.1 ... Raise and carry out scientific investigations of various types, SC.5.N.1.4 Identify a
control group and explain its importance in an experiment.

Set a Purpose

What will you better understand about plants after doing this experiment?

_____

_____

_____

State Your Hypothesis

Write your hypothesis, or testable statement.

_____

_____

_____

Think About the Procedure

What parts of your experiment stay the same for each test group?

_____

_____

_____

Why is it important to establish a control in your experiment?

_____

_____

_____

What part of the experiment did you change?

_____

_____

_____

Name _____

Record Your Data

Record your observations in the table below.

Plant Observations	
Cup A	
Cup B	
Cup C	
Cup D	
Cup E	

Draw Conclusions

Was your hypothesis supported? Why or why not?

_____

_____

What conclusions can you draw from this investigation?

_____

_____

Claims • Evidence • Reasoning

1. What natural conditions did Cup A and Cup E represent? Explain your reasoning.

_____

_____

_____

2. Did the plants in the cups that got the most water do the best? What inference can you claim, based on your results?

_____

_____

_____

3. Suppose you are studying pea plants. You have evidence that half of the individual pea plants are able to survive in mild drought conditions. Why might this data be important?

_____

_____

_____

_____

4. How would you set up an experiment to test the following hypothesis: The amount of fertilizer does not affect how quickly plants grow. Draw and label a picture that shows your setup.

Name _____

Vocabulary Review

Use the terms in the box to complete the sentences.

> environment
> pollution
> ecosystem
> extinction

1. A community of organisms and the environment

   in which they live is called a(n) _____.

2. All of the living and nonliving things that surround you

   make up your _____.

3. The disappearance of an entire kind of living thing is known

   as _____.

4. Harmful substances that get into the air, ground, and water are

   forms of _____.

Science Concepts

Fill in the letter of the choice that best answers the question.

5. Twenty years ago, Mr. Jackson planted four trees in his front yard. The thickness of the bark on each tree is given in the table below.

Tree	Bark thickness (cm)
A	3.5
B	5.2
C	4.1
D	4.5

In Mr. Jackson's back yard, woodpeckers are nesting. Woodpeckers can damage a tree if they drill all the way through the bark. Based on these data, which tree is most likely to not be damaged by the woodpeckers?

(A) Tree A

(B) Tree B

(C) Tree C

(D) Tree D

6. The state bird of Florida is the mockingbird. Mockingbirds eat many types of food, including insects, berries, and seeds. Insects and seeds have hard coverings, but berries are soft.

If the plants that make berries don't grow well one year, which individual mockingbirds are most likely to survive?

(F) those who sing the loudest

(G) those with the strongest beaks

(H) those with the longest tail feathers

(I) those that lay eggs with the most spots

7. When the environment changes, differences between individuals allow some plants and animals to survive while others die or move to new locations. Which of these statements best describes how this happens?

Ⓐ Environmental changes cause variations in animals that lead to adaptations.

Ⓑ All animals are able to survive when the environment changes, which leads to their variations and adaptations.

Ⓒ Animals have variations, and when the environment changes, these variations allow populations to adapt and survive.

Ⓓ Animals have different adaptations that allow them to survive when the environment changes, which leads to variation.

8. Some zebras are taller, and some can run faster. Some have longer hair, and some have longer tails. What is the most important reason for a population to have individual variation?

Ⓕ Variation helps individuals recognize each other.

Ⓖ Variation ensures that every individual will survive.

Ⓗ Variation determines how large a population can be.

Ⓘ Variation ensures that at least some individuals may be able to survive if the environment changes.

9. Environmental changes happen all the time. Some of these changes are easy to spot. For example, the figure below shows a sign that you might see while riding along a road in Florida.

What can you conclude about environmental changes after seeing this sign?

Ⓐ Changes in the environment happen in cycles.

Ⓑ All changes to the environment happen naturally.

Ⓒ This environment will soon be changed by human activity.

Ⓓ Any change made to the environment will lead to extinction.

Name _____

10. Beach mice live on the Gulf coast of Florida's barrier islands. Despite their name, these beach mice are found in inland areas as well as along the beach. However, the beach mice that live inland are usually darker in color than those that live on the sandy beaches along the coast. Which of these statements explains this color difference?

F The mice are not related to each other.

G The mice that live inland are colored by the mud.

H The mice have adapted to living in their specific environment.

I The mice on the sandy beaches have become lighter in the sun.

11. In a science experiment, soil was placed in four different beakers. The following diagram shows the conditions of the soil for each beaker.

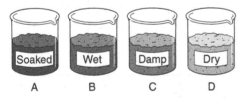

| Soaked | Wet | Damp | Dry |
| A | B | C | D |

Which of the following beakers models drought conditions?

A Beaker A

B Beaker B

C Beaker C

D Beaker D

12. The following picture shows a wetland in Florida and the plants that grow there.

Which of the following conditions do the plants shown have to cope with?

F wet soil

G low rainfall

H drought conditions

I very cold temperatures

Apply Inquiry and Review the Big Idea

Write the answers to these questions.

13. A farmer plants corn every year. One year, the farm experiences a drought and receives some rainfall, but much less than is normal during the growing season. Make a claim about what is likely to happen to the corn plants. Explain your reasoning.

_____

_____

_____

14. Ricardo planted 50 grass seeds in three identical pots of soil. He watered one pot every day, watered one pot every third day, and gave one pot no water. He observed each pot and recorded the number of seeds that had sprouted after 30 days. The following table shows his results.
What conclusion can you draw from the data? How does the data support your conclusion?

Pot	Watered	Number of seeds sprouted
A	every day	36
B	every third day	25
C	not watered	0

_____

_____

_____

_____

Plant and Animal Adaptations

FLORIDA BIG IDEA 17

Interdependence

Alligators hide in the water.

I Wonder Why

Look at the location of the alligator's eyes Look and nostrils. Why are they where they are? *Turn the page to find out.*

521

Here's Why

Living things, including alligators, have characteristics that help them survive in their environment. The location of the alligator's eyes and nostrils allow it to see and breathe while nearly completely submerged.

Essential Questions and Florida Benchmarks

Science Notebook

Before you begin each lesson, write your thoughts about the Essential Question.

SC.5.L.17.1 Compare and contrast adaptations displayed by animals and plants that enable them to survive in different environments such as life cycles variations, animal behaviors and physical characteristics.

ESSENTIAL **QUESTION**

What Is Adaptation?

 Engage Your Brain

Find the answer to the following question in this lesson and record it here.

Watch out! Don't get bit by that... caterpillar? What type of adaptation does this caterpillar have?

_____

_____

_____

 ACTIVE **READING**

Lesson Vocabulary
List the terms. As you learn about each one, make notes in the Interactive Glossary.

_____

_____

_____

Signal Words: Details
This lesson gives details about how living things are suited to where they live. Signal words link main topics to added details. For *example* and *for instance* are often used as signal words. Active readers look for signal words that link a topic to its details.

A Place to Call Home

Where are living things found on Earth?
They can be found deep underground, high
up in the air, and everywhere in between!

ACTIVE **READING** As you read this page, put a
star next to the main idea of each paragraph.

Think about all the different kinds of living things on Earth.
They each live in a different location. The place where a living
thing lives is called its **habitat**. There are many different kinds
of habitats. Some habitats are hot and dry. Other habitats are
frozen. Still other habitats are found deep under
the ocean.

All of a living thing's needs must be met
within its habitat. Because of this, only
certain kinds of living things can live in
certain habitats. For example, an animal
that has gills for breathing under
water cannot live in a dry habitat.
A plant that needs very little water
cannot live in a wet habitat.
As you look at the different
types of habitats shown on
this page and the next, ask
yourself why each plant
or animal is found in a
certain kind of habitat.

mountain

jungle

Where Do I Live?
Write the type of habitat in which these animals are found.

_____ _____ _____ _____

Habitats on Earth

Each type of habitat is home to different plants and animals. Which type of habitat shown here is most similar to a habitat found where you live?

polar

ocean

desert

grassland

Adaptations

Living things have many similarities. They also have many interesting differences.

ACTIVE **READING** As you read this page, underline the definition of *adaptation*.

Deserts are home to many kinds of snakes. This is because snakes have characteristics that help them survive in a desert. For example, snakes have tough, scaly skin that keeps them from drying out.

A characteristic that helps a living thing survive is called an **adaptation**. Suppose an animal is born with a new characteristic. If this characteristic helps the animal survive, the animal is likely to reproduce and pass on the characteristic to its young. As long as the animal's habitat doesn't change, young that have this characteristic are also likely to survive and reproduce. Over time, the adaptation becomes more common in the population. In this way, populations of plants and animals become adapted to their habitats.

These rabbits live in very different habitats. Because of this, they have different adaptations.

An arctic hare lives in a cold habitat. It has thick fur to keep it warm and small ears that keep heat from being lost.

A jackrabbit lives in a hot habitat. Jackrabbits have large ears that help keep their blood cool.

Ostriches, rheas, and emus all live on different continents. Even though they live very far from each other, they look almost the same! Their habitats are very similar, and so they share similar adaptations. These birds are all adapted for running fast. Ostriches are the fastest flightless birds on Earth. They can reach speeds of 72 km/hr (45 mi/hr)!

ostrich

emu

rhea

▶ Vines and trees are both plants, but they are very different from each other. What adaptations can you see in these plants, and how do you think these adaptations help them survive?

_____

_____

_____

_____

_____

_____

Physical Fitness

Whether blending in or standing out, physical adaptations help organisms survive.

Can you see the owl in this picture? The owl is camouflaged to look like bark.

The bright color of this rose attracts pollinators, but the thorns keep plant-eating animals away.

Some adaptations are differences in the bodies of plants and animals. These are called physical adaptations. For example, sharp teeth, webbed feet, and large eyes are physical adaptations.

Some physical adaptations protect living things from being eaten. For example, roses have sharp thorns that help keep their stems from being eaten. Other physical adaptations help to keep an animal hidden. This type of adaptation is called *camouflage* [KAM•uh•flazh]. Green lizards hiding in green grass are camouflaged.

Catching Flies

Bright coloring on an animal is often a warning that an animal is dangerous. Many animals know that paper wasps, like the one shown below, have a painful sting. The black and yellow hoverfly doesn't have a stinger. It is completely harmless. But because it looks like a wasp, animals will think twice before trying to eat it. This adaptation is called *mimicry*.

▶ Draw a line from the chameleon's tongue to the insect it would most likely eat.

paper wasp

hoverfly

house fly

Chameleons have many adaptations that help them catch insects. They have long, sticky tongues that capture an insect in the blink of an eye. They have eyes that move in all directions, helping them see not only food but also possible danger. They also have feet and a tail that wrap around branches, making them excellent climbers. With all of these adaptations, a tasty fly must look like a wasp to avoid being eaten by a chameleon!

Animals that hunt, such as eagles, have adaptations that help them catch food. Eagles have very good eyesight. They also have sharp claws on their feet, which they use to capture their food.

Many plants have adaptations that help spread their seeds. Some seeds can be carried by the wind. Other seeds are inside berries. When the berries are eaten, the seeds are carried to a new location.

On Your Best Behavior

The way living things act is called behavior. Some behaviors are adaptations that help animals survive.

ACTIVE **READING** As you read the paragraph below, circle examples of instinctive behavior and underline examples of learned behavior.

Some things that animals do seem to come naturally. Babies do not have to be taught how to cry. Spiders are not taught how to spin webs. Behaviors that animals know how to do without being taught are called **instincts**. Animals have to learn other types of behaviors. For example, a lion cub is not born knowing how to hunt. It learns to hunt by watching its mother. Raccoons learn to wash food by watching other raccoons.

Many animals have behaviors that help protect them from predators. When an octopus is frightened, it releases ink into the water. If the octopus is being attacked, the animal attacking it will not be able to see, and the octopus can escape.

Some bats are *nocturnal*. This means they are active at night and sleep during the day. This allows bats to hunt insects that are active only at night.

Each year, millions of snow geese migrate south in autumn and north in spring.

DO THE MATH

Interpret Data in a Bar Graph

Ground squirrels hibernate. They must eat a lot during the spring, summer, and fall to store up enough energy to survive hibernation. Study the graph below.

Ground Squirrel Body Mass

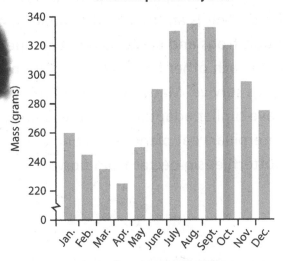

Mass (grams)

340
320
300
280
260
240
220
0

Jan. Feb. Mar. Apr. May June July Aug. Sept. Oct. Nov. Dec.

About how much mass does a ground squirrel have in March?

_____

During which month do ground squirrels start to hibernate? How do you know?

_____

_____

Some animals move to different locations at certain times of the year to find food, reproduce, or escape very cold weather. This instinctive behavior is called *migration*. Many birds, butterflies, and some bats migrate long distances.

Other animals hibernate. *Hibernation* is a long period of inactivity that is like sleeping. But hibernation is not the same as sleeping. When an animal hibernates, its body processes slow down and it stays inactive for months. Can you imagine taking a three-month nap?

The way that animals act toward other animals of the same type is called *social behavior.* Honeybees have very complex social behavior. They communicate using movements called the "waggle dance." A bee that finds food will return to the hive and do a waggle dance. The pattern of the dance gives other bees a lot of information! The dance communicates which direction to go, how far away the food is, how much food there is, and even what kind of food it is!

The Circle of Life

All living things grow and develop. The way that living things develop can be an adaptation.

ACTIVE **READING** Circle two different examples of organisms whose life cycles keep adults and young from competing for food.

Living things go through stages of growth and development called a *life cycle*. A living thing's life cycle is related to its habitat. Because of this, differences in life cycles are a type of adaptation.

Most frogs are adapted to live near water. A frog's life cycle starts when its eggs are laid in water. When the eggs hatch, tadpoles emerge. Tadpoles live in water until they grow legs and lungs. At this point, they are ready to live on land. In places where water tends to dry up quickly, tadpoles develop more quickly. This difference, or variation, in frog life cycles helps tadpoles survive.

Tadpoles and adult frogs live in different places, and they eat different foods. This is another kind of adaptation. Adult frogs and tadpoles don't compete with each other for food. This helps more frogs survive. Many other living things have similar adaptations. For example, caterpillars eat plant leaves and adult butterflies sip nectar from flowers.

salmon eggs

Adult salmon live in the ocean, which is a dangerous place for young salmon. Adults migrate from the ocean to shallow rivers to lay eggs. More young salmon are able to survive in rivers.

A female impala has one or two calves and then spends months feeding and protecting them. A female salmon lays thousands of eggs and then returns to the ocean. What are some advantages of each type of life cycle?

_____

_____

_____

_____

_____

_____

_____

_____

_____

Some animals can adjust their life cycle to changes in their habitat. In a very dry year, a pregnant impala can wait up to a month, until rain falls, to give birth. This life cycle variation helps make sure there is enough food and water for the young impalas to survive.

luna moth caterpillar

adult luna moth

It does not rain very often in the desert. When it does rain, the seeds of desert wildflowers, such as those shown below, immediately begin to grow. The plants bloom, make new seeds, and complete their whole life cycle within a few weeks! Explain how the life cycle of desert wildflowers helps them survive in the desert.

_____

_____

_____

_____

Sum It Up »

**The outline below is a summary of the lesson.
Complete the outline.**

I. Habitats: The place where a living thing lives is called its habitat. Earth has many different types of habitats.

    A. Example: _____

    B. Example: _____

    C. Example: _____

    D. Example: _____

II. Adaptations: A characteristic that helps a living thing survive is called an adaptation. Kinds of adaptations include:

    A. Physical Adaptations

        1. Example: _____

        _____

        2. Example: _____

        _____

    B. Behavioral Adaptations

        1. Example: _____

        _____

        2. Example: _____

        _____

    C. Life Cycle Adaptations

        1. Example: _____

        _____

        2. Example: _____

        _____

Brain Check

Name _____

Vocabulary Review

1 Use the words in the box to complete each sentence.

1. An adaptation that helps a living thing hide in its environment is called. _____.

2. The place where an animal lives is its _____.

3. An animal that is active at night is described as being _____.

4. All of the stages a living thing goes through as it develops are called its _____.

5. An example of _____ is birds flying south for the winter.

6. An _____ is any characteristic that helps an animal survive.

7. _____ is a behavior that causes an animal to be inactive for a long period of time.

8. A behavior that an animal doesn't learn is an _____.

adaptation	camouflage	habitat	hibernation
instinct	life cycle	migration	nocturnal

Apply Concepts

2 Draw a picture of three habitats described in this lesson. Underneath each drawing, label the habitat.

_____   _____   _____

3 Circle the camouflaged animal.

4 In winter, ground squirrels retreat into burrows and do not come out until spring. Circle the term that bests describes this behavior.

Communication   *Hibernation*
Migration   *Nocturnal hunting*

5 A narrow-mouthed frog's eggs do not hatch into tadpoles. Instead, they hatch directly into tiny frogs. What type of habitat would you expect the narrow-mouthed frog to live in? Explain your answer.

_____

_____

_____

Take It Home! See *ScienceSaurus®* for more information about animals.

SC.5.L.17.1 Compare and contrast adaptations displayed by animals and plants that enable them to survive in different environments such as life cycles variations, animal behaviors and physical characteristics. SC.5.N.1.6 Recognize and explain the difference between personal opinion/interpretation and verified observation. SC.5.N.2.1 ... explanation must always be linked with evidence.

INQUIRY LESSON 2

Name _____

Why Do Bird Beaks Differ?

EXPLORE

Birds have adapted to eat different kinds of food. Because of this, there are many different kinds of beaks. In this activity, you'll investigate which beaks work best for each kind of food.

Before You Begin—Preview the Steps

① Look at the tools you will use to model beaks. Discuss how you use each tool and how each tool is different.

② Place one of your food choices next to the beak that you think will work best to "eat" the food. CAUTION: Do not eat any of the foods in this investigation.

③ Try to "eat" each type of food using each of the different tools.

④ Record your observations.

Materials

chopsticks
dropper
large pliers
needle-nose pliers
slotted spoon
forceps
shredded lettuce in
  a bowl of water
juice in a graduated
  cylinder
rice in plastic foam
gummy worms in
  sand
sunflower seeds
walnuts

Set a Purpose

Why do you think different birds have beaks with different shapes?

_____

_____

_____

Write a statement summarizing what you plan to investigate.

_____

_____

_____

_____

Think About the Procedure

What will you be modeling in this investigation?

_____

_____

_____

_____

Name _____

Record Your Data

In the space below, make a table in which you record your observations.

Draw Conclusions

Did some beaks work for more than one kind of food? What might this suggest about the bird's ability to survive?

_____

_____

_____

Did one kind of beak work for eating all of the different foods?

_____

_____

Claims • Evidence • Reasoning

1. Based on your model, which bird's beak would be best for eating flower nectar? Which beaks would be best for picking insects out of wood and worms out of sand?

_____

_____

_____

_____

2. A toucan is a bird that eats very large, tough tropical fruit. Write a claim about how you expect a toucan's beak to look. Explain your reasoning.

_____

_____

3. Look at the bird beaks below. Based on your model, make a claim about which tool in the investigation was most similar to each of the beaks. Explain your reasoning.

hummingbird

finch

macaw

_____   _____   _____

shorebird

woodpecker

duck

_____   _____   _____

4. Think of other questions you would like to ask about how adaptations relate to the food an animal eats.

_____

_____

SC.5.L.17.1 Compare and contrast adaptations displayed by animals and plants that enable them to survive in different environments such as life cycles variations, animal behaviors and physical characteristics.

LESSON **3**

ESSENTIAL **QUESTION**

What Are Some Adaptations to Life on Land?

 Engage Your Brain

Find the answer to the following question in this lesson and record it here.

Is that a pine cone with eyes? No, it's a pangolin! Pangolins have strong claws for climbing and digging, and their strong tail wraps around objects. Where might you find a pangolin?

_____

_____

_____

 ACTIVE **READING**

Lesson Vocabulary
List the terms. As you learn about each one, make notes in the Interactive Glossary.

_____

_____

_____

Visual Aids
This lesson has many photographs of animals and plants that live on land. Active readers pause their reading to review the photographs and captions and decide how the information in them adds to what is provided in the running text.

Take a Walk
in the Woods

Forests are habitats filled with trees. Many living things call forest habitats their home.

ACTIVE **READING** As you read this page, circle the types of organisms found in a forest.

Some of the largest forests in the United States are temperate forests. Temperate forests have warm summers and cold winters. Trees that grow in a temperate forest have wide leaves that absorb a lot of sunlight. Many kinds of plants grow beneath the trees. These plants are adapted to live with less light than plants that are not shaded. Vines, such as ivy, climb the trees to reach light.

Many animals live in a forest. Some of them have adaptations that help them climb or live in trees. Birds are common in forests. Many forest birds have feet that help them perch on branches. Insects are also common in forests. Many of them have special mouth parts that let them bore into wood. These insects can live under a tree's bark. Woodpeckers are adapted to eat insects that burrow into wood.

Describe the Temperate Forest	Describe Adaptations for Living Here

Woodpeckers eat insects that live in trees. They use their hard, pointy beak to drill holes in the tree.

Young deer, called fawns, have spots on their fur. When a fawn is curled up on the forest floor, the spots help camouflage it.

Most trees in temperate forests are *deciduous*. Their leaves change color as nights become longer in the fall. They lose their leaves before winter begins to help prevent water loss in the cold, dry air. Before the leaves fall, deciduous trees pull important nutrients from the leaves into the trunk and stems. When the weather becomes warmer in spring, the trees sprout new leaves.

Rain, Rain Every Day

Deep in the jungles live amazing plants and animals that can't be found anywhere else on Earth.

ACTIVE **READING** As you read this page and the next, underline plant adaptations and circle animal adaptations.

Tropical rain forests, often called jungles, are warm and rainy all year. As a result, many different kinds of plants live there. The tallest trees reach out over the top of the forest to get sunlight. Another layer of trees spreads below those giants. With so many trees, not much light reaches the forest floor. A third layer of plants live close to the ground. These are adapted to low light. Some plants, called *epiphytes* [EP•ih•fyts], have adapted to reach light by living in the trees.

Daily rain washes dirt into rivers. As a result, the soil is very thin in a tropical forest. Because their roots cannot grow very deep, large trees in tropical forests have special adaptations that help keep them from falling over. Some trees have roots that grow down from the branches to prop the tree up. Other trees have roots that make walls that spread out around the tree.

Buttress roots form walls at the base of trees. This helps keep the tree from falling over in shallow soil.

Describe the Tropical Forest	Describe Adaptations for Living Here

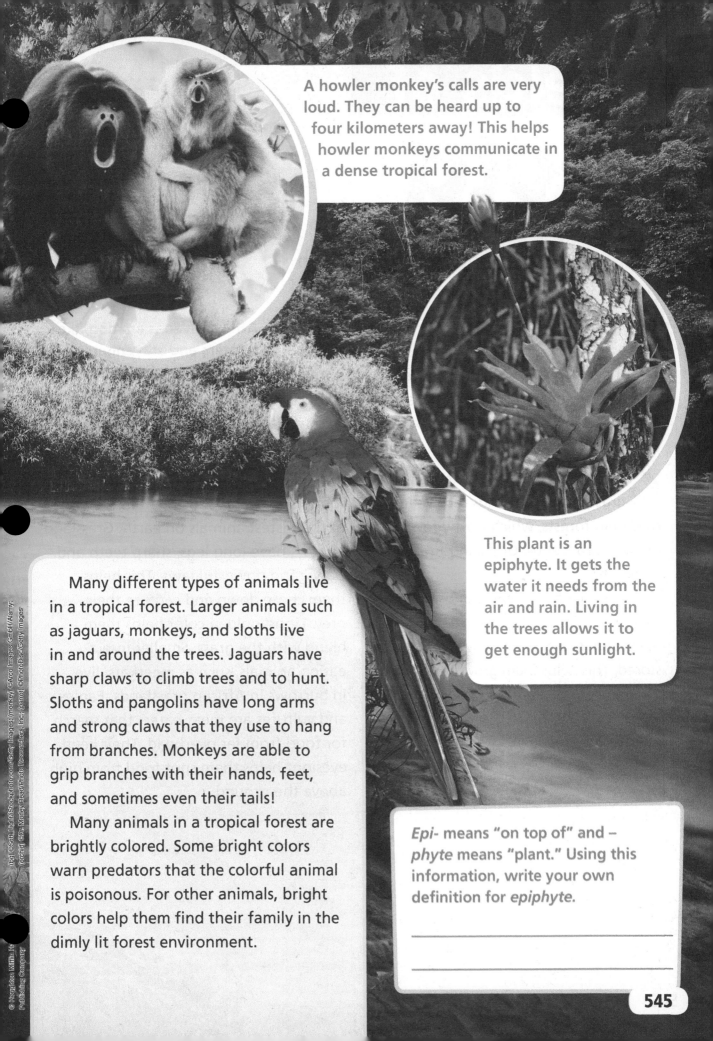

A howler monkey's calls are very loud. They can be heard up to four kilometers away! This helps howler monkeys communicate in a dense tropical forest.

This plant is an epiphyte. It gets the water it needs from the air and rain. Living in the trees allows it to get enough sunlight.

Many different types of animals live in a tropical forest. Larger animals such as jaguars, monkeys, and sloths live in and around the trees. Jaguars have sharp claws to climb trees and to hunt. Sloths and pangolins have long arms and strong claws that they use to hang from branches. Monkeys are able to grip branches with their hands, feet, and sometimes even their tails!

Many animals in a tropical forest are brightly colored. Some bright colors warn predators that the colorful animal is poisonous. For other animals, bright colors help them find their family in the dimly lit forest environment.

Epi- means "on top of" and –*phyte* means "plant." Using this information, write your own definition for *epiphyte*.

_____

_____

Fields of Gold

In some habitats, there is not enough rain for many trees to grow. What grows in place of trees?

ACTIVE READING As you read this page and the next, underline the types of animals that eat plants. Circle the types of animals that eat meat.

African hyenas are dog-like hunters and scavengers. They have powerful, bone-crushing jaws and live in packs with complex social behavior.

Grasses are the main plant life in a **grassland**. Grasslands receive less rain than forests, which is why few trees grow in grasslands. Grassland fires are common.

The long, narrow leaves of grasses keep them from losing very much water. Grasses have large root systems in which energy is stored. This helps them grow back quickly after a fire or after they've been eaten. Plant eaters in African grasslands, shown here, include elephants, zebras, giraffes, and gazelles. They have flat teeth that help them chew grass.

Many grassland animals are very fast runners. Gazelles and cheetahs are two of the fastest animals on earth. Grassland hunters have long legs, sharp teeth and claws, and powerful jaws. This helps them chase down and capture their prey. Lions' golden color helps them blend with the grass. Smaller insect-eating animals, such as meerkats, live in burrows in African grasslands. Eagles and vultures are meat eaters that search for food from far overhead. Their keen eyesight helps them spot food from high above the ground.

Describe the Grasslands	Describe Adaptations for Living Here

In North America, grasslands are also known as prairies. Bison, shown below, were once very common on the prairies. Like elephants and zebras, bison have flat teeth that help them chew grass. Bison also have more than one stomach. This helps them digest the tough fibers in grass.

Coyotes also live in prairies. They hunt small animals such as rabbits and prairie dogs. These small animals have strong front paws that help them dig. Since there are few hiding places in grasslands, living underground in burrows helps protect these animals from grassland hunters.

Thorny trees called acacias are found in African grasslands. Giraffes eat the leaves of these trees. Their mouths are tough, so the thorns don't bother them. A giraffe's long neck helps it reach leaves high up in a tree.

Some Like It Dry

Some habitats get almost no rain all year. Few plants and animals can live in such dry places.

ACTIVE READING As you read this page, circle signal words that alert you to details about the main idea.

Sandy. Rocky. Dusty. DRY! These words describe a **desert**, which is a place that receives very little rain. Lack of water makes a desert a hard place to survive. Some deserts are very cold. Other deserts are the hottest places on Earth. Plants and animals must have special adaptations to live in deserts.

Many desert plants, such as these Arizona cactuses, have thick bodies that store a lot of water. Their stems and leaves have a tough, waxy coating. They often have very small leaves. This helps keep water from escaping into the dry air.

Desert animals also have adaptations that help them conserve water. For example, many animals in hot deserts are nocturnal. They sleep during the heat of the day and only come out at night, when the desert is much cooler.

Describe the Desert	Describe Adaptations for Living Here

In the North African and Middle Eastern deserts, camels are common animals. Camels have wide feet for walking on sand. They are able to drink large amounts of water and go a long time without drinking. Camels store all of their fat in their humps. This helps their bodies cool more easily. A camel's long lashes protect its eyes from blowing sand. A camel can also close its nostrils during a sandstorm to keep sand out of its lungs.

This American sidewinder rattlesnake is adapted to move over the smooth desert sand. It takes sideways "steps" with its body, so that it doesn't slip in the sand.

DO THE MATH

Make a Bar Graph

Deserts that are very hot during the day often cool down quickly after sunset. This happens because there is no cloud cover to trap the heat. In the Sahara, in Africa, daytime temperatures may reach as high as 55°C (131°F). The temperature may drop to 10°C (50°F) at night. Plot this information on a bar graph below.

Some Like It Cold

A tropical forest isn't the only place where trees are green all year round. Some trees are tough enough to stay green even when they're covered with ice!

ACTIVE READING As you read this page, find and underline the meanings of *conifer* and *taiga*.

Pines, firs, and spruces are evergreen trees—they stay green all year long. They live in the **taiga** [TY•guh], a far northern habitat with very cold winters and short, warm summers. Trees called conifers are common in the taiga. *Conifers* are evergreen trees that grow seeds inside of cones.

Conifers are well adapted to the taiga. They have pointed tops and flexible branches. This helps them shed snow and allows them to bend without breaking when they're weighed down with ice. They are also dark green in color. This helps them absorb more light from the sun. In addition, the cones that contain seeds are hard. This helps protect the seeds inside from harsh weather and hungry animals.

lynx

Describe the Taiga	Describe Adaptations for Living Here

Most conifers have needle-like leaves.

Animals that live in the taiga have many cold-weather adaptations. Animals such as wolverines and lynxes have thick fur coats. The color of their fur helps camouflage them among the trees.

During the summer, many birds live in the taiga. These birds feed on berries and insects that are abundant during the summer months. Most of these birds migrate south in autumn. This helps the birds avoid the harsh winter months when few berries and insects can be found. The birds that stay in the taiga during the winter have thick layers of feathers. These feathers insulate the birds from the cold.

A moose grows a thicker coat of fur for the long winter.

This crossbill's beak is adapted to open pine cones. The bird can then eat the seeds hidden inside the cones.

Life on Ice

Some habitats are winter wonderlands all year long!

ACTIVE READING Look at the photos and read the captions on this page and the next page. Place a star next to the animal that changes color.

This arctic willow plant has very fuzzy leaves. The fuzz stops snow from collecting on the leaves.

Habitats that are near the North Pole and South Pole are called **polar** habitats. In some areas, called the *tundra,* snow on the surface of the ground melts during the summer. The ground below stays frozen, but the thin layer of soil on top is just enough to allow plants to grow. These plants must grow and reproduce before the ground freezes again in late summer. The arctic willow, shown above, is one example of this kind of plant. It is a small, woody plant that is dormant all winter. When summer arrives it sprouts furry leaves , grows flowers, and makes seeds all in a few short months.

In places closest to the poles, the ground is always fozen. No plants can survive here. Plantlike organisms called *lichens* [LY•kuhns] live on the rocks. Many animals, including reindeer, eat lichens in polar habitats.

Describe Polar Habitats	Describe Adaptations for Living Here

Polar habitats that are covered with ice year-round are home to many animals. Penguins, like the emperor penguins shown here, live near the South Pole. They are excellent swimmers and dive for fish in the icy ocean. These amazing hunters have thick layers of fat and a layer of water-proof feathers.

Polar bears live near the North Pole. They hunt seals and are excellent swimmers. Both polar bears and seals can close their nostrils. This keeps water from entering their noses when they swim.

A willow ptarmigan has white feathers in winter. This camouflages the bird in the snow. The feathers on its legs and feet help to keep it warm.

In the summer, ptarmigans shed their white feathers and grow brown feathers. This camouflages them against the brown soil and tundra plants.

Sum It Up »

Read the summary statements below. Each one is incorrect. Change the part of the summary in blue to make it correct.

(1) Most of the trees in a temperate forest stay green in winter.

(2) Many animals in a tropical forest are very loud so that they can hide from predators.

(3) A habitat dominated by grass is called a taiga.

(4) Desert plants have waxy stems and tiny leaves so that they can use more water.

(5) Many birds in the taiga become nocturnal before the winter comes.

(6) Animals that live in polar habitats often have black fur for camouflage.

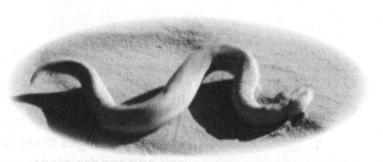

554

©Photoshot Holdings Ltd /Alamy

© Houghton Mifflin Ha[...] Publishing Company

Brain Check

Name _____

Vocabulary Review

1 Draw lines to match the words in the column on the left to the correct picture on the right.

1. polar

2. conifer

3. deciduous

4. desert

5. epiphyte

6. grassland

7. taiga

A

B

C

D

E

F

G

Apply Concepts

2 Beside the picture of each living thing, write the name of the habitat where it would be found and two adaptations it has that help it survive in that habitat.

Habitat: _____

Adaptations: _____

_____

Habitat: _____

Adaptations: _____

_____

Habitat: _____

Adaptations: _____

_____

Habitat: _____

Adaptations: _____

_____

3 How is a camel adapted for life in the desert?

_____

_____

_____

_____

4 Write the adaptation from the list next to the animal that it belongs with.

_____   _____   _____

_____   _____   _____

furry leaves

strong beak

loud call

camouflage

waxy leaves

buttress roots

Take It Home ! Research an animal that lives in a habitat you learned about in this lesson. Draw the animal in its habitat. Label your drawing with at least three adaptations the animal has for surviving in its habitat.

556

SC.5.L.17.1 Compare and contrast adaptations displayed by animals and plants that enable them to survive in different environments such as life cycles variations, animal behaviors and physical characteristics.

PEOPLE **IN SCIENCE**

Meet the Environment Detectives

Erika Zavaleta

Erika Zavaleta is an ecologist in California. She studies the links between the environment and people. Cities grow and climates change. These changes make it hard for some plants and animals to survive. Part of Erika Zavaleta's job is figuring out good ways for people, plants, and animals to live in harmony.

Recently, Erika Zavaleta has studied oak trees. Fires and other disasters can kill a whole forest of these trees. She is studying the best ways to help new trees grow after such a disaster.

Peter & Rosemary Grant

Peter and Rosemary Grant study animal adaptation. On the Galápagos Islands off the coast of South America, they study how birds called finches change over time. They are most interested in changes in the birds' beaks. The Grants have found that beak shape and size change when the environment changes.

During severe droughts many birds die of starvation. When the only seeds remaining on the ground are large, hard seeds, only the birds with the biggest beaks can crack them. They survive and the small-beaked birds die. The next year, the big-beaked birds produce big-beaked young like themselves.

557

Now You Look For Clues

Answer the questions below about the scientists you just read about.

What kind of problems in the environment does Erika Zavaleta study?

_____
_____
_____
_____

What measurements do you think the Grants made as part of their studies?

_____
_____
_____
_____
_____

What have these scientists learned about plant and animal adaptation?

_____
_____
_____
_____
_____

SC.5.L.17.1 Compare and contrast adaptations displayed by animals and plants that enable them to survive in different environments such as life cycles variations, animal behaviors and physical characteristics.

LESSON **4**

ESSENTIAL **QUESTION**

What Are Some Adaptations to Life in Water?

Engage Your Brain

Find the answer to the following question in this lesson and record it here.

Can you spot the sea horse? Pygmy sea horses are adapted to blend with their brightly colored habitat. Where would you find a pygmy sea horse like this one?

_____

_____

_____

📖 ACTIVE READING

Lesson Vocabulary
List the terms. As you learn about each one, make notes in the Interactive Glossary.

_____

_____

Problem-Solution
You can think of differences in habitats as problems, or challenges. You can think of adaptations as solutions to these problems. Active readers keep track of problems and solutions as they read. This helps them stay focused on the way information is organized.

Life in Lakes and Ponds

There are many kinds of water habitats. Some are salty and some are not. Water found on Earth that is not salty is called *fresh water*, but ocean water is just as "fresh."

ACTIVE READING As you read the text below, circle the descriptions of the three zones of a lake.

Ponds and lakes are examples of freshwater habitats. Lakes and ponds are wide bodies of water that do not flow very much. These habitats are divided into zones. The zone close to the shore has many living things in it. Many kinds of water plants grow near the shore. Their roots grow in the soil at the bottom, but the water is shallow enough that their leaves get plenty of sunlight. Other plants, such as water lilies and water hyacinth, float near the shore. Many animals, including ducks, snails, and fish, eat water plants.

Further away from the shore is the open-water zone. Floating plants and plantlike organisms called algae can grow here. But the water is usually too deep for non-floating plants to reach light. The deep part of a lake or pond, where light does not reach, is called the deep-water zone. No plants can grow here. Catfish, worms, and bacteria are found in the deep-water zone. They feed on dead plants and animals that fall down from above.

> ▶ What are two meanings for the word "fresh"?
>
> _____
>
> _____

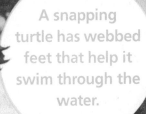

A snapping turtle has webbed feet that help it swim through the water.

Water lilies have air-filled pockets in their leaves. This helps them float on the surface of the water.

Catfish spend much of their time in the dark near the bottom of a pond or lake. Their whiskers are adapted to sense chemicals, which helps catfish find food in the dark.

▶ **Which living thing shown on this page has an adaptation that helps it find food in the dark?**

_____

Go with the Flow

Unlike lakes and ponds, the water in rivers and streams is always on the move. How do living things keep from being washed away?

ACTIVE READING As you read this page, put brackets [ ] around the sentences that describe a challenge for living things in rivers and streams. Underline the sentences that describe an adaptation that living things have for life in rivers and streams.

The kind of living things found in a river or stream depends on how fast the water is moving. The faster the water moves, the harder it is for living things to make a home. Because of this, fast-moving streams are often clear. Very few plants and animals live there.

In places where the water slows down, more living things will be found. Many plants can grow near the banks of rivers and streams. Tiny plants called mosses make a fuzzy green carpet on rocks in and around rivers and streams. Mosses have hair-like structures that cling to rocks. This keeps them in place. Insects also live in flowing water. They can often be found floating on the surface, clinging to plants, or living under rocks in shallow water.

Of course, many fish are also found in rivers and streams. Fish must constantly swim upstream so that they are not carried away by the current.

▶ If a filter in a fish tank creates a stream of flowing water near the edge of the tank, what might happen?

_____

_____

_____

Why aren't any plants growing in this stream?

_____

_____

_____

River otters have webbed feet for swimming and streamlined bodies that glide easily through water.

Many stream-dwelling fish and tadpoles have suction disks. These disks can hold on to rocks to help keep the animal from being washed away.

Plantlike living things called green algae attach firmly to rocks. This helps keep the algae from being washed away. Algae also have very flexible bodies. This allows them to bend with the flowing water instead of being broken.

Soggy Bogs

What do a bog beast and a swamp creature have in common? These imaginary creatures are adapted to live in muddy, wet habitats.

ACTIVE **READING** Underline the phrases that explain why wetlands are important habitats.

A **wetland** is an area of land covered by a shallow layer of water for most of the year. Bogs, swamps, and marshes are three types of wetlands. Bogs tend to be covered in a layer of thick mud. Swamps, like the one shown here, are forested wetlands. The trees often have roots both above and below the water. *Marshes* are wetlands without trees. Grasses and reeds are common marsh plants. Wetland plants have special tissues that carry air from the plant's leaves to its roots. Marshes on ocean coasts are covered with salt water. Plants here also have adaptations to get rid of excess salt.

Wetlands are very important habitats. Many kinds of birds make their nests in wetlands. Migrating water birds use shore wetlands as rest areas on their journeys to spend winter in warmer habitats. Wetlands are also home to many different kinds of plants and animals, such as carnivorous plants, insects, fish, snakes, alligators, frogs, and even giant water rodents!

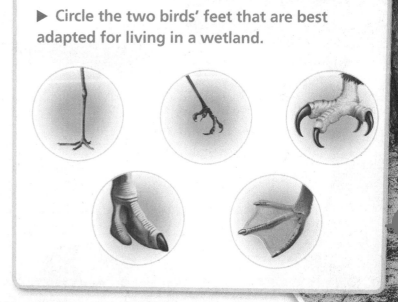

▶ Circle the two birds' feet that are best adapted for living in a wetland.

Herons have very long legs. These legs blend in with wetland reeds, so fish don't notice herons hunting from above.

Pitcher plants grow in many bogs. Bogs tend to lack certain nutrients in the soil. Pitcher plants get these nutrients by trapping and digesting insects.

Alligators live in American wetlands. Their eyes and nostrils are raised to enable them to hide in shallow water while hunting.

Between a Rock and a Hard Wave

One of the harshest habitats on Earth is found on the edge of the ocean along coastlines.

ACTIVE READING As you read this page, underline challenges faced by living things in the intertidal zone. Circle adaptations for living in the intertidal zone.

The place where the ocean meets the coast is called the **intertidal zone**. Every day the tide comes in and covers the intertidal zone in salt water. Then the tide goes out and the intertidal zone is exposed to air and bright sunlight. Between high tide and low tide, the intertidal zone is constantly bashed by waves. Living things in the intertidal zone have adaptations that protect their bodies from being crushed, washed away, or dried out. Seaweed, sea stars and sea urchins, barnacles, clams and oysters, tube worms, and anemones [uh•NEM•uh•neez] call the intertidal zone home.

▶ Put an *H* next to what the sea anemone and clam look like during high tide. Put an *L* next to what they look like during low tide.

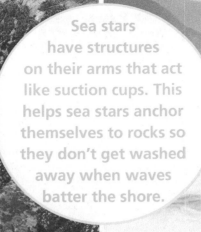

Sea stars have structures on their arms that act like suction cups. This helps sea stars anchor themselves to rocks so they don't get washed away when waves batter the shore.

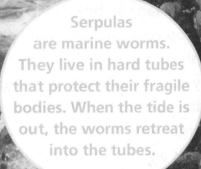

Serpulas are marine worms. They live in hard tubes that protect their fragile bodies. When the tide is out, the worms retreat into the tubes.

Air pocket

Seaweeds have strong, flexible bodies that can endure constant waves. They attach to rocks to keep from being washed away. Many have air pockets that help the tops of the seaweed float and stay in the sunlight when the tide is in.

Out to Sea

The ocean is the largest habitat on Earth! Life can be found all the way from its edges down to its deepest depths.

ACTIVE READING Read the text below and circle the names of the two major zones of the ocean.

Like lakes, the ocean can be divided into zones. Light reaches the top zone, known as the photic [FOH•tik] zone. Close to shore, corals and seaweeds live. Colorful fish and pygmy sea horses blend with brightly colored coral reefs. In the open ocean, floating seaweed and tiny plantlike organisms use the sun to make food. The photic zone is also full of animal life, including jellyfish, squid, fish and sharks, dolphins, and whales.

Underneath the sunlit zone is the part of the ocean where light does not reach. This part is called the aphotic [ay•FOH•tik] zone. It is very dark and very cold. Some animals move back and forth between the photic and aphotic zones.

The ocean floor is covered with mountains, valleys, and canyons, much like on land. There are undersea volcanoes and hot springs called vents. Hot water full of minerals shoots out of these deep-sea vents. Many living things depend on the heat and use the minerals to make food. Animals living here are very different from other ocean animals. Their bodies are adapted to living under extreme water pressure. Most cannot survive closer to the surface.

Coral reefs are found near many coasts. They are filled with a great diversity of sea life.

▶ Match each zone with its description.

APHOTIC ZONE	Seaweeds and corals live here.
DEEP OCEAN FLOOR	Mid-ocean level where no light reaches.
PHOTIC ZONE	Animals that glow are found here.

Large floating mats of a seaweed called sargassum provide a safe habitat for many animals, including young sea turtles.

dolphins

Jellyfish float in the open ocean, catching fish that accidentally wander into their tentacles.

shark

Deep-sea fish live in total darkness. Some have adaptations that allow them to produce light. They use this light to lure food or find mates.

Some marine tube worms live near the hot vents at the bottom of the ocean. They filter tiny organisms out of the water for food.

Oceans in Peril

Most living things are very well adapted to their habitats. When their habitats change, living things can be put in danger.

ACTIVE READING As you read this page, find and underline three problems sea life faces.

Today, many changes are taking place in ocean habitats. Large areas of coral reef are losing their color, a process called *coral bleaching*. Many bleached patches are dying. Possible reasons for coral bleaching include rising water temperatures and ocean pollution.

People take too many fish out of the sea. Animals that depend on these fish for food do not have enough to eat. The fish that are left cannot reproduce fast enough to rebuild their population. It is possible that the fish we and many other animals depend on for food could become extinct.

Some countries dump their garbage in the ocean. This harms sea life. Chemicals from the trash are harmful. Living things in the ocean easily get caught in trash, such as the plastic rings used to package drink cans. Recently, a giant patch of garbage has been discovered floating in the middle of the ocean. Ocean currents have brought garbage from many countries to one area, and now the Great Pacific Garbage Patch is about twice the size of the state of Texas!

▶ Draw an X where coral bleaching has occurred in the picture.

⊞ DO THE **MATH**

Understand Fractions

About 75 percent of Earth's surface is covered by oceans. Change this percentage into a fraction. Then complete the circle graph and label the amount of Earth's surface covered by land and the amount covered by water.

Sum It Up »

Read the summary statements. Then match each statement with the correct image.

1 Many animals in wetlands have adaptations that allow them to blend with grasses while they hunt for food.

_____

A

2 Seaweed such as sargassum lives near the surface of the ocean.

_____

B

3 Because rivers and streams flow, plants that live in them must have adaptations that keep them from floating away.

_____

C

4 Many animals living in lakes and ponds have webbed feet to help them swim.

_____

D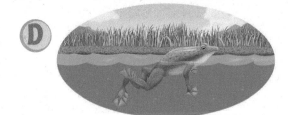

5 In intertidal areas, many animals have protective shells or casings that they retreat into during low tide.

_____

E

Name _____

Vocabulary Review

1 Use words from the lesson to complete each sentence.

1. The ocean has salt water, but rivers and streams have __ __ __ __ __ water.

2. Animals that live at the edge of the ocean are adapted to life in the
   __ __ __ __ __ __ __ __ __ __ __ zone.

3. A swamp and a bog are both examples of a __ __ __ __ __ __ __.

4. An area of land with many grasses and reeds that is covered by water is
   known as a __ __ __ __ __.

5. About 75% of Earth's surface is covered by __ __ __ __ __ __.

6. A reef may lose its color due to __ __ __ __ __ bleaching.

7. The many rows of sharp, jagged teeth on some sharks is an example
   of an __ __ __ __ __ __ __ __ __ __ __ for catching food.

Figure out how to place the answers in the boxes below so that the letters
in the red boxes answer the riddle.

Riddle: Who am I? You may have seen my latest blockbuster movie. It's
playing now in underwater theaters. I am a __ __ __   __ __ __ __.

Apply Concepts

2 What adaptations would a plant living in a river need that a plant living in a pond would not need?

_____

_____

_____

3 Circle the animal that is best adapted to live in an intertidal zone.

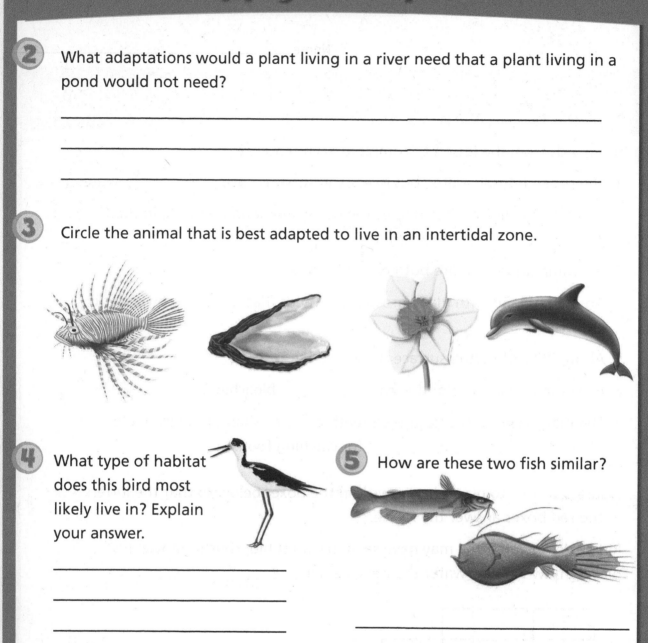

4 What type of habitat does this bird most likely live in? Explain your answer.

_____

_____

_____

_____

5 How are these two fish similar?

_____

_____

 **Take It Home!**
Walk with your family at a local body of water. Observe living things in the water and list the living things that you see. Talk with your family about how these living things are adapted to their habitat.

SC.5.N.1.1 Define a problem, use appropriate reference materials to support scientific understanding, plan and carry out scientific investigations of various types such as: systematic observations, experiments requiring the identification of variables, collecting and organizing data, interpreting data in charts, tables, and graphics, analyze information, make predictions, and defend conclusions.

S.T.E.M.

ENGINEERING & TECHNOLOGY

How It Works:

Tracking Wildlife

Tracking animals helps scientists learn the animals' patterns of movement. Researchers fit animals with a variety of devices that send back information. Mammals often wear tracking collars. Toads can wear tracking belts. Fish can swallow tiny devices that work inside their bodies!

This lion is fitted with a GPS collar. Sometimes collars like these also have cameras that send back video.

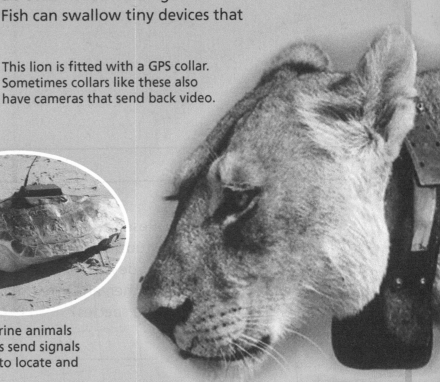

Tracking devices are attached to marine animals with glue or suction cups. The collars send signals to GPS satellites, enabling scientists to locate and track the collars over time.

TROUBLESHOOTING

Describe how an animal's body, its movement, and its environment determine the design of a tracking device.

_____

_____

_____

S.T.E.M. continued

Animal tracking devices help scientists understand the behaviors of animals within their natural habitats.

Choose an animal. Draw a diagram of how a tracking device might be attached to the animal. Explain how the device is attached and what information it captures.

_____

_____

Research an animal species that has been studied using a tracking device. Which kind of device was used? What kind of data did it gather, and what did scientists learn about the species?

_____

_____

_____

_____

_____

Make a Process:
Mimicking an Adaptation

There's a branch of engineering that's based on imitating adaptations. It's called biomimicry.

If you've ever used a hook-and-loop fastener, you've seen an example of biomimicry. Hook-and-loop fasteners were invented by an engineer who examined seeds that stuck to his dog's fur. He discovered that the "stickiness" of the pod was produced by tiny hooks that became entangled with the hair.

Based upon his observations, he created a hook-and-loop fastening system. One half of the system is a patch with hooks. The other half is a patch with tiny loops that get snagged on the hooks.

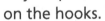

DESIGN PROCESS STEPS

1 Find a Problem
2 Plan & Build
3 Test & Improve
4 Redesign
5 Communicate

What to Do:

1 Learn more about biomimicry. In the chart, list three examples of products that are based upon natural adaptations.

Natural Adaptation	Product

2 For each example, use two pages in your Science Notebook. On the left side page, describe the plant or animal adaptation. On the right side page, describe the product based on that adaptation.

3 Find out more about other plant and animal adaptations. From what you learn, brainstorm new products that are based on biomimicry.

4 For each product you propose, use the two-page layout that you followed in Step 2.

5 Discuss your ideas with classmates. Use their feedback to choose and improve one of your designs. Identify the natural adaptation on which you based your design.

6 Draw your final design below.

7 Keep a record of your work in your Science Notebook.

Name _____

Vocabulary Review

Use the terms in the box to complete the sentences.

desert
adaptations
habitats

1. An area that gets very little precipitation is

   classified as a _____.

2. Animals that have white fur often live in cold,

   snowy _____.

3. An organism's _____ help it survive in its
   environment.

Science Concepts

Fill in the letter of the choice that best answers the question.

4. Catfish can live in rivers and lakes where
   the water is not very clear. The following
   picture shows a catfish.

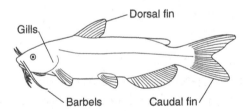

   Dorsal fin
   Gills
   Barbels   Caudal fin

   What do the barbels most likely help the
   catfish do in muddy water?

   (A) grab objects   (C) dig holes

   (B) sense objects   (D) breathe better

5. Rivers and streams are sometimes fast
   moving. What adaptations would help
   plants live in swiftly moving water?

   (F) stiff stems and broad leaves

   (G) shallow roots and long stems

   (H) thin leaves and large flowers

   (I) flexible stems and the ability to cling
   to rocks

6. The picture shows an alligator that lives
   in the Florida Everglades.

   What advantage does this swimming
   position give the alligator?

   (A) It keeps its skin from drying out.

   (B) It keeps it away from muddy water.

   (C) It keeps it mostly hidden under water,
   but the alligator can still see prey.

   (D) It keeps its body temperature from
   getting too high.

7. Sharks can smell very small amounts of
   substances in ocean water. What does this
   adaptation **most likely** let sharks do?

   (F) sense water temperature

   (G) find a place to lay eggs

   (H) find a safe place to hide

   (I) find food that is far away

8. Compared to other marine habitats, very few kinds of fish live on the ocean floor. To live in the deep ocean, what condition do fish need to be adapted for?

Ⓐ lack of food

Ⓒ high pressure

Ⓑ low salt levels

Ⓓ lots of light

9. The following picture shows a mother deer and her baby, called a fawn.

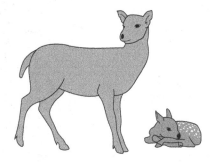

The markings on the fawn's fur are different from the markings on the mother. How does the pattern in the fawn's fur help it survive?

Ⓕ It helps the fawn stay warm in cool weather.

Ⓖ It helps the fawn stay cool in warm weather.

Ⓗ It helps the fawn blend in with the forest background.

Ⓘ It helps the fawn stand out against a forest background.

10. Bryce drew the picture on the right. It is a tree commonly found in a tropical forest.

How do buttress roots help this tree survive in the ecosystem in which it lives?

Ⓐ They keep the tree from freezing during a very cold winter.

Ⓑ They help support the tree in shallow soil so it does not fall over.

Ⓒ They help the tree make sugars from carbon dioxide and sunlight.

Ⓓ They help the tree reach deep into sandy soil for nutrients and groundwater.

11. A pitcher plant is a carnivorous plant—a plant that traps and digests insects. The American pitcher plant lives in bogs.

Insects that fall into the slippery opening of the pitcher plant get trapped inside. The plant digests the insect and absorbs the nutrients. Which of the following is a characteristic of bogs that pitcher plants are adapted to?

Ⓕ Bogs get little sunlight, so plants compete with insects for sunlight.

Ⓖ Bog soil is low in nutrients so some plants are adapted to digest insects.

Ⓗ Bogs are filled with plant-eating insects that plants need to defend against.

Ⓘ Bogs get little rain, so plants need to store water to live through dry periods.

Name _____

12. Camouflage is coloring or texture that helps a living thing blend in with its environment. Which describes an animal with camouflage that is best suited for a grassland ecosystem?

Ⓐ solid, dark black

Ⓑ solid, bright white

Ⓒ light brown, vertical stripes

Ⓓ bright, colorful patterns

13. A ptarmigan is a bird that walks on the ground. Ptarmigan feet are completely covered with tiny white feathers.

How are the ptarmigan's feet adapted for living in its environment?

Ⓕ The feathers help keep its feet warm in the cold.

Ⓖ The feathers keep fish from noticing the ptarmigan's feet in marshes.

Ⓗ The feathers help the ptarmigan walk quietly so it can sneak up on prey.

Ⓘ The feathers help protect the ptarmigan's feet from sharp cactus spines.

14. The diagram below shows how an antlion catches its food.

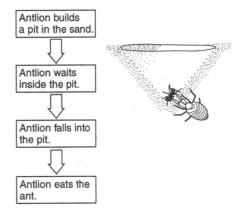

Antlion builds a pit in the sand.
↓
Antlion waits inside the pit.
↓
Antlion falls into the pit.
↓
Antlion eats the ant.

What does the diagram suggest about the antlion?

Ⓕ The antlion is not adapted to its habitat.

Ⓖ The antlion has a diet of both plants and animals.

Ⓗ The antlion survives by hunting and chasing food.

Ⓘ The antlion has behavioral adaptations for its environment.

15. Which behavioral adaptation below allows the alligator to control its body temperature?

Ⓐ Alligators mate in April and May.

Ⓑ The alligator basks in the sunlight.

Ⓒ Alligators lay between 20 and 50 eggs at one time.

Ⓓ The alligator eats turtles, small mammals, and birds.

Apply Inquiry and Review the Big Idea

Write the answers to these questions.

16. The coloring of the rough green snake allows it to blend in with its background. Make a claim about what type of adaptation the rough green snake's color is. Support your claim with evidence and explain your reasoning.

_____

_____

_____

17. Many desert plants, such as the welwitschia, have long central roots called taproots. Taproots grow deep underground to reach groundwater. Explain how a taproot is a useful adaptation for a desert ecosystem.

_____

_____

18. It is estimated that fewer than 100 Florida panthers are still living. Florida now has a protected habitat for the panther. Make a claim about how protecting the habitat will affect the panther population. Provide reasoning to support your claim.

_____

_____

_____

_____

Don't Wait

Tick...tick...tick. Time is wasting. Don't wait until the last minute. Start your research and planning now!

What kind of project is it?

What is the goal of the project? Is it an experiment, an engineering challenge, or something entirely different? Find out about the rules and expectations.

Projects in

Science

by Michael DiSpezio

Since you're reading this section, there's probably a science project in your future. Right?

Don't worry, we're here to guide you along. Whether you were given specific steps to follow or want to create your own totally awesome project, you've come to the right place. We'll show you how to put it together.

What topic should I pick?

You'll be spending quite a bit of time on this undertaking, so select a topic that you're interested in.

What's the plan?

When you know your goals, formulate a plan. Make a calendar that shows completion dates for various steps. Try to stick to that schedule, but update it as needed.

What materials do I need?

Make sure you use materials that are safe, available, and affordable.

The first step in any project is to learn as much as you can about the subject.

Gathering
Information

You'll need to fine-tune your research skills to help you complete your project. As you learn more about your topic, you'll be able to design a better project. You may even change your topic based on what you uncover.

Home   A Search Engine for Kids
                          Search

These days, it's easy to access a global library of information. All it takes is an Internet connection and the ability to use a search engine. A search engine is a tool that scours the Internet and locates web pages containing documents, images, and videos. All you have to do is enter keywords or phrases that relate to your subject. The search engine does the rest and generates a list of relevant links. Click on a link, and a new web page opens that contains information related to your search.

▶ Suppose the subject of your project is hurricane damage. Write down five keywords or phrases that you would enter into a search engine to learn more about this subject.

_____

_____

_____

_____

_____

Print References

A library has books, magazines, pamphlets, and other kinds of print references. If you still need a topic for your project, you might try flipping through some of the references. You can ask a librarian for assistance.

Computerized Catalog

Many libraries have computerized their catalog of books. Enter keywords or phrases into the catalog search engine. In response, the computer screen displays an assortment of books and references that are part of the library's holdings.

Interview Questions

You might want to interview a local expert. Find out which individuals are likely to have knowledge of your topic. Politely ask to set up an interview. Before you speak with an expert, make sure that you have your questions thought out and written down.

Tell It or Type It...
Transmit Information!

The world is at your fingertips! Communication is important at every step of a science project, from working with members of a team to sharing your results with others. Technology makes sending and receiving information easier than ever before.

Sandy's Science Site

Home　　　About　　　Search |　　GO

Report Your Findings

Report Your Data

Recent posts

Bug of the week

Books on Nature

Archives

　　June

　　July

Can you help us find this butterfly?

Friends might use cell phones to communicate, but text messages aren't always clear. Are there better ways to communicate scientific information? ▶

Here's a ? 4 U. What's the 411 with our project? Are we meeting L8R? Give me a shout. TTFN :o)

▲ Scientists used to communicate by writing books and journal articles. This process could take several months or even years. Today, you can communicate instantly using the Internet.

Say What?

What message was sent on the cell phone?

_____

_____

_____

_____

_____

SCIENCE BLOG SITES

Search

Home | About | Video

Blogs and Websites

The Internet is a great tool for communicating with others. You can send e-mails about a project to team members. You can make a website to post your results and share them with others. You can read blogs to find out what projects others are doing. Computers keep records, so it's easy to track the progress of your project.

Internet Safety Tips

▶ Your parents or teacher should know when you are using the Internet.

▶ Never enter personal information on websites.

▶ If something makes you uncomfortable, tell your parents or teacher immediately.

▶ Just like you shouldn't talk to strangers on the street, you shouldn't communicate with strangers on the Internet.

Share Your Results

Tell Your Story

Field Reports

Internet a global system of computers that are connected together

Website a collection of online pages that a person, an organization, or a company puts on the Internet for others to view

Blog an online diary where people post information about hobbies or experiences

Science Fair Projects

Is your school going to stage a science fair? You'll have several weeks to prepare an award-winning project. But where should you start? The answer is easy—right here!

Experimental Design

Design an investigation to answer your question. Keep it simple and to the point. Most questions will lead to an investigation that explores how one factor affects a subject. For example, "How does temperature affect seed germination?"

Begin with a Question

Most science fair projects answer a question. A good question can be solved by an investigation. To come up with a good question, you may need to do some research about your topic.

Scientific Methods

Write a hypothesis about how you think things will turn out. During your investigation, make sure you are using scientific methods.

Keeping Notes

Keep a notebook that describes everything about the project. Make sure that it stays up-to-date with descriptions of your materials, experimental setup, steps, and collected data. You can transfer this information to a computer so it can be printed out later.

Crunching Numbers

Collected data needs to be analyzed. Tools such as calculators and computers can help you examine and evaluate your results. Can you observe any patterns in the data? If so, what might they suggest?

▶ Write the numbers 1–6 on these two pages in the correct order next to the main steps.

Repeatability

Are your results repeatable? Find out. Perform your experiment several times to make sure that your data is valid. If your results don't repeat, you may need to redesign your experiment.

Communicate What You've Learned

When you're finished with your project, it's time to communicate your findings at a science fair. Chances are the event will be held in a cafeteria, gym or other large space. Here, you'll have the opportunity to present your project to other students, teachers, parents, and judges.

Drawing Conclusions

Once you've analyzed your data, it's time to evaluate your hypothesis. Do the collected measurements agree with your educated guess? If so, describe this relationship and how it is supported by your data. If not, describe how your hypothesis is disproved by your findings.

Show It Off

You may want to take pictures to document your project.

FINISH

Before you talk about your project, know what to say. Have your key points written down or memorized. Practice in front of a mirror or before friends and family.

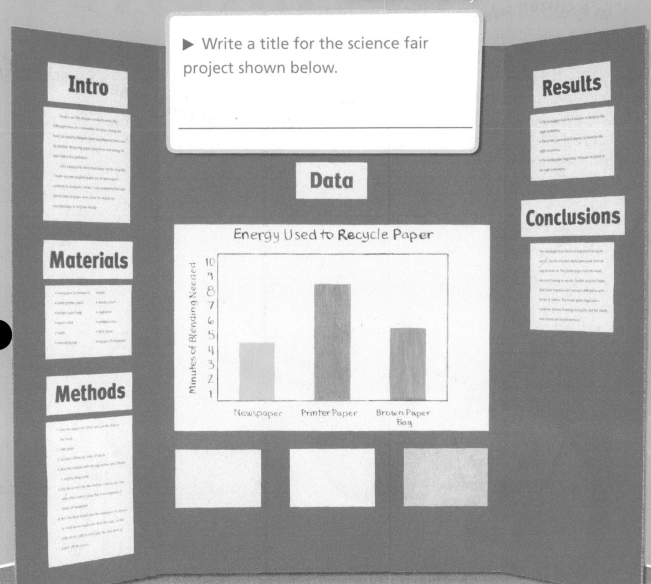

▶ Write a title for the science fair project shown below.

_____

Intro

Materials

Methods

Data

Energy Used to Recycle Paper

Results

Conclusions

For display and judging, you'll probably set up an exhibit on a tabletop. Most often, science fair projects are communicated using a self-standing display made of cardboard. You can buy a tri-fold display or make your own. If a single sheet is too small, try taping three large pieces together. Each section of the display shows a different part of the project. In addition to a poster, you might want to exhibit materials, parts of the setup, or models of what you investigated.

Citizen Science:
Get Involved

In a citizen science project, you can collect data that can be used by scientists.

Hey, Robin. I've been having this strange feeling that someone's been watching us. It started a few days ago when those students first appeared with binoculars. Be honest. Am I just being paranoid, or do they keep staring at us?

Listen, bird brain, of course they're looking at us. They're doing a bird count. It's part of a citizen science project. That's when ordinary folks collect data and share it with scientists. Using all the collected data, scientists can perform more extensive research.

When people participate in citizen science, scientists can quickly gather a lot of data.

Did you know that there are other citizen science projects? One involves analyzing local water samples to help monitor pollution. Another project has volunteers making local weather observations. To find out more, do a web search.

I see six crows and one robin. We'll e-mail the data to the local bird preserve. They'll post it online and share it with scientists and other bird watchers.

Field Guide to Humans

▶ Make a list of materials you'd need to participate in a local bird count.

_____

_____

_____

_____

Engineering a Challenge

Get out your thinking cap and your hard hat!

Classroom engineering challenges are like real-world construction projects. Are you up for the challenge?

Engineering challenges offer the opportunity to plan, test, and improve original designs. To start, learn as much as you can about the challenge and its associated science.
Be familiar with the rules before you begin to brainstorm ideas.

Creativity

Be creative! Have fun! At this point, don't worry if your ideas are perfect. Brainstorm and generate a list of all design options. Later on, you'll select and test your best ideas.

Materials

Consider what sort of materials would be best to use. Make sure that you are aware of the guidelines for the challenge. There may be limits to kinds of materials or to the cost of supplies used to assemble your entry.

594

Blueprints

As you start to think up a design, draw simple diagrams or blueprints on paper. It's much easier to change a drawing than an assembled project, so this is the perfect time to update your plans.

Teamwork

If you're working with others, make sure that each person has a specific responsibility. Share what you know. Work together to engineer a design based on the entire team's understanding and experience.

Test and Redesign

Once you have a model assembled, test it. Does it perform as you imagined? Test it again. From what you observe, can you improve your design? Continue making improvements until it's time to show off your completed project.

A Better Design?

How would you change one element in this wacky design?

_____

Try These
Challenges

Would you like to challenge your classmates
to a friendly design competition?
Here are some suggestions.

Bridge Building

When it comes to engineering, bridges
offer an "inside" view of design. Unlike
buildings, whose beams are concealed
by outer walls, the structural framework
of bridges is often exposed. How would
you build a bridge using craft sticks and
white glue? How much weight could
you add to the bridge before the
structure collapsed?

Solar-Powered Racers

Fill 'er up—with sunshine, that is!
Here's your chance to build a solar-
powered vehicle. The energy to run
the car's motor comes from a solar
cell. Beyond the motor and cell, the
design is up to you! Should it have
four wheels or three? Where
should you place the motor and
cells? What style of car body will
you design?

596

Parachute Drop

3...2...1...Release! Can you design a soft lander that will prevent a dropped egg from cracking? To meet this challenge, you might use a parachute or bumpers that cushion impact.

Towering Towers

How high can you build a tower using only 20 straws and modeling clay? Draw a blueprint to show how you would design your tower.

Robotic Challenges

Robot competitions offer a more difficult challenge. To assemble a robotic device, you'll need construction materials that include motors and other electronic parts. Your entry's design will be guided by the contest's specific task. Perhaps, it will compete in some sort of robotic basketball game? Score!

My Project Plan

Title of project: _____

Type of project: _____

Teammates (if any): _____

Describe the project.

_____

_____

List the goals of the project.

_____

_____

What materials are needed for the project?

_____

_____

The safety issues (if any) are:

_____

What are some sources of background research?

_____

_____

_____

How will you communicate or display your project?

_____

_____

How will you evaluate the project?

_____

_____

_____

21st Century Skills
Technology and Coding

The first popular video games were created in the 1970s. They had simple single-color graphics and could not play music. Compare this to today's video games, which have colorful 3D graphics, high-quality music, and Internet connectivity. Advances in computer technology led to this rapid change in how video games look, sound, and behave.

If you are interested in computer technology and how it works, you might like computer science. *Computer science* is the study of computer technology and how data is processed and stored by computers.

ACTIVE READING
As you read, underline examples of tools and devices that use computer technology.

Hello world!

A computer is any device that receives, stores, processes, and outputs data. In the 1940s and 1950s, early electronic computers were used by militaries and research laboratories. These computers were very large and could only complete limited tasks. The invention of the integrated circuit led to smaller, faster, and more affordable computers. Personal computers (PCs) were popularized in the 1980s, and became essential household devices in the 2000s. And since then, computer technology has developed even further. Today's computers can connect to the Internet wirelessly and process hundreds of millions of instructions per second!

What technology led to the development of smaller personal computers in the 1970s?

_____

_____

_____

Computers in the 1950s were the size of the entire room.

By 2015, a cell phone could store as much data and run as fast as a personal computer from 1995. A cell phone can fit in the palm of your hand!

Computer scientists work to solve real-world problems with computer technology. Some computer scientists develop and test technical hypotheses. Others use computer science concepts to create software. Many professional computer scientists became interested in computer technology at a young age. Learning how to make a website or create simple electronic devices can be fun and rewarding.

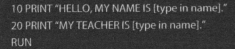

```
10 PRINT "HELLO, MY NAME IS [type in name]."
20 PRINT "MY TEACHER IS [type in name]."
RUN
```

What materials and skills would be required to create a simple circuit like the one pictured here?

Materials	Skills

Computers at Work

Whether for work or for play, computer science requires certain skills and habits of mind. Computer science is applicable to many fields, from medicine to business to art. Collaboration is an important skill in computer science. Computer scientists must be able to think logically and creatively, too.

Motion capture technology is used for special effects in film and to make realistic video games. It tracks the movement of an actor using special electronics, cameras, and computers. This kind of work requires the collaboration of computer scientists, engineers, actors, and artists.

Why is collaboration important in computer science?

_____

_____

_____

_____

Proteins found in the body fold up into unique shapes. Knowing these structures can help scientists develop treatments for certain diseases. However, the folding patterns are complex and can be very difficult to solve. A team of biochemists and computer scientists collaborated on a unique idea for solving these structures. They created a video game that lets players work together to solve protein structures.

Computers carry out tasks by following instructions, or programs, that people design. Examples of computer programs include websites, word processors, and digital photo editors. Computer programs are sometimes called "software," "applications," or "apps."

Computer software can help us to learn more about our world. It can be useful for business. It can retrieve and store information. It can also simply entertain us. Whatever its purpose, computer software should fulfill some human want or need. But how is it made?

1. Identifying a need
   What real-world problem could I solve by creating a computer program?

2. Brainstorming
   What should my computer program do?
   What features should it have?

3. Creating
   How can I write instructions for the computer to achieve my desired goals?

4. Testing and revising
   How can I identify errors and improve my computer program? Do others find my program easy to use and understand?

Writing Computer Code

The instructions that make up video games, word processors, and other kinds of software are not written in human language. They are written in a programming language, or *code*. Ruby, C, and Java are examples of programming languages. Programming languages—like human languages—must follow certain rules in order to be understood. A series of instructions written in a programming language is called *source code*.

Tools allow programmers to test their programs during development.

```
Run ↵

89 /* Check to see if game is over */
90 if ( timeremaining == 0 ) {
91 printf( "Game over" );
92 }
93 else {
```

Attention to detail is needed for writing code. If the spelling and order of commands are incorrect, the computer will not be able to follow the instructions given.

Comments are notes left by the programmer to help organize and explain the code. The computer does not interpret comments.

This is *source code* for a video game. What do you think this code does?

_____

_____

_____

_____

Computer Safety

Take care when using computers and other electronic devices.

1. Be cautious when handling and transporting computers and other electronic devices. Dropping them could cause serious damage.

2. Keep computers away from dirt, dust, and moisture.

3. Balance computer time with other activities, including plenty of exercise.

4. Sit upright with your shoulders down, or stand up, when using a computer.

5. Observe electrical safety when working with electric circuits or components.

Talk to your family about rules for Internet use. Do not share private information such as photographs, your phone number, or your address. Do not open emails or links from people you don't know.

It is important to treat others with respect when communicating online. Unfortunately, not everyone follows this rule. You do not need to reply to someone who sends you an unwanted contact online. Alert a trusted adult instead.

Propose an idea for improving health and safety in your school computer lab.

_____

_____

_____

_____

_____

_____

Careers in Computing

What question would you ask a robotics specialist?

_____

_____

_____

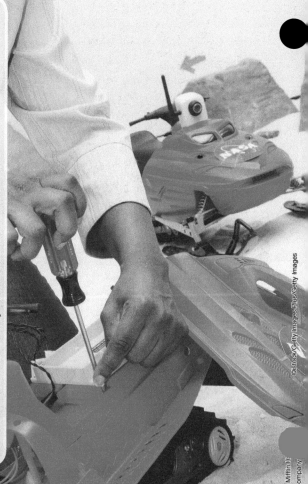

Dr. Ayanna Howard is an engineer specializing in robotics at Georgia Tech. She developed a series of robots named SnoMotes, which contained weather sensors. Dr. Howard's team could program the robots' routes in dangerous parts of the Arctic using computers. Computer software was then used to analyze the data and track changes in the climate of the area.

608

Interactive Glossary

As you learn about each term, add notes, drawings, or sentences in the extra space. This will help you remember what the terms mean. Here are some examples.

fungi [FUHN•jee] A group of organisms that get nutrients by decomposing other organisms

 A mushroom is an example of fungi.

physical change [FIHZ•ih•kuhl CHAYNJ] Change in the size, shape, or state of matter with no new substance being formed

When I cut paper in half, that's a physical change.

Glossary Pronunciation Key

With every glossary term, there is also a phonetic respelling. A phonetic respelling writes the word the way it sounds, which can help you pronounce new or unfamiliar words. Use this key to help you understand the respellings.

Sound	As in	Phonetic Respelling	Sound	As in	Phonetic Respelling
a	bat	(BAT)	oh	over	(OH•ver)
ah	lock	(LAHK)	oo	pool	(POOL)
air	rare	(RAIR)	ow	out	(OWT)
ar	argue	(AR•gyoo)	oy	foil	(FOYL)
aw	law	(LAW)	s	cell	(SEL)
ay	face	(FAYS)		sit	(SIT)
ch	chapel	(CHAP•uhl)	sh	sheep	(SHEEP)
e	test	(TEST)	th	that	(THAT)
	metric	(MEH•trik)		thin	(THIN)
ee	eat	(EET)	u	pull	(PUL)
	feet	(FEET)	uh	medal	(MED•uhl)
	ski	(SKEE)		talent	(TAL•uhnt)
er	paper	(PAY•per)		pencil	(PEN•suhl)
	fern	(FERN)		onion	(UHN•yuhn)
eye	idea	(eye•DEE•uh)		playful	(PLAY•fuhl)
i	bit	(BIT)		dull	(DUHL)
ing	going	(GOH•ing)	y	yes	(YES)
k	card	(KARD)		ripe	(RYP)
	kite	(KYT)	z	bags	(BAGZ)
ngk	bank	(BANGK)	zh	treasure	(TREZH•er)

A

accurate [AK•yuh•ruht] **Very close to the actual value** (p. 55)

anemometer [an•uh•MAHM•uht•ER] **A weather instrument that measures wind speed** (p. 178)

adaptation [ad•uhp•TAY•shuhn] **A trait or characteristic that helps an organism survive** (p. 526)

asteroid [AS•ter•oyd] **A chunk of rock or iron less than 1,000 km (621 mi) in diameter that orbits the sun** (p. 122)

air mass [AIR MASS] **A large body of air that has similar temperature and humidity throughout** (p. 194)

astronomy [uh•STRAHN•uh•mee] **The study of objects in space and their properties** (p. 138)

air pressure [AIR PRESH•er] **The weight of the atmosphere pressing down on Earth** (p. 192)

atmosphere [AT•muhs•feer] **The mixture of gases that surround a planet** (p. 159)

R2

atom [AT•uhm] The smallest unit into which an element can be divided and still retain all the properties of that element (p. 326)

barometer [buh•RAHM•uht•er] A weather instrument used to measure air pressure (p. 179)

atomic theory [uh•TAHM•ik THEE•uh•ree] A scientific explanation of the structure of atoms and how they interact with other atoms (p. 288)

bioengineering [by•oh•en•juh•NIR•ing] The application of the engineering design process to living things (p. 96)

B

balance [BAL•uhns] A tool used to measure the amount of matter in an object, which is the object's mass (p. 52)

biotechnology [by•oh•tek•NAHL•uh•jee] A product of technology used to benefit organisms and the environment (p. 97)

balanced forces [BAL•uhnst FAWRS•iz] Forces that cancel each other out because they are equal in size and opposite in direction (p. 396)

bladder [BLAD•er] Organ in the excretory system that stores and releases urine (p. 477)

bone [BOHN] A hard organ that has a spongy layer inside and that may help support the body or protect other organs (p. 450)

circuit [SER•kuht] A path along which electric charges can flow (p. 370)

brain [BRAYN] The organ in the human body that processes information (p. 432)

climate [KLY•muht] The pattern of weather an area experiences over a long period of time (p. 210)

C

chemical change [KEM•ih•kuhl CHAYNJ] A change in one or more substances, caused by a reaction, that forms new and different substances (p. 251)

climate zone [KLY•muht ZOHN] An area that has similar average temperatures and precipitation throughout (p. 212)

chemical energy [KEM•ih•kuhl EN•er•jee] Energy that is stored in matter and that can be released by a chemical reaction (p. 315)

comet [KAHM•it] A chunk of frozen gases, rock, ice, and dust orbiting the sun (p. 123)

compound [KAHM•pownd] **A substance made of two or more different atoms that have combined chemically** (p. 292)

control [kuhn•TROHL] **The experimental setup to which you will compare all the other setups** (p. 33)

condensation [kahn•duhn•SAY•shuhn] **The process by which a gas changes into a liquid** (p. 160)

criteria [kry•TEER•ee•uh] **The standards for measuring success** (p. 76)

D

conductor [kuhn•DUK•ter] **A material that readily allows electric charges to pass through it and therefore carries electricity well** (p. 501)

desert [DEZ•ert] **An area of land that is very dry** (p. 548)

conservation [kahn•ser•VAY•shuhn] **The preserving and protecting of an ecosystem or a resource** (p. 501)

dwarf planet [DWORF PLAN•it] **A nearly round body, slightly smaller than a planet, whose orbit crosses the orbit of another body** (p. 122)

ecosystem [EE•koh•sis•tuhm] A community of organisms and the environment in which they live (p. 495)

electromagnet [ee•lek•troh•MAG•nit] A device in which electric current is used to produce magnetism (p. 349)

electric current [ee•LEK•trik KER•uhnt] The flow of electric charges along a path (p. 332)

element [EL•uh•muhnt] Matter that is made of only one kind of atom (p. 290)

electric motor [ee•LEK•trik MOHT•er] A device that changes electrical energy into mechanical energy (p. 346)

energy [EN•er•jee] The ability to cause changes in matter (p. 306)

electrical energy [ee•LEK•trih•kuhl EN•er•jee] Energy caused by the movement of electric charges (p. 313)

engineering [en•juh•NEER•ing] The use of science and math for practical uses such as the design of structures, machine, and systems (p. 71)

environment [en•vy•ruhn•muhnt] All the living and nonliving things that surround and affect an organism (p. 248)

exoskeleton [eks•oh•SKEL•uh•tuhn] A hard outer covering, found in many types of animals, that supports and protects the body (p. 453)

equator [ee•KWAYT•er] An imaginary line around Earth, equally distant from the North and South Poles (p. 212)

experiment [ek•SPAIR•uh•muhnt] A procedure carried out under controlled conditions to test a hypothesis (p. 27)

evaporation [ee•vap•uh•RAY•shuhn] The process by which a liquid changes into a gas (p. 159)

extinction [ek•STINGK•shuhn] The death of all the organisms of a certain kind of living thing (p. 505)

evidence [EV•uh•duhns] Information collected during a scientific investigation (p. 6)

F

force [FAWRS] A push or a pull, which may cause a change in an object's motion (p. 392)

friction [FRIK•shuhn] A force that acts between two touching objects and that opposes motion (p. 395)

generator [JEN•er•ayt•er] A device that makes an electric current by converting kinetic energy to electrical energy (p. 351)

front [FRUHNT] The border where two air masses meet (p. 194)

grassland [GRAS•land] An area of land covered mostly with grasses that generally receives less rain than a forest (p. 546)

G

galaxy [GAL•uhk•see] A group of billions of stars, objects that orbit those stars, gas, and dust (p. 141)

gravity [GRAV•ih•tee] The force of attraction between two objects, such as the attraction between Earth and objects on it (p. 394)

gas [GAS] The state of matter in which a substance does not have a definite shape or volume (p. 236)

groundwater [GROWND•waw•ter] Water that is stored underground. (p. 162)

H

habitat [HAB•ih•tat] **The place where an organism lives and can find everything it needs to survive** (p. 524)

heart [HART] **A muscular organ that pumps blood through the rest of the circulatory system** (p. 451)

humidity [hyoo•MID•uh•tee] **The amount of water vapor in the air** (p. 179)

I

instinct [IN•stinkt] **A behavior that an organism inherits and knows how to do without being taught** (p. 530)

insulator [IN•suh•layt•er] **A material that resists the flow of electric charge and therefore does not conduct electricity well** (p. 368)

intertidal zone [in•ter•TYD•uhl ZOHN] **The area between the land and the ocean that is covered by water at high tide and uncovered at low tide** (p. 566)

investigation [in•ves•tuh•GAY•shuhn] **A procedure carried out to carefully observe, study, or test something in order to learn more about it** (p. 4)

K

kidneys [KID•neez] **Organs in the human excretory system that remove waste materials from the blood** (p. 477)

kinetic energy [kih•NET•ik EN•er•jee] The energy an object has because of motion (p. 308)

lungs [LUNGZ] The largest organs in the respiratory system that bring oxygen from the air into the body and release carbon dioxide (p. 454)

L

latitude [LAT•ih•tood] A measure of how far north or south a place is from the equator (p. 212)

M

matter [MAT•er] Anything that has mass and takes up space (p. 232)

liquid [LIK•wid] The state of matter in which a substance has a definite volume but no definite shape (p. 236)

mechanical energy [muh•KAN•ih•kuhl EN•er•jee] The total energy of motion and position of an object (p. 314)

liver [LIV•er] A large organ that makes a digestive juice called bile (p. 473)

microscopic [my•kruh•SKAHP•ik] Too small to be seen without using a microscope (p. 49)

mixture [MIKS•cher] A combination of two or more different substances in which the substances keep their identities (p. 271)

molecule [MAHL•ih•kyoo] A single particle of matter made up of two or more atoms joined together chemically. (p. 292)

muscle [MUHS•uhl] An organ made of bundles of long fibers that can contract to produce movement in living things (p. 451)

organ [AWR•guhn] A body part that is made of smaller parts that work together to do a certain job (p. 430)

organ system [AWR•guhn SIS•tuhm] A group of organs that work together to do a job for the body (p. 430)

organism [AWR•guh•niz•uhm] A living thing (p. 430)

O

opinion [uh•PIN•yuhn] A personal belief or judgment that does not need to be backed up with evidence (p. 9)

P

pancreas [PAN•kree•uhs] An organ that makes a digestive juice and insulin (p. 473)

parallel circuit [PAIR•uh•lel SER•kit] An electric circuit that has more than one path for the electric charges to follow (p. 373)

pollution [puh•LOO•shuhn] A waste product that harms living things and damages an ecosystem (p. 500)

physical change [FIZ•ih•kuhl CHAYNJ] A change in which the form or shape of a substance changes but the substance still has the same chemical makeup (p. 250)

potential energy [poh•TEN•shuhl EN•er•jee] Energy that an object has because of its position or its condition (p. 308)

planet [PLAN•it] A large, round body that revolves around a star (p. 114)

precipitation [pree•sip•uh•TAY•shuhn] Water that falls from the air to Earth's surface (p. 161)

polar [POHL•er] Near Earth's North Pole or South Pole (p. 552)

prototype [PROH•tuh•typ] The original or test model on which a product is based (p. 74)

R

reaction [ree•AK•shuhn] The process in which new substances are formed during a chemical change (p. 251)

series circuit [SIR•eez SER•kit] An electric circuit in which the electric charges have only one path to follow (p. 373)

runoff [RUN•awf] Water that does not soak into the ground and that flows across Earth's surface (p. 163)

skin [SKIN] The human body's largest organ, which covers the outside of the body (p. 438)

S

science [SY•uhns] The study of the natural world through observation and investigation (p. 5)

solar system [SOH•ler SIS•tuhm] A star and all the planets and other objects that revolve around it (p. 114)

scientific methods [sy•uhn•TIF•ik METH•uhds] Different ways that scientists perform investigations and collect reliable data (p. 26)

solid [SAHL•id] The state of matter in which a substance has a definite shape and a definite volume (p. 237)

solution [suh•LOO•shuhn] A mixture that has the same composition throughout because all the parts are mixed evenly (p. 272)

stomach [STUHM•uhk] A baglike organ in which food is mixed with digestive juices and squeezed by muscles (p. 472)

spring scale [SPRING SKAYL] A tool used to measure forces (p. 53)

T

taiga [TY•guh] Land that is very cold in winter and that is covered mostly with conifers (p. 550)

star [STAR] A huge ball of very hot, glowing gases in space that produces its own light and heat (p. 138)

technology [tek•NAHL•uh•jee] The use of scientific knowledge to solve practical problems (p. 72)

static electricity [STAT•ik ee•lek•TRIS•uh•tee] The buildup of electric charges on an object (p. 329)

temperature [TEM•per•uh•cher] The measure of the energy of motion in the particles of matter, which we feel as how hot or cold something is (p. 234)

unbalanced forces
[uhn•BAL•uhnst FAWRS•iz] Forces that cause a change in motion because they act on an object and don't cancel each other out (p. 396)

universe [YOO•nuh•vers] Everything that exists, including galaxies and everything in them (p. 140)

variable [VAIR•ee•uh•buhl] Any condition that can be changed in an experiment (p. 33)

volume [VAHL•yoom] The amount of space something takes up (p. 232)

water cycle [WAWT•er SY•kuhl] The process in which water continuously moves from Earth's surface into the atmosphere and back again (p. 173)

weather [WETH•er] What is happening in the atmosphere at a certain place and time (p. 176)

weather map [WETH•er MAP] A map that uses symbols to show weather data (p. 196)

wetland [WET•land] An area of land covered with shallow water for most of the year (p. 564)

wind [WIHND] Air that is moving (p. 192)

Index

electric current, 332, 334–335, 337–338, 348–349, 352
  sources of, 332–334
  uses of, 333
electricity, 333, 352–353
  conserving, 350–352, 354
  and magnetism, 348–349
  static, 239–330, 333–335, 338
  uses of, 344–347
electricity generating station, 332–335, 350, 354
electric motor, 346, 349, 352–353
electromagnet, 348–349, 352–353
electronics, 599–608
  safety, 606–607
electron microscopes, 49
electrons, 289, 326–327, 329–330, 334–336
  moving through wire, 332–333
electrostatic discharge, 334, 338
elements, 290–291
elliptical galaxies, 142
embryo, 480
energy, 306–307, 318–319
  chemical, 314–316, 318–320
  electrical, 309, 313–314, 317–320, 333, 337, 344, 346–347, 350–354
  from food, 315
  heat, 316, 319

  in hot–air balloon, 311
  kinds of, 305
  kinetic, 308–311, 314–315, 318–320, 351
  light, 312–313, 316–317, 319–320, 325–354
  in machines, 314
  mechanical, 314–316, 318–320, 344, 346–347, 350, 352, 354
  potential, 308–309
  record data, 323
  roller coaster car, 308–309
  solar, 351
  sound, 310, 316, 318–320, 344, 347, 352–354
  in stage production, 316–317
  from sun, 307, 312
  thermal, 311, 313–315, 318–320, 344, 352–354
  transfer in trumpet, 310
engineering, 71. *See also* **design process**
Engineering and Technology. *See also* **STEM (Science, Technology, Engineering, and Mathematics)**
  animal tracking, 575–576
  artificial hearts, 467–468
  benefits and risks, 94–95

  carbon fiber, 245
  code, 604–605
  coding, 604–605
  space tools, 147–148
  sports safety gear, 409–410
environment, 248
  biotechnology and, 97
  biotic and abiotic parts of, 248–249
  change, 496–497, 504–504, 508
  and climate, 216–217
  conservation, 501, 506–507
  effect of beaver, 498, 509
  effect of fire ant, 499
  effect of harvester ant, 499
  effect of human, 500, 510
  forest fire, 493, 497
  habitat destruction, 500
  in ice age, 496–497
  nonliving, 494–495
  pollution, 500, 506–507
  resources, 508
equator, 212, 219
esophagus, 472–473, 482–484
Europa, 122
evaporation, 159, 238–239, 275
evidence, 6–7
excretory system

heart beat, 458–459
heat energy, 316, 319.
See also **energy**
hibernation, 531, 534–536.
See also **migration**
high pressure, 192–193, 200
Higinbotham, William, 11
Hubble, Edwin, 141
humans
bones, 431, 450
circulatory system, 458–459, 463–464
digestive system, 472–473, 482–483
excretory system, 436–467, 482
heart, 451, 458–459
integumentary system, 431, 438–439, 442–443
life cycle, 480
lungs, 454–456, 463
muscles, 430, 450–451, 462–465
muscular system, 451
nervous system, 432–434, 442–443
reproductive system, 480, 482–483
respiratory system, 454–455, 462–463, 465
senses, 429–430, 432, 434–435, 442
skin, 431, 438–439
urinary system, 476–477, 482–484
humidity, 179, 185
hurricane, 198, 202.
See also **weather**

hydroelectric dam, 350
hydrologist, 223–224
hygrometer, 179. *See also* **science tools**
hypotheses, 32–33, 35, 207, 267, 323

ice, 252
ice age, 496–497
identify, 179
inferences, 8–9
Inquiry Skills
analyze and extend, 19, 41, 59, 85, 103, 133, 171, 205, 265, 283, 321, 339, 363, 413, 417, 445, 513, 537
claims, evidence, and reasoning, 22, 44, 63, 88, 106, 136, 174, 208, 268, 286, 324, 342, 366, 416, 420, 448, 516, 540
classify, 180–181
communicate, 531, 545, 554
compare, 211, 493
contrast, 182
draw conclusions, 21, 22, 44, 62, 88, 106, 136, 174, 208, 268, 286, 323, 324, 342, 366, 416, 419, 447, 516, 540
hypothesize, 207, 267, 325
identify, 179
investigations, 540
measure, 182

predict, 196–197, 202, 215
record your data, 21, 35, 43, 61, 87, 105, 135, 173, 179, 207, 267, 285, 323, 341, 365, 415, 419, 447, 515, 539
set a purpose, 20, 21, 35, 42, 43, 60, 86, 87, 104, 134, 135, 172, 206, 266, 284, 285, 322, 340, 364, 414, 415, 418, 419, 446, 514, 515, 538
sequence, 343–344, 477
state your hypothesis, 86, 87, 266, 284, 285, 322, 414, 419, 446, 514, 515
think about the procedure, 20, 21, 42, 43, 60, 86, 87, 104, 134, 135, 172, 206, 266, 284, 285, 322, 340, 364, 414, 415, 418, 419, 446, 514, 515, 538
insects
caterpillar, 523, 532–533
cicada, 453
fire ant, 409
fly, 6–7, 436–478
harvester ant, 499
house fly, 529
life cycle of, 481
maggot, 6–7
moth, 437

moose, 551
pangolin, 541
river otter, 563
seal, 453
sloth, 545
squirrel, 531, 536
Tasmanian wolf, 505, 508
wolverine, 551
zebra, 547
Mars, 117
Mars Rover, 402–403
mass, 52
conservation of, 256–257
forces and, 400–401
matter and, 232, 235
matter, 232–241
changes of state, 238–239
chemical changes in, 251, 257–258
gases, 236–241, 253
liquids, 236–241, 252
mass and, 232, 235
mixtures, 270–277
physical changes in, 250, 256
properties of, 232–235, 240–241
solids, 236–241
states of, 236–237
temperature and, 234, 238–239, 252–255, 270
volume and, 232, 234
measure, 182
of force, 53
of length, 50
of mass, 52
of temperature, 51
of time, 51
tools, 50–55
of volume, 54–55
rain, 182
mechanical energy, 314–315, 318–320, 344, 346–347, 350, 352, 354. *See also* **energy**
melting, 238–239, 254
Mendeleev, Dmitri, 290
meniscus, 55
Mercury, 116
mercury (element), 290
mesh screens, 275
meteorites, 123
meteoroids, 123
meteorologist, 176, 194, 196, 199
use tools, 197
meteors, 123
meter (m), 50
metric system, 50
Miami Heat basketball, Florida, 427
microscopes, 49
migration, 531, 534–535, 554
Milky Way, 140–141
mixtures, 270–277
alloys, 276–277
separating, 274–275
solutions, 272–273
models, 27, 30–31
molecules, 292–293
moon, (of earth)
impacts upon, 124
moons, 114–115, 122
motion
forces and, 329–393
motion capture technology, 602
mountain breeze, 204
mouth, 431, 454, 484
muscles
animals, 453, 464
function of, 451, 465
humans, 430, 450–451, 462–465
types of, 451
muscular system, 451

N

Nakamura, Shuji, 355–356
neon, 290
Neptune, 119
nerves, 432–434, 442
nervous system, 432, 442–443
brain, 432, 434, 442–443
nerves, 432–434, 442
spinal cord, 432–433
neutrons, 290, 326–327, 334–336
North Atlantic Ocean
water temperature in, 214
niches, 252, 253
nocturnal animal, 530, 535
nose
animals, 437
humans, 434–435, 442, 454
olfactory bulb, 435
numbers, 48
nutrients, 458–459, 472, 474–476, 479
nutrition information, 474–475

warm front, 194
washboard, 72—73
water
  boiling, 238—239, 275
  condensation and
    evaporation,
    238—239, 254—255,
    275
  habitats, 560—574
  melting and freezing,
    238—239 252—254
  molecular composition
    of, 292
  precipitation, 182, 184
  using, 506
water cycle, 173—174
weather, 176—177, 185,
  219
  blizzard, 198
  change, 156, 194
  data, 196
  in desert, 210
  Doppler radar, 196—197,
    202
  frost, 175
  hurricane, 198
  map, 196
  meteorologist, 176, 194,
    196—197, 199
  predict, 196—197, 202

  report, 176, 196
  satellite, 196—197
  station, 196, 201—202
  thunderstorm, 176
  tornado, 198
  vs. climate, 210—211, 218
  wind, 192—193
weather balloon, 178. *See
  also* **science tools**
weather forecaster, 195
weather map, 196—197, 201
weight, 53, 393
wet climate, 220
wetland, 564, 572—574
  animals in, 564—565
  bog, 564—565
  marsh, 564
  plants in, 564—565
  swamp, 564
white blood cells, 458, 466
Why It Matters, 36—37,
  78—79, 96—97,
  124—125, 198—199,
  216—217, 259—260,
  276—277, 316—317,
  330—331, 350—351,
  402—403, 456—457,
  474—475, 504—505,
  570—571

wildflower, life cycle of,
  533
wildlife surveyors,
  511—512
wind, 192, 201
  weather, 192—193
windmills, 351
windpipe, 454
wind vane, 178. *See also*
  science tools

**Yellowstone National
  Park,** 28

Zavaleta, Erika, 557—558
zoologist, 17—18, 61—62